I0616399

Kai Tuchmann (ed.)
Postdramatic Dramaturgies

Kai Tuchmann graduated in directing from Hochschule für Schauspielkunst Ernst Busch in Berlin. He works as a dramaturge, director, and academic. He is a visiting professor at The Central Academy of Drama in Beijing – for which he has developed, together with Li Yinan, the curriculum for the first dramaturgy program in Asia. He is also a member of the Theatre Management Faculty at Frankfurt's University for Music and Performing Arts. He has held fellowships at The Graduate Center, CUNY (Fulbright), the Academy for Theatre and Digitality, Germany, and the Mellon School of Theater and Performance Research at Harvard University.

Kai Tuchmann (ed.)

Postdramatic Dramaturgies

Resonances between Asia and Europe

[transcript]

Bibliographic information published by the Deutsche Nationalbibliothek
The Deutsche Nationalbibliothek lists this publication in the Deutsche National-bibliografie; detailed bibliographic data are available in the Internet at http://dnb.d-nb.de

This work is licensed under the Creative Commons Attribution-NonCommercial-NoDeri-vatives 4.0 (BY-NC-ND) which means that the text may be used for non-commercial pur-poses, provided credit is given to the author. For details go to
http://creativecommons.org/licenses/by-nc-nd/4.0/
To create an adaptation, translation, or derivative of the original work and for commercial use, further permission is required and can be obtained by contacting rights@transcript-publishing.com

Creative Commons license terms for re-use do not apply to any content (such as graphs, figures, photos, excerpts, etc.) not original to the Open Access publication and further permission may be required from the rights holder. The obligation to research and clear permission lies solely with the party re-using the material.

First published in 2022 by transcript Verlag, Bielefeld
© Kai Tuchmann (ed.)

Cover concept: Kordula Röckenhaus, Bielefeld
Cover illustration: Jiang Fan in RED, Photography by Richy Wong
Copy-editing: Nora Kauffeldt
Proofread: Graeme Currie
Typeset: Nora Kauffeldt

Print-ISBN 978-3-8376-5997-9
PDF-ISBN 978-3-8394-5997-3
https://doi.org/10.14361/9783839459973
ISSN of series: 2700-3922
eISSN of series: 2747-3198

Content

III POSTSCRIPT

Following Chinese usage, all Chinese names transliterated in this book are given with the family name first.

Acknowledgments

A book is never the sole work of its author, and this is all the more true for an anthology like this, which is a site of intersection for so many collective practices. So it is inevitable that any attempt at acknowledgments will be incomplete. Nevertheless, this attempt must be made because, without very specific people, this book would most certainly not be available in this form today.

First, my thanks go to all the contributors. Without their commitment and open-mindedness, this volume would have been unthinkable. Like them, however, my big thanks also go to the dramaturgy class of 2017 of the Beijing Topography Seminar at the Central Academy of Drama. Their interest and inquiries played a major role in creating the framework in which the contributors acted. I especially thank Xu Li in this context. I would also like to thank the organizers and translators without whose help this seminar could not have been held, namely Pu Wenyan, Huang Yiping, Gao Feng, and Gao Yinfu. And I have to make a special mention of my colleague and head of the Dramaturgy Faculty of the Central Academy of Drama, Li Yinan, who had such a deep trust in me, that sometimes surprised me, but which certainly helped me to identify and develop my strengths in educating students.

Conversations with dear friends and colleagues such as Anuja Ghosalkar, Thomas Schmidt, Soumyabrata Choudhury, Chris Connery, Jochen Kiefer, Su Wei, Fabrizio Massini, and Rustom Bharucha also influenced this book quite a bit, and I am very thankful for that.

A Fulbright research stay at the Theatre Department of the Graduate Center of the City University of New York was an important time for developing the scaffolding of this publication. My thanks go to the German-American Fulbright Commission (Antje Outhwaite) and to the theatre faculty at the Graduate Center. The regular conversations with Marvin Carlson and Frank Hentschker provided a lot of food for thought, but I am particularly indebted to Peter Eckersall. Not only has he encouraged me a lot, but his rich expertise in the field of dramaturgy combined with his intellectual generosity also had a major impact on this volume.

A fellowship at the Mellon School of Theater and Performance Research at Harvard University also helped significantly in thinking through this collection of texts. In this context, I would especially like to thank Martin Puchner for his incredibly selfless sharing of experiences.

I am deeply grateful and honored that Hans-Thies Lehmann has supported this publication with all his energy and has given it the distinction of providing it with his foreword.

Essentially, at the end of this acknowledgment, I would like to thank the transcript Verlag, as well as Graeme Currie, who undertook the English-language proofreading and did so with precision and speed that was breathtaking and indispensable to the process of completion.

The final thanks go to my partner Nora Kauffeldt, who also undertook the proofreading and editorial review of this publication. Because of her tireless efforts and always fair and precise criticism, as well as through her faith in this project and in me, she deserves probably the greatest share in completing this volume! Thank you, Nora. And forgive me for being so nervous at times.

It goes without saying that all errors appearing in this publication are mine alone.

Kai Tuchmann
Berlin, January 2022

Foreword

If, over the last few decades, one had given credence to the Cassandras among the clan of theatre critics, one would have had to conclude that "good theatre," "theatre of value," in which the text—spoken by well-trained actors and displaying "literary quality"—demands concentration, attention and patience in the audience, was terminally ill. The disease took the form of a many-headed Hydra, diagnosed as postmodern and performance, physical theatre, abstract theatre, theatre of the real, and many other supposed ailments. Evidently, this was a conflict in the tradition of the age-old struggle between young and old. It is important to remember these polemics, because they tend to be overshadowed by the very positive and enthusiastic response that my book *Postdramatisches Theater* found among theatre people right from the start. Nevertheless, this critique accompanied the book's immediate reception like a constant chorus for roughly a decade following its publication in 1999. Then these voices quietened down a lot, especially since the book was a success in Germany. This was paralleled by an unexpectedly intense resonance in a multiplicity of divergent milieus of theatre discourse and practice: Latin America and the US, Russia as well as Eastern Europe, even in Iran and India. Kai Tuchmann's book deals with one especially fascinating aspect of this worldwide reception: the resonance *Postdramatisches Theater* found in East Asia.

In fact, the Japanese version was the first translation, even before the French, and Li Yinan's Chinese translation came out only a few years later. This translation was welcomed by young Chinese theatre people, though there was also a certain academic resistance towards the book. (I remember the moment in Shanghai Theatre Academy on my first visit to China, where I taught about *Rimini Protokoll* and all the students were very interested. But after the lecture two teachers from the Academy came to me and said: "But this is only presentation—not representation.")

Li Yinan has played a great role in the reception of postdramatic theatre. She even introduced some of the pedagogical aspects of Germany's Giessen School to China, thereby expressing guiding principles for postdramatic theatre practice that have given rise to interesting debates and changes. One was the tendency to stay close to the real of experiences in society. The notion of the "real" here should not be mistaken for the concept of realism, but rather has everything to do with a

Lacanian notion of the Real: that which evades both the symbolic structure and the imaginary. So even Hans-Werner Kroesinger, for example, and his documentation of the real, digs into the underground of the society. It is less his intention to inform the spectator at the level of consciousness, but rather to create an awareness of the Real, which is always concealed.

Another important element is of course the dimension of the political. Wherever postdramatic theatre is held, debate is created. Postdramatic theatre took on the role of opposition to depoliticized theatre. But soon it became clear that theatre as such cannot be judged as politics. It remains true that theatre is never directly political, it has a specific relation to the political dimension. This dimension is carried out in postdramatic theatre essentially by opening theatre space to the audience—thus redefining theatre as something that is not representation for spectators but an event created with the spectators. In this respect, the artists, many of them groups, have displayed remarkable creativity in developing postdramatic dramaturgies. I here allow myself to adapt the definition given by Kai Tuchmann, who understands dramaturgy not as a traditional craft of adapting drama to the stage but rather a practice and a theory for enlarging, opening, and transforming the theatre.

Hans-Thies Lehmann
Athens, October 2021

I
POSTDRAMATIC RESONANCE
BETWEEN EUROPE AND ASIA

Introduction

Kai Tuchmann

> From the clay of life abandoned on the ground grow no lofty trees, only wild grass. [...]
>
> Wild grass strikes no deep roots, has no beautiful flowers and leaves, yet it imbibes dew, water and the blood and flesh of the dead [...]. As long as it lives it is trampled upon and mown down, until it dies and decays.
>
> But I am not worried; I am glad. I shall laugh aloud and sing.
>
> Lu Xun, Wild Grass

The contributions to this publication originate in the *Beijing Topography* project, which was held under my co-direction at the Faculty of Dramaturgy and Applied Theatre at the Central Academy of Drama in Beijing in the winter semester of 2018/19. The *Beijing Topography* project, initiated by Li Yinan, gives BA Dramaturgy students the task of exploring the past and present of Beijing. The project promotes the general goal of understanding how theatre performances can be generated from real materials. I invited several Asian and European artists who are pioneers of the postdramatic theatre in their specific theatre landscapes and have worked in this field for decades. I asked them to give our students an insight into their work and working methods in the form of impulse lectures, panels, and workshops. At the center of every invitation stood my request to the artists to share the fundamental convictions underlying their dramaturgies and working methods. Most of the invited artists began their seminars with introductory lectures and then presented and commented on some of their most influential works. They encouraged the students to conduct their own experiments along the lines of the questions posed in the *Beijing Topography* project and evaluated the students' scenic experiments together with them. The structure of the project is reflected in the form of the contributions published here. Most of the invited artists are represented by a transcription of their opening lecture (together with a video link) and a script of a performance piece that is representative of their approach. It is essential to be aware that the latter are not classical drama texts and that they thus only acquire their actual function when performed.

By making these lectures public, I wish to provide a broader audience with a unique insider's impression of postdramatic theatre's artistic thinking and working methods together with a sense of the variety of its manifestations.

The theatre-thinking of all the invited theatre-makers originates from a dramaturgical impulse because it has been developed, defended, and matured *against* the established theatre landscapes in their countries. These works utilize one dramaturgical field of action in particular: the development of performance situations.[1] This is an original dramaturgical activity that deals with the questions of who gathers where, with whom, and—above all—how. Each performance creates a theatrical public sphere in its specific way,[2] one whose members are produced by the design of the performance situation. The works of the artists collected in this book are typified by the utilization of this ephemeral theatrical public performance sphere to de-familiarize the everyday public sphere, which is constituted through media representations of social and political processes. This everyday public sphere is considered less as a place than a specific set of rules that individuals who want to appear and act publicly must fulfill and reproduce. These rules are de-familiarized through the performance situations of the works represented in this volume.

The development of performance situations is one of the most important fields of dramaturgical activity, especially if, like us at the Beijing Dramaturgy Department, one understands dramaturgy as an artistic practice primarily concerned with expanding the possibilities of theatre. The permanent search for extensions of our understanding of theatre differentiates dramaturgy from the practice of directing, which rather tries to exert effects on an audience derived from an already existing canon of performance and reception.

One thing the artists presented in this book have in common is that all their works seek to break the cycle of reality construction, within which "nature" and "history" are constantly confused. By such a motion, their theatre produces aesthetic procedures that grasp reality in a complex way that classical dramatic theatre cannot create. The theatre-makers presented here do not stop at a mere gesture of deconstructing reality but rather attempt to turn beyond it—towards the fragile and non-subsumable particular of the lived experience. This attempt

---

1   The theatre scholar Jochen Kiefer argues for a conception of dramaturgy as a practice that expands the possibilities of theatre and encompasses five fields of action. In addition to the mentioned practice of developing performance situations, Kiefer also lists narration, economics, curation, and knowledge critique as dramaturgical fields of action. Cf. Jochen Kiefer, "Re-Vision Dramaturgie" (Zurich, February 21, 2019).

2   Cf. Christopher B. Balme, *The Theatrical Public Sphere* (Cambridge: Cambridge University Press, 2014).

resonates with the program of postdramatic theatre, as described and developed by Hans-Thies Lehmann in his 1999 publication *Postdramatisches Theater*.³ The non-mimetic approaches towards reality discussed in Lehmann's book became the starting point for the experiments of numerous theatre-makers and theatre-thinkers in Europe and Asia. While the book has meanwhile been translated into many languages, the 2002 Japanese translation of *Postdramatisches Theater* by Michiko Tanigawa and Masaya Honda was among the first. It came out even before the English translation by Karen Jürs-Munby in 2006. The Chinese translation by Li Yinan appeared only four years later, in 2010. It has become a point of reference for all those theatre-makers and theatre-thinkers who felt not entirely at home in their national aesthetics, which have been strongly influenced by Western-style mimetic theatre.

Initially, postdramatic theatre grew out of a critique of the dramatic assumption that reality can be unambiguously depicted, narrated, and morally evaluated. This dramatic assumption and the theatre that emerges from it, stretching from Aristotle to Hegel, has set up a particular regime of representation and dramatic literature that historically has privileged certain artistic strategies and political perspectives in unambiguous ways. Thus, most drama has been constructed and performed from the center of a heteronormative, Western-colonial gaze, which expresses itself in a dramaturgy that centers around the conflicts of dramatic characters. The postdramatic dramaturgies of the works presented here attempt to break free of this assumption and its techniques—and to do so in different places and times. For this very reason, they have been produced outside the mainstream, and are usually associated with the foundation of their own groups, new forms and modes of production, and the emergence of their very own audience structure.

By archiving the lectures given at the Central Academy of Drama in Beijing, this volume seeks to show that the concept of postdramatic theatre is not a static one. Rather, it changes over time and is also highly dependent on its translation into the specific situations of different theatre cultures. Dramaturgy is of decisive importance for this translation process, since it is essentially identical to expanding the possibilities of theatre.

As dramaturgy scholar Jochen Kiefer points out, such an emphatic understanding of dramaturgy appears for the first time in Lessing's *Hamburgische Dramaturgie* (Hamburg Dramaturgy), in which "dramaturgy" becomes a signifier for a theatre that has yet to be developed. Lessing's aim in setting up a discourse around an entity he called "dramaturgy" was to turn actors into independent artists who critically distance themselves from the prevailing rules of the drama and performance canon. Thus, even at this early stage, dramaturgy is already closely interlinked with performativity and can therefore not exclusively be related to

---

3 Hans-Thies Lehmann, *Postdramatisches Theater* [Postdramatic Theatre] (Frankfurt/Main: Verlag der Autoren, 1999).

how theatre texts are constructed. Saying this is not to deny the existence of dramaturgies before Lessing's *Hamburgische Dramaturgie*. But these belonged rather to the world of poetics, and their primary purpose was the codification of certain narrative patterns.[4] With Lessing, however, dramaturgy emerges as an independent realm of artistic thinking that starts precisely with the absence of any poetological rules. Dramaturgy is no longer the reflection of an existing *dispositif* but rather transforms itself into one.[5] Dramaturgy, as I understand it, is an action that expresses itself in the practices of narration (selection and montage of materials, discourses, and texts) and the development of performance situations. These dramaturgical practices are then aligned with the needs of the respective theatre form in which they are situated. Thus, roughly speaking, dramatic, epic, and postdramatic theatre each have their very specific modes of narration and performance development. Particularly in dramatic theatre, but also in epic theatre, the development of performance situations is not the focus of dramaturgical activity, since both strongly adhere to the classical proscenium situation (often parodied in German as the *Guckkastenbühne* or "peep-show theatre") and display of dramatic characters as a means of theatrical communication. By contrast, postdramatic theatre, because of its explicit emphasis on the reality generated between spectators and performers in the course of a performance, is permanently required to reflect on and experiment with the performance situation. Since the works and lectures gathered here repeatedly problematize theatre as a site of visualization as much as the idea of drama based on dramatic characters, the works of the artists presented here can be described as postdramatic dramaturgies.

With this collection, I wish to provide the framework for exploring the resonance that postdramatic dramaturgy has created between Europe and Asia.

On the Structure of this Book

The book is divided into three sections. The **first section** sets out to unpack the resonance of the postdramatic theatre. It contains the panel discussion ***Rethinking Theatricality—A Conversation on Postdramatic Theatre and the Chinese Juchang***, held on October 13, 2018, at the Goethe Institute Beijing and Li Yinan's essay ***Hans-Thies Lehmann's Postdramatic Theatre and the New Aesthetics of Juchang***. These two texts point to the resonance that the translation of Lehmann's *Postdramatisches Theater* has had on Chinese theatre scholarship.

---

4   Kiefer thus suggests reading these earlier dramaturgies "as representations of prevailing social *dispositif*." He defines the concept of the *dispositif*, in reference to Foucault, as a network between heterogenous elements, which encompasses linguistic and non-linguistical realms, such as discourses, institutions, laws, philosophies, etc. Cf. Jochen Kiefer, "Re-Vision Dramaturgie" (Zurich, February 21, 2019).

5   Cf. Jochen Kiefer, "Re-Vision Dramaturgie" (Zurich, February 21, 2019).

The **second section** includes the artists' lectures, which are followed by a script representative of their work, supplemented with a QR code linking to a video excerpt. Since Wen Hui gave a physical dance workshop instead of a lecture, the script of her dance piece *RED* is not introduced by means of a lecture but rather followed by a postscript written by the author of *RED*, Zhuang Jiayun.[6]

Since none of the materials in this section have been published before, I aim to place the foundation stone of an archive of postdramatic resonance between the German-speaking theatre landscape and that of Asia. Of course, such an archive will be a living one, and the resonances have already started to reinforce themselves mutually. Productions of Wen Hui's *RED*, Zhao Chuan's *World Factory*, and Kyung Sung Lee's *Love Story* are touring worldwide. In addition, students of the *Beijing Topography* seminar have now started to pursue their MA degrees in Europe. Among them is Gao Yinfu, who studies at the Institute for Applied Theatre Studies of the Justus Liebig University Giessen. These performances and students will alter the initial sound of the postdramatic.

Since the discourses about theatre and its relationship to reality are in constant flux, the materials collected here cannot be more than a still image from a certain place at a particular time. However, to deal with this situatedness, this book's **third and final section** invites its key contributors to reflect on their lectures and works at a temporal distance. To this end, I asked them in May 2021 to reevaluate their contributions from 2018. This final conversation, titled ***Shame and Power. A Critical Conversation on the Postdramatic Condition***, explores how the postdramatic aesthetic itself is subject to changing interpretations. Through an algorithmically controlled digitization of our communication, common reference points of reading and understanding reality are becoming more and more contested. Under this quite new condition, contemporary configurations of the postdramatic tend to overemphasize the role of the individual—often by highlighting the performer's identity as the only possible framework of meaning. This anthology seeks to intervene in the course of this development by archiving modes of postdramatic theatre dramaturgies that still value the idea of difference. Only through this approach of difference can a theatre refer to what is not there: the dead, the other, the past, the future. This perspective of difference is essential for facilitating an aesthetics that allows the audience's perception to swing back and forth between the irreducible individual *and* reality—as something historically grown and thus something that is contingent and alterable.

To ease the reader's access to the lectures and scripts printed here, I will now introduce each artist and their work with a specific focus on what kind of relationship the dramaturgies of the discussed performances have with the

---

6   The production *RED* is the result of an intensive collaboration between the performers and the other production participants, who lived and worked together at the *Living Dance Studio* in Beijing during a large part of the rehearsals. The original credits for this production identify Wen Hui as its choreographer, Zhuang Jiayun as its author, and Kai Tuchmann as its dramaturg.

postdramatic paradigm. In particular, I will highlight how their working method-
ologies and aesthetics are situated in the (recent) history of their theatre
landscapes and how their underlying dramaturgies set out to develop performance situations that intervene in the routines of the public sphere. In the second
part of this introduction, I will give a very brief overview of the emergence of
postdramatic theatre in Germany and the context of its resonances in China.

CONTRIBUTORS

Zhao Chuan, born in 1967, is one of the most important *juchang* theatre-makers
in China. His lecture ***There Is No Empty Space on Earth*** was held on November
6, 2018, at the Dramaturgy and Applied Theatre Faculty of the Central Academy
of Drama in Beijing. This was the first time that he had conducted a seminar in a
Chinese state-run theatre academy. In his lecture, Zhao Chuan described the guiding ideas underlying the work of his theatre collective *Grass Stage* (*Caotaiban*),
which is an independent amateur theatre group that has been operating in Shanghai since 2005. Their theatre performances are created under simple conditions
and with limited financial means. Since the collective was founded, it has been
engaged in creative work in a range of alternative spaces, where it has given free
performances and held discussions. Over the years, *Grass Stage* performances and
other artistic projects have become meeting points for people from different social milieus; they represent a public space that is constantly in motion. This
artistic flexibility in dealing with space is one of the most outstanding features of
Grass Stage. The change of performance venues typical of the collective has to do,
on the one hand, with their idea of bringing theatre to communities away from
the large and developed cities of the east coast, and on the other hand, the refusal
to perform within institutionalized theatres is the only way to undermine the censorship system, to the degree that this is possible. An important term in the
context of Zhao's approach to theatre is "post-performance theatre". This concept,
coined by Zhao, means that the discussion that also unfolds within the audience
after the performance has the quality of a play itself. One could say that Zhao conceives *Grass Stage* performances as a trigger for these discussions between its
audience members.[7] The production of a discursive public sphere in the works of
Zhao Chuan thus becomes a counterweight to consumerism, which is currently
being transfigured in the form of the ideology of the *Chinese Dream* as propagated
by Xi Jinping. Since the amateurs in the cultural sector are freed from this production order, they have the opportunity to renegotiate hegemonies. It is this
opportunity that the theatre of Zhao Chuan wants to make radical use of. Thus

---

7   Cf. Zhao Chuan and Tao Qingmei, "Feldmanöver," [Field manoeuvre] *Theater der Zeit*,
    2015/12 (2015). See also Zhao Chuan, "There Is No Empty Space on Earth" in this volume.

one could speak of his theatre as an amateur practice with the aim of awaking from the *Chinese Dream*.

As a theatre-maker who is working in Shanghai and has many international contacts, Zhao Chuan is repeatedly confronted with the canonical thinking of the European theatre avant-gardes. Moreover, their concepts are often copied without hesitation in the institutions of the Chinese cultural industry. In his contribution, Zhao Chuan sharply criticizes the basic assumptions of Eugenio Barba's theatrical anthropology and Peter Brook's idea of an empty space. He sees in them the expression of a typical Western theatre of the 1980s that appropriates non-European theatre cultures to produce aesthetic innovations. Above all, Zhao Chuan refuses the construction of a universal performative body that lacks historical and social dimensions—something that is constitutive of Barba's theatre anthropology. Criticism of the same de-historicizing premise of human socialization lets Zhao also reject Brook's concept of an empty space. The central theme of the theatre Zhao Chuan creates is precisely the filling of spaces with experience and history and the constant struggle for public spaces. He contrasts the utopian ideas of an empty space and a timeless human expressiveness with his concrete way of working, which has developed from collective production to a process that focuses especially on the individual and contradictory solos of the group members. This method, which Zhao Chuan calls the "comprehensive method," is characterized by the fact that it does not reconcile the conflicting solo performances of the group members into a single narrative but combines them in such a way that a complex panorama of Chinese society becomes visible.

Aesthetically, *Grass Stage* attempts to revive, among other things, the performative aspects of the marginalized traditional Chinese opera. Recently, *Grass Stage* has also been experimenting more and more with circus-like techniques.

World Factory (*Shijie gongchang*) is one *of Grass Stage's* most important productions. It critically intervenes in the foundational myth of the Chinese Republic, according to which the workers are an essential element of the nation and its history. By focusing on the living conditions of migrant workers, the production questions the actuality of this foundational myth. At the beginning of their research for *World Factory*, Zhao Chuan and *Grass Stage* gave theatre workshops for the Foxconn workers in Shenzhen, which has given rise to a number of Foxconn worker theatre groups that continue to operate and self-organize to this day.

The starting point of the production was Zhao Chuan's visit to the city of Manchester, formerly known as the "World Factory," and his assumption that although capitalism has entered the age of consumerism more than 200 years after its emergence, the phenomenon of the "World Factory" has not yet disappeared.

To develop the performance of *World Factory*, *Grass Stage* used, in addition to the workshops already mentioned, a variety of classic documentary sources, from historical and sociological material to first-person testimonials, such as the personal story of *Grass Stage* member Wu Jiamin, who is one of the tens of millions of children who left their rural homes to find a paid job in urban industry. The staging and design of the script are not limited to the gesture of presenting documents. Rather the classical strategies of documentary theatre are complemented by other theatrical means, ranging from clown play to revue-like musical numbers and Beijing *xiqu* opera parodies.

The spirit of collaboration directly impacted the performance situation of the Shenzhen showcase of *World Factory*, which was held in November 2014 at the OCAT Contemporary Art Terminal in Shenzhen as part of a symposium organized by Zhao Chuan. The performances of *World Factory* were attended not just by the usual middle-class theatre-going public and students from the local university, but also by the very workers from Foxconn who participated in the workshops.

Since 2010, Foxconn, the company that does much manufacturing for Western companies such as Apple, has repeatedly been mentioned in connection with instances of suicide among its workers, who are often poorly paid migrant workers and students. Right at the beginning of this performance, two clowns enter the stage, grotesquely exaggerating the suicides of the Foxconn workers. One of the two clowns slips into the role of the (invented) psychology professor Lü, who evaluates the psychological resilience of Foxconn workers and makes prognoses about how many of them will commit suicide in a given period. The Shenzhen showcase exemplify the strong *juchang*[8] quality of Zhao Chuan's work, which is almost always aimed at creating temporary public spaces rather than simply presenting the group's latest theatre works. If one further considers Zhao Chuan's conception of performance as a trigger for what he calls "post-performance theatre," *World Factory* is decidedly about creating a performance situation in which theatre-goers of different classes are supposed to meet: The class of the middle bourgeoisie, significant for the Chinese cultural industry, confronted with the migrant workers, otherwise banished from society's sight. The performance situation of *World Factory* thus offers a possibility of confrontation and dialogue between these classes that does not occur in the protocols of everyday public life. However, I would like to point out that the political circumstances that led to the symposium in Shenzhen were extremely favorable. Nowadays, censorship and other state interventions into the work of Zhao Chuan (and other Chinese *juchang* theatre-makers) have become more frequent.[9]

---

8   For the concept of *juchang*, see Li Yinan "Hans-Thies Lehmann's Postdramatic Theatre and the new aesthetics of *juchang*" in this volume.

9   For example, guest performances curated by *Grass Stage* in Beijing planned for the spring of 2019 by Foxconn workers' theatre troupes, which were established in the course of the work on *World Factory* and were directed by *Grass Stage* members, could not be shown there. This probably has to do with the interest of the authorities in keeping the degree of organization of non-governmental workers' organizations as low as possible and, above all, in preventing them from forming networks between different cities.

Hans-Werner Kroesinger and Regine Dura have been working together since 2000 and are considered among the most important independent documentary theatre-makers in Germany. They were both invited to the Central Academy of Drama, but Regine Dura had to cancel her participation at the last moment. Given the permanence and intensity of their collaboration, however, Kroesinger and Dura are nevertheless consistently discussed here as an artistic duo. Their productions are created after extensive material research, undertaken together with their actors as part of play development, on topics such as the genocide in Rwanda, the European border agency Frontex, and the South-Eastern European front of the First World War.

To this book, Kroesinger/Dura contribute the lecture *How to Work With Things That Really Happened,* which provides a detailed description of the techniques and contexts of the documentary theatre play *Q&A—Questions & Answers,* which Kroesinger made in 1996, and which was completely based on documents related to the Eichmann Trial. This lecture about the foundation of their documentary way of working is deepened by the script of their joint work *Stolpersteine Staatstheater.* [10]

Hans-Werner Kroesinger was born in Bonn in 1962. He studied drama, theatre, and media from 1983 to 1988 with Andrzej Wirth and Hans-Thies Lehmann at the Institute for Applied Theatre Studies of the Justus Liebig University Giessen. While still a student, Kroesinger began working as assistant director and dramaturg to Robert Wilson, who held a guest professorship at the Giessen Institute. Another formative encounter for Kroesinger was with Heiner Müller, who also taught as a guest professor in Giessen. Kroesinger worked as an artistic collaborator in Müller's legendary 1989 production of *Hamlet/Hamletmaschine* at the Deutsches Theater in East Berlin. This production is significant, not least because the state of the GDR dissolved during its development. This intervention of reality and history in the rehearsal process had a lasting effect on Kroesinger's aesthetic search. In his 1996 work *Q&A—Questions & Answers,* which Kroesinger developed while he held a scholarship at the Akademie Schloss Solitude in Stuttgart, he succeeded in translating this search into his later typical style. This work also marks the revival of the tradition of documentary theatre in Germany and its continuation under the entirely new conditions of the turn of the century. Since then, he has directed his own productions at prestigious municipal and state-funded theatres and on the independent scene, above all at Hebbel am Ufer (HAU) in Berlin.

---

10 Stumbling blocks (Stolpersteine), also sometimes referred to as "stumbling stones," are gold paving or cobble stones set into the pavements of cities in Germany, Austria and throughout parts of Europe where the Nazis once ruled that mark where Jews and other victims of the National Socialists lived before being persecuted, transported to concentration or extermination camps and/or murdered. The project was initiated by the artist Gunter Demnig in 1992.

Regine Dura studied political science, theatre, film and media studies, German language and literature, and art education in Marburg and Frankfurt/Main. as well as video at the Berlin University of the Arts. Since 1996 she has been working as a freelancer in the field of feature and documentary film, including for the European Film Academy and Wim Wenders Produktion in Berlin. Kroesinger/ Dura's theatre projects usually focus on political issues and events—especially violent conflicts—and consider the role of theatre in such contexts to be one of facilitating negotiation within society.

Their work is deeply connected to questions that are constitutive to the discourse of history and their aesthetics follow the canonical definition of documentary theatre, as laid down by Erwin Piscator. For Piscator, documentary theatre is theatre in which "the political document forms the sole basis, both textually and scenically"[11] of the performance. Peter Weiss defined it in the same spirit:

> Documentary theatre is a theatre of reportage. Records, documents, letters, statistics, market-reports, statements by banks and companies, government statements, speeches, interviews [...] are the basis of the performance.[12]

Kroesinger/Dura's performances and dramaturgy deeply connect with the protocols and procedures of this tradition of documentary theatre, but they also alter them to a significant extent. In contrast to Piscator's and Weiss's theatre, the document is no longer exclusively regarded as a truthful and trustworthy account of the past but rather as something that co-produces the past to the same extent as it records it. From this perspective, Weiss's formulation of a documentary theatre that "presents authentic material unchanged in content but edited in form"[13] can no longer be maintained. Kroesinger/Dura articulate their doubt about the document's neutrality through the act of montage, which in their work always facilitates a bringing together of conflicting truth claims. In contrast to Peter Weiss's documentary theatre, in which various documents are assembled to generate *one* consistent (counter-)narrative of a historical issue, Kroesinger/Dura are concerned with developing a multi-perspective view on historical or current facts.

The disbelief in the document's capacity to represent the historical truth "as it was" is typical of representatives of the third period of documentary theatre.[14]

---

11 Erwin Piscator, *Das Politische Theater* [Political Theatre] (Berlin: Henschelverlag, 1968), 63. Translation by Kai Tuchmann.

12 Peter Weiss, "The Material and the Models: Notes Towards a Definition of Documentary Theatre," *Theatre Quarterly*, no. 1 (1971): 41.

13 Weiss, "The Material and the Models: Notes Towards a Definition of Documentary Theatre," 41.

14 Documentary theatre in Germany is divided into three periods. The first period is dated 1924–1929 and is closely linked to the works of theatre director Erwin Piscator. The second

While most of the third period theatre-makers, as a consequence of this disbelief in the document, have banished trained actors from their stages, Kroesinger/Dura stand out in so far as they are the only ones who vehemently adhere to the use of professionally trained actors. That is very much in contrast to the works of *Rimini Protokoll*, perhaps the most famous representatives of this third period, in whose works all actors are replaced by actual people ("experts of the everyday") who tell their personal stories on stage. The documentary truth claims in their works are thus usually limited and legitimized by the emphasis on the subjective perspective of the performers. Instead of textual documents, the individual bodies of the performers and their memories, stories, movements take the place of documents. Kroesinger/Dura, by contrast, want to demonstrate how precisely the linguistic composition of documents reflects power relations and constructions of reality. For this work on language, they need actors who can work out the linguistic peculiarities and argumentations of documents and offer them to the audience for critical reflection.

For their play **Stolpersteine Staatstheater**[15], commissioned by the Staatstheater Karlsruhe, and invited to the 2016 edition of Germany's most important theatre festival "Theatertreffen," Kroesinger/Dura have reconstructed the details of how anti-Semitic discrimination worked after 1933 from the personnel files of the Staatstheater Karlsruhe. Jewish actors, a Jewish prompter, and the artistic director were dismissed, arrested, driven into exile, or committed suicide in Karlsruhe. In this performance, actors sit together with the audience at a large work table and read files, newspaper reports, memoirs, and interviews with contemporary witnesses. Again and again, the actors enter and—after a short period—exit the characters they portray. The bureaucratic procedure that legally regulated social exclusion transforms the performance into a lesson about the functioning of state bureaucracy. The performance situation conceived by

---

period is dated 1963–1970 and is characterized by playwrights such as Rolf Hochhuth, Peter Weiss, and Heinar Kipphardt, whose works have in common a critical approach to German Nazi and post-war history. Documentary theatre reemerges in a third period around the turn of the millennium and is deeply linked with the works of Hans-Werner Kroesinger, She She Pop, and Rimini Protokoll. This third wave has been explicitly described as postdramatic in: Andreas Tobler, "Kontingente Evidenzen: Über Möglichkeiten Dokumentarischen Theaters," [Contingent Evidence. On the Possibilities of Documentary Theatre] in *Dokument, Fälschung, Wirklichkeit: Materialband zum Zeitgenössischen Dokumentarischen Theater* [Document, Fake, Reality. Materials of Contemporary Documentary Theatre], ed. Boris Nikitin, Carena Schlewitt and Tobias Brenk (Berlin: Theater der Zeit, 2014) 147-63.

15 Stumbling blocks (Stolpersteine), also sometimes referred to as "stumbling stones" are gold paving or cobble stones set into the pavements of cities in Germany, Austria and throughout parts of Europe where the Nazis once ruled that mark where Jews and other victims of the National Socialists lived before being persecuted, transported to concentration or extermination camps and/or murdered. The project was initiated by the artist Gunter Demnig in 1992.

Kroesinger/Dura in *Stolpersteine Staatstheater* transforms the history of the performance site into an essential element of the performance. The history of the Karlsruhe theatre's involvement in National Socialism, reconstructed from archival material, thus becomes an omnipresent frame for the encounter between spectators and performers, who meet in the very institution whose collaboration with the NS regime is elaborated in the performance. Dramaturgy thus also reveals itself here as a specific way of thinking about theatre art, in this case as a reflection on its history, since dramaturgy in German theatre owes much to the widespread introduction of dramaturgical offices at German municipal theatres during the Nazi period. These dramaturg positions were established with the sole purpose of bringing theatres into line with the Reich Ministry of Propaganda.[16] The selection of the play *Stolpersteine Staatstheater* for this book is also due to the fact that this production was invited to the 2017 edition of "Theatertreffen in China" and thus led to a strengthening of interest in documentary forms in Chinese theatre.[17]

At this point, it might be interesting to speak about the very different starting points of Kroesinger/Dura's and Wen Hui's documentary theatre. Kroesinger/ Dura's documentary theatre rejects the discourses on authenticity of the first two periods of German documentary theatre. Yet, the contemporary theatre-makers share with the practitioners of these two earlier periods their stock of material, which consists mainly of published texts from newspapers, essayistic articles, or archive material. Thus, the material backbone of Kroesinger/Dura's work consists of the products of the free press and freely accessible archives. Wen does not find this kind of material in the People's Republic of China. Her documentary theatre cannot be text-based, since neither counter-narratives nor multi-perspective reflections would arise from published texts in China. Archives are not easily accessible to the public in China either. Furthermore, the official relationship of the People's Republic to its history is a very special one: For example, in the opening ceremony of the 2008 Olympic Games, there is not a single reference to any event of the 20th century.[18] This absence of a published historical discourse almost inevitably leads to a preoccupation with personal and embodied histories, as these are the only freely accessible, uncontrolled archives in China. The two documentary approaches of Kroesinger/Dura and Wen thus stand almost crosswise to each other: Kroesinger/Dura are taking textual documents but believe in their

---

16 Cf. Evelyn Deutsch-Schreiner, *Theaterdramaturgien von der Aufklärung bis zur Gegenwart* [Theatrical Dramaturgies from the Enlightenment to the Presence](Köln: Böhlau Verlag, 2016).

17 The "Theatertreffen in China" was founded in 2016 as a cooperation between the Goethe-Institut China and the Berliner Festspiele. As part of this program, which is curated by experts from the culture sector, two to three productions from the Theatertreffen are invited to China each year.

18 I owe this observation to Peter Eckersall.

representational possibilities only to a limited extent, while Wen regards the body and its experiences as a document, and she follows its claim to truth without reservation.

Wen Hui was born in 1960 and is regarded worldwide as the leading representative of modern dance in China. She studied dance and choreography at the Beijing Dance Academy and was especially influenced by her collaborations in the 1990s with Trisha Brown and Pina Bausch. As a form of increased liveliness, her understanding of art is the focus of the *Living Dance Studio* (*Shenghuo Wudao Gong-zuoshi*) that she founded in 1994 in Beijing.

The documentary dance performance **RED** (*Hong*) serves as a paradigmatic example of Wen's theatrical approach. *RED* premiered on December 25, 2015, at Shanghai Power Station of Art and takes its point of departure from *The Red Detachment of Women,* which was one among the eight model operas (*yangbanxi*) during the time of the Cultural Revolution in China (1966–76).

The Red Detachment of Women takes place on the southern Chinese island of Hainan. It tells the story of the peasant girl Wu Qinghua, who is kept as a slave by the landowner Nanbatian. Wu manages to escape and joins the battalion of an army led by General Hong Changqing, which consists only of female soldiers. After some entanglements, the all-decisive battle between the women's battalion and Nanbatian's army takes place on the island. The battalion wins. It is worth mentioning that a battalion stationed on Hainan Island consisting exclusively of women very likely did exist in the 1930s. Liang Xin wrote a novel about this army, which again became the basis for a film adaptation under the personal aegis of Prime Minister Zhou Enlai. Novel and film were then the sources from which the plot of the ballet, which premiered in 1964, was assembled. Interesting discoveries can be made by comparing these different representations of history, such as the fact that the figure of a male commander of the Women's Army was only developed for the model opera version. *RED* has dealt with all these different historical representations of the material and has incorporated them in the rehearsal and staging process.

I want to give some brief remarks on the historical context and concept of the model opera, as they will deepen the understanding of an existing dramaturgy *avant la lettre* in mainland China. In 1963, in reaction to the de-Stalinization that was taking place in the Soviet Union under Khrushchev, Mao gave a speech in which he expressly warned against a "counter-revolutionary restoration" in China that would completely change China's essence and, of course, threaten his power base.[19] To counter this fear of China's "drifting" into capitalism, Mao, in the

---

19 Chen Xiaomei, "Performing the 'Red Classics.' From 'The East Is Red' to 'The Road to Revival'," in Li; Zhang, *Red Legacies in China*, Cultural Afterlives of the Communist Revolution (Leiden, Boston: Brill, 2016) 151.

same year, launched the socialist education campaign, whose battle cry was "Never forget class struggle!" This campaign became the starting point of cultural production on a massive scale, especially of works that were later called "Red Classics," such as *The East is Red* (*Dongfang Hong*, 1964) and *The Red Detachment of Women* (*Hongse Niangzi, Jun* also 1964). This state-controlled planning and execution of artistic production that goes hand in hand with the intertwining of political campaigns and cultural production can be very well described with the term "dramaturgy in the mode of policing" [*polizeiliche Dramaturgie*], a phrase coined by the theatre scholar Nikolaus Müller-Schöll.[20] Such dramaturgy safeguards narratives that privilege a few groups in society while simultaneously preventing the entry of certain other groups and their experiences into the public sphere. Opposed to such police dramaturgy is political dramaturgy that seeks to use theatre to change the dynamics of public space by initializing a new "distribution of the sensible".[21] Chinese theatre has been deeply affected by the approach of police dramaturgy since the founding of the People's Republic in 1949, as it has assured the state authorship and control over the products of the theatre. *RED* rejects this claim of police dramaturgy and sets out to use the production and performance of theatre to collect, interpret, and publish alternative perspectives on the Cultural Revolution.

The Cultural Revolution itself had one of its starting points in a controversy over Wu Han's play *Ha Rui Dismissed from Office*, which was published in 1961 and then read years later by Yao Wenyuan as a critical commentary on Mao's responsibility for the Great Famine. In defense of Mao, Yao published an article criticizing the play. This criticism led to the imprisonment of Wu Han and the first campaigns against so-called right-wing extremists. This circumstance alone shows how relevant theatre was in the political debates of the 20th century in China. The model operas that emerged from the Cultural Revolution probably reflect an attempt to regulate performances that was unprecedented in theatre history. The selection and dramaturgy of these model operas was carried out by Mao's wife Jiang Qing, who herself had been an important actress in the 1930s and who, in the context of the introduction of socially critical naturalism and spoken theatre in China, played the leading role in Ibsen's *Nora*, among others. The dramaturgy of these plays, typical of the Cultural Revolution, is based on the "Three Prominences" concept. This concept states that of all the characters, the positive ones should be emphasized; among these positive characters, in turn, those with a heroic character should be highlighted; and among the heroic characters, the most heroic figure should be emphasized. Overall, the dramaturgy of

---

20 Nikolaus Müller-Schöll, "Polizeiliche und politische Dramaturgie," [Policing and Political Dramaturgy] in *Postdramaturgien* [Postdramaturgies], ed. Sandra Umathum and Jan Deck (Berlin: Neofelis, 2020).

21 For a discussion of the concept of the political understood as a particular distribution of the sensible, see: Jacques Rancière, *The Politics of Aesthetics: The Distribution of the Sensible* (London: Continuum, 2011).

Revolutionary Model Theatre aims to create beautiful, fully developed worker-peasant-soldier figures. In terms of staging, the positive figures brought into focus by the dramaturgy should be further emphasized by being presented in the middle of the stage with full lighting. In contrast, the negative characters should be placed in the corners of the stage in the shadows.[22] The dramaturgy of the model opera was fixed. Acting, sets, and costumes were so detailed that they hardly offered the performers any room for improvisation.

It is important to emphasize that Chinese society in 1966–76 was largely a rural society, and that media such as radio and television were not widespread at that time. For ten years, therefore, the state-directed performance practice across the whole country, from urban factories to village communities, made these model operas the privileged tool of political propaganda and the cultural-ideological symbol of the Cultural Revolution period. It is estimated that 36 million people were sentenced alone in rural areas, of whom between 750,000 and 1.5 million were killed. The same number of people suffered life-long injuries during this time.[23] Phenomena of denunciation, self-incrimination rituals, and even public torture/killing characterized the public life of the Cultural Revolution, as shaped by the Red Guards. The Red Guards were usually composed of young urban men and women who had never experienced a political period other than Mao's China. Taking Mao's doctrine of the permanent revolutionization of all cultural institutions literally, these young people rebelled violently against any form of authority, both Confucianist and right-wing. It was thanks to the emergence of the Red Guards that Mao's rule could be maintained after his disastrous experiment of the so-called Great Leap Forward (1958–62).

In the decade after Mao's death in 1976, the Cultural Revolution became an important subject of literature, art, and cinema. Still, these unofficial historiographies of the arts always remained controlled by censorship and were therefore never able to deal with the essential questions of guilt and responsibility. The increasing criticism of the effects of China's market reforms under Deng then even prepared the ground for a posthumous Mao cult in the late 1980s and early 1990s, and commodification of the memory of the Cultural Revolution period began.[24] At the same time, the Central Propaganda Department in Beijing had explicitly prohibited the publication of further works on the Cultural Revolution. This has resulted in the absence of debate about the reasons for the Cultural Revolution, marked by censorship and commodification of memory.

RED opposes this absence of debate about the reasons for the Cultural Revolution by publicly discussing the different experiences of the performers. In

---

22 See the script of *RED* in this volume.

23 Cf. Andrew G. Walder and Yang Su, "The Cultural Revolution in the Countryside: Scope, Timing and Human Impact," *The China Quarterly*, no. 173 (2003).

24 Cf. Li Jie, "Introduction: Discerning Red Legacies in China," in Li; Zhang, *Red Legacies in China*, 3.

contrast to the Scar Literature[25] of the 1980s, however, the focus is not exclusively on the personal accounts of eyewitnesses but also includes how the time of the Cultural Revolution is interpreted in the cultural products of *The Red Detachment of Women* and their equivalents in popular culture. This question is all the more relevant because our current moment marks the time in which, in Aleida Assman's terms, the communicative memory of the Cultural Revolution is transformed into cultural memory.

The performance situation of *RED* is significantly shaped by the casting practices underlying the dance performance. Thus, with the dancer Liu Zhuying, who danced *The Red Detachment of Women* several hundred times during the Cultural Revolution, a person enters the stage whose specific experiences with the Cultural Revolution hardly receive any attention in today's China. In addition, Li Xinmin, a migrant worker, tells her life story by unfolding it in associative proximity to the title heroine of *The Red Detachment of Women*. In the context of this cast, Wen Hui's choreography technique is significant. It understands the dancer's body as an archive of forgotten stories and suppressed history—and attempts to tap into these memories to facilitate their public communication to an audience.

Despite all the influences of modern dance, Wen Hui's relationship to dance is strongly influenced by the physical imprint of Maoism on her body. She has talked about this ambivalent relationship to Maoism on several occasions.[26] For Wen Hui, this experience of a body that is the agent of her own identity and yet at the same time is always ideologically overwritten becomes the starting point and the aesthetic foundation for all her productions. Wen Hui tries to discover personal and social stories from her body and its memories. Her rehearsal design and theatre work are derived from exactly this understanding—diametrically opposed to the dramaturgy of the "Three Prominences." In the *Living Dance Studio*, the guiding principle is that no characters are embodied, no roles are played, and

---

25 The term *Scar Literature* refers to works written immediately after the Cultural Revolution, in which the crimes of the Cultural Revolution are settled/recounted. It is often claimed that the name for this literary movement is derived from the story *Scars* (*Shanghen*), by Lu Xinhua.

26 "Back in the 1960s and 1970s, it was a common sight for us kids to express our admiration and appreciation for various political leaders through our bodies; it was even a source of pride. As a kid, I remember, in our yard each morning and evening, young and old alike gathering around a portrait of Chairman Mao to pay our respects. After we gathered in front of that portrait and reflected on all the bad things we had done that day, we would then perform an affectionate song in Mao's honour. And that's how I began dancing, with this 'Loyalty Dance'. At that time in China, everyone danced more or less the same type of dance; there was no real distinction between the individual sense of body and the collective body [...] In other words, any sense of an individual body vanished." Wen Hui, "Female Memory Begins with the Body," in *The Body at Stake: Experiments in Chinese Contemporary Art and Theatre*, ed. Jörg Huber and Zhao Chuan (Bielefeld: transcript, 2013), 133.

therefore no one is highlighted. Everyone brings their identity, memory, and personality equally onto the stage. Performing means sharing the rehearsal experience with the audience.

The script of *RED* will be followed by the essay ***From the Red Detachment to the Women: A Postscript*** by the author of *RED*, **Zhuang Jiayun**. The impulse for this postscript was Zhuang's regret that the last part of *RED* "could not be developed as planned, due to inadequate initiatives, opportunity, budget, and rehearsal time". In her text, Zhuang especially highlights the feminist potential associated with the afterlife of *The Red Detachment of Women.*

Boris Nikitin, born in 1979 in Basel, where he is also currently based, is the son of Ukrainian-Slovakian-French-Jewish immigrants. He is active as a director within the international independent theatre scene and at German-language municipal theatres. As an author, director and essayist, he has been exploring the representation and production of identity and reality since he graduated from the Institute for Applied Theatre Studies in Giessen in 2008. His production *Hamlet* received the greatest acclaim and toured worldwide. Nikitin is also the founder and curator of the international festival "It's the real thing," which devotes itself to exploring documentary works. In his contribution, ***Don't Be Yourself. Notes on the Impossibility of the Documentary***, Nikitin is primarily concerned with how mutual observation generates reality in everyday life and theatre. I see Nikitin's aesthetic importance in the unique way his theatre criticizes and plays with what Roland Barthes calls "reality effects," which are a fundamental constituent of certain branches of documentary art. Barthes defined this notion, with regard to literature, as follows:

> By "effect of the real" I mean: language fading into the background, to be supplanted by a certainty of reality: language turning in on itself, burying itself and disappearing, leaving bare what it says.[27]

As characteristics of this transparency of linguistic signs, Barthes mentions their brevity and simplicity as they are given in the form of the *haiku*. Through its literary means, the *haiku* virtually forces the signified to flash. The reality effect is understood by Barthes as a specifically receptive experience: The certainty of an evident given. Applied to the theatre situation, the reality effect can be understood as a moment of reception in which the sign system of the theatre seems not to represent something else (a fictitious role, historical figure, place, etc.), but recedes in favor of "real" being (the concrete performer, this concrete place here and now, etc.). The relevant theatrical means of producing this reality effect are hardly different from the literary means discussed by Barthes in connection with

---

27 Roland Barthes, "February 17, 1979," in *The Preparation of the Novel: Lecture Courses and Seminars at the Collège De France, 1978–1979 and 1979–1980* (New York: Columbia University Press, 2011), 70.

the *haiku*: Brevity, simplicity, and above all, focus on details (not essential to the plot).[28] Therefore, in documentary theatre works, detailed accounts of intimacy are often shared between performers and spectators.

Nikitin's works create performance situations that intervene in the naïve belief in reality as something self-evident by displaying reality construction as an effect of perceptual biases. Nikitin expresses this very clearly when he puts documentary theatre and illusionary theatre in a surprisingly direct relationship:

> Every reality report reproduces its own premises. Premises and norms are collectively recognized fictions, which in their repetition create the illusion of reality. Precisely when documentary theatre claims to represent reality, it must be considered a radical form of illusion theatre, even more so than fictional theatre, in which the fictional character of what is shown and said is always revealed.[29]

So for Nikitin, there is no doubt that human perception, and thus aesthetic experience, is determined by social and historical factors. Therefore, reality effects are always socially and historically situated experiences and depend on a sensibility shared by the theatre-makers and the audience. It is this sociological foundation of perception and aesthetic experience around which Nikitin's theatre circles.

The premiere of **Hamlet** took place on September 24, 2016, at Kaserne Basel and it has since been performed over 60 times worldwide. *Hamlet* is not a retelling of Shakespeare's material but rather an attempt to develop a theatrical vision concerning identity, illness, and reality. At the center of this vision is the performer and electric musician Julia*n Meding, who, as the dazzling Hamlet figure, exposes themselves, their body, and biography to the audience's gaze. For the spectator, the central experience in *Hamlet* is usually one of initially rejecting Meding because their address is perceived as a never-ending, self-referential monologue by a weird, narcissistic person. According to Nikitin's statements, this beginning leads almost a third of the audience to mentally or even physically drop out of the evening. For the rest, after about 45 minutes, something gradually sets in that even they had not expected: Namely, empathy and identification. *Hamlet* stages a temporal experience that gradually turns something foreign into something familiar. The same reality—that of Meding—is experienced twice. *Hamlet*

---

28 In *The Reality Effect,* Barthes explicitly explores the narrative significance of the seeming insignificance of "*détails inutiles*" (useless details) as a means of constructing the reality effect. Cf. Roland Barthes, "The Reality Effect," in *The Rustle of Language* (Berkeley: University of California Press, 1989), 143.

29 Boris Nikitin, "Der unzuverlässige Zeuge: Zwölf Behauptungen über das Dokumentarische," [The Unreliable Witness. Twelve Assertions about the Documentary] in *Dokument, Fälschung, Wirklichkeit: Materialband zum Zeitgenössischen Dokumentarischen Theater* [Document, Fake, Reality. Materials of Contemporary Documentary Theatre], ed. Boris Nikitin, Carena Schlewitt and Tobias Brenk (Berlin: Theater der Zeit, 2014), 14. Translation by Kai Tuchmann.

intends to create permanent doubts about the authenticity of its performer and their biography.

Hamlet creates a performance situation that questions the general condition of the possibility of communication situations and investigates the dynamics of stepping into the public eye, the breaking of social taboos, and the vulnerability that arises when people start to make themselves visible and audible. It is not least a plea for a utopia of a vulnerability that is not a deficiency of being human but a revolutionary ability.

Lee Kyung-Sung was born in Basel in 1983 and studied directing at Chung-Ang University in Seoul before completing his postgraduate studies at the Central School of Speech and Drama in London. In 2007, he founded the theatre company *Creative VaQi* and has been its artistic director ever since. He and his troupe are among the most influential representatives of the "younger" South Korean theatre-makers that have increasingly drawn attention to themselves since the turn of the century. This generation has permanently shifted the coordinates of South Korean theatre by clearly breaking away from the questions and working methods of their predecessors, whose works were primarily determined by the struggle to reconcile the concept of drama imported from the West with traditional Korean performative practices, such as the *gut* (shamanic rites). Lee's artistic generation has replaced this approach, which revolves around one's own artistic identity, with a rigorous exploration of contemporary issues. Lee explains his artistic approach in his contribution **Practice of Theatre—Rehearsal of Life** and comments on some of his works, such as *Let Us Move Your Sofa* (2010), which deals with the commercialization and anonymization of Seoul's public space, and his examination of the Sewol ferry disaster in *Before After* in 2015. This work focuses not so much on a documentary re-enactment of the ferry disaster but rather on the question of how pain turns into narration and eventually ends up being a commodity. The tragedy, in which 304 people lost their lives in April 2014, becomes a starting point for investigating the specific vulnerability of the modern human condition, which results from its increasing entanglement with technological agencies. The production pays special attention to the impact the mass media's handling of such technological catastrophes has on the social consciousness. In *Before After,* a fundamental component of Lee's work becomes visible: It repeatedly deals with questions of the ethics of perception and representation—especially in the face of the pain of others.

Lee's first works took place at sites of everyday life, such as pedestrian crossings, public squares, and hotel rooms. Since the production *Namsan Documenta* in 2014, which was based on research into the history of the Namsan Arts Center, he has increasingly conceived his works for the more concentrated situation of the theatre. A salient characteristic of these works is the intensive research that the *Creative VaQi* collective undertakes in developing their plays. This research goes far beyond desk work. It almost always involves the entire ensemble and takes the form of long-term on-site visits. The impressions gained in this way are evaluated as autonomously as possible by the performers and processed aesthetically by them trying to develop a personal attitude to the material. In this way, the rehearsals become a process in which an attempt is made to work out the lines of connection between the different materials and the performers' views of them. The rehearsal thus becomes a method that is not concerned with developing a generalized reading but, on the contrary, with discovering the contradictions in the material and finding ways to let them coexist unreconciled. The aim is thus to produce a social panorama of contradictions rather than a smoothed-out reading. Lee understands his role as that of a mediator, which is very similar to Zhao Chuan's working method.

Love Story by Lee and his collective dates from 2018. It illustrates very well how the collective research work leads to the development of a performance piece. Moreover, *Love Story* shows how Lee never relies merely on the reality effect but always irritates or intensifies it through revealed acts of imagination and fiction.

Love Story tells the stories of relationships among North/South Korean couples from the time when South Korean companies were still operating in the Kaesong Industrial Complex. The Kaesong Industrial Region in North Korea served as a symbol of collaborative economic development with South Korea. In 2016, this park was closed in protest against a North Korean missile launch, and all South Korean companies had to leave. The play tells the story of the suddenly separated tragic couples, who are also a symbol for the situation of the two Koreas. Developed from research and interviews with South Korean businesspeople, among others, the play attempts to bridge the irreducible distance between the couples and states by means of the imagination. A central aspect of this is the invention of North Korean characters with whom the audience is supposed to empathize on a personal level. To do this, the cast members have developed a performance style that constantly enters and exits the characters to provide information about how their background knowledge of the characters was researched and where their own fantasies were incorporated into the performance.

The performance situation of Love Story is that the South Korean actors demonstrate to their audience in South Korea how they imagine their neighbors in North Korea. The transformation of the actors into their North Korean characters is revealed, and the research underlying this acting process is also made visible. Through this performance situation, which relies on strong alienation effects, the very mechanism of projecting oneself onto the other is made visible and placed in the context of the South's North Korea policy.

RESONANCES

In physics, the term resonance (from Latin *resonare*: to reverberate) refers to the relationship between two bodies, where one excites the other to vibrate. The essence of the resonance phenomenon is that the reverberation of this other body takes place in its *own* frequency. Resonance is therefore a response to another *expressed in a body's own frequency*, as opposed to an echo, where the body would reverberate in the same frequency of the body that excited it.

This volume aims to depict a specific theatrical resonance by tracing how the ideas of the postdramatic and dramaturgy stimulated the theatre scenes in Korea and, especially, in mainland China. I will show that the institutional and aesthetic beginnings of discourses around dramaturgy and postdramatic theatre in China and Germany are closely interwoven.

When it comes to postdramatic theatre in China, the Faculty of Dramaturgy and Applied Theatre at the Central Academy of Drama in Beijing is the driving force of its practice. Li Yinan founded the faculty in 2015 and oriented it from the beginning towards a German model of dramaturgy that would work radically on expanding the possibilities of theatre. That is very much in contrast to the Anglo-Saxon understanding of the dramaturg, which is identified with the figure of a literary manager. Since Li, as the translator of Lehmann's book into Chinese,[30] introduced the concept of postdramatic theatre into the Chinese theatre discourse, postdramatic dramaturgy played a leading role in the faculty from the very beginning. This concept of a specifically postdramatic dramaturgy has been translated into Chinese theatre studies and theatre practice by Li with the term *juchang*. *Juchang* has thus become the central term of resonance of the postdramatic in China. Li originally established the term in the course of her translation of Hans-Thies Lehmann's *Postdramatisches Theater*. In 2010, she translated the title and term as *Houxiju Juchang*. The word *juchang*, which was neglected in mainland Chinese theatre studies at the time, served primarily as a counter-term to the established term for drama, *xiju*. The term *juchang* thus had the purpose of pointing to the dimension of theatricality/performativity. Since then, Li and I have also repeatedly emphasized the dramaturgical practices of narration and the development of performance situations as crucial aspects of *juchang* within our artistic and academic activities. In this regard, certain Chinese theatre-makers working since the late 1990s, such as Wen Hui and Zhao Chuan, have been a particularly prominent point of reference for us. Our pedagogy results from an experiment with a certain form of German theatre that has resonated with artists, scholars, and students from China.

In physics again, resonance can also lead to mutual amplification of vibration, and in fact, such amplification of postdramatic thought is what has been going on

---

30 Hans-Thies Lehmann, *Houxiju Juchang* [Postdramatic Theatre] (Beijing: Beijing daxue chuban she [Beijing University Press], 2010).

in the last decade between Europe and Asia. The appropriation of postdramatic dramaturgical thought by Asian theatre-makers will surely significantly alter the sound of postdramatic practice in the world.

Postdramatic Theatre in Germany

The beginning of the institutionalization of postdramatic theatre in the German-speaking world is, on the one hand, linked to the revival of the genre of documentary theatre in the 1990s and, on the other hand, to the foundation of the Institute for Applied Theatre Studies at the Justus Liebig University Giessen in 1982 by Andrzej Wirth and Hans-Thies Lehmann. Lehmann highlighted the Institute's basic aesthetic assumptions in dialogue with a detailed analysis of avant-garde theatre in the 1980s and 1990s in his publication *Postdramatisches Theater* in 1999. It is no coincidence that the representatives of the latest period of documentary theatre in Germany are mostly graduates of the Giessen Institute for Applied Theatre Studies. This Institute has made a significant contribution to expanding the formal language of classical documentary theatre. This can be traced back to the specific research practiced at the Giessen Institute, which sought to discover "theatre forms beyond drama and beyond acting".[31] This research approach was accompanied by an absence of actors and classical theatre repertoire during training. The students in Giessen were therefore referred back to themselves as material and performers from the very beginning, and they experimented early on with alternative forms of text and authorship. Schlewitt and Brenk write about the methods used by the students of the Giessen Institute:

> Early on, experiments were carried out with documentary material, among other things; pieces were developed on the basis of specially collected interview material; the students, as performers, used their biographies as material. Rimini Protokoll's theatre, which can function entirely without actors, is rooted in the structures of the Giessen rehearsal stage.[32]

This educational practice explains the paradigmatic concept of the body as an archive of personal memory that took the place that documents had in the classical documentary theatre of Piscator and Weiss.

These developments, strongly connected to changes in theatre education, have found buyers in the theatre market and have thus been able to spread. In the Berlin HAU under the directorship of Matthias Lilienthal (2003–2012), the grad-

---

31 Boris Nikitin, Carena Schlewitt, and Tobias Brenk, "Vorwort," [Preface] in *Dokument, Fälschung, Wirklichkeit: Materialband zum Zeitgenössischen Dokumentarischen Theater* [Document, Fake, Reality. Materials of Contemporary Documentary Theatre], ed. Boris Nikitin, Carena Schlewitt and Tobias Brenk (Berlin: Theater der Zeit, 2014) 8. All translations by Kai Tuchmann.

32 Nikitin, Schlewitt and Brenk, "Vorwort," 8.

uates of the Giessen school have found a production and performance venue that has effectively implemented their new way of dealing with reality. Lilienthal's dictum of the "hysterical addiction to reality"[33] has been the programmatic guideline that has bound groups and artists such as Hans-Werner Kroesinger, Rimini Protokoll, She She Pop, and Boris Nikitin to itself for a long time. The networking of production sites on the independent scene then led to a multiplication of these forms. In addition to the HAU, this network consists of TAT (Frankfurt/Main), Mousonturm (Frankfurt/Main), Kampnagel (Hamburg), Podewil Berlin, Sophiensäle (Berlin), FFT (Düsseldorf), and Gessnerallee (Zurich) as well as a diverse range of festivals. However, this narrative only represents one (if probably the most powerful) line of tradition in Germany's younger postdramatic theatre. Since then, new theatre schools such as Hildesheim have joined the Giessen Institute. Furthermore, the history of theatre in the GDR also provided important impulses for the development of postdramatic theatre. In the production *Dreamland* (*Traumland,* 1985), the East Berlin theatre group *Zinnober* presented their dreams—after months of dealing with them—as a personal document, an "imprint" of their subjective state of mind with all the anxieties typical of GDR society.[34]

The presence of postdramatic theatre on the stages of the independent theatre scene in the last twenty years has also had a major impact on the German municipal theatre system (*Stadttheater*). This influence is manifested in the rapid increase in documentary procedures and the exploration of new ways of collaborating, such as play development (*Stückentwicklung*). The critique of representation, which is constitutive of postdramatic theatre, is also moving into the municipal theatre system, which is reflected in the increase in debates about diversity and inclusion in theatre.

One can conclude that in Germany, postdramatic theatre works have long since found their way out of the independent scene and embarked on a march through the institution that eventually will lead to new hybrid forms. Even the aesthetics of realism, and the ways of acting based on it, have been lastingly changed by the arrival of postdramatic theatre in Germany.

Dramaturgy in China

Dramaturgy *avant la lettre* in China started already with the *Movement for a New Culture* (*Xin wenhua yundong*), which was active in the 1910s and 20s. The movement's affection for and involvement with Western spoken theatre was an important building block for the modernization movement in China. As early as 1918, the movement dedicated a special issue of its journal to Ibsen's realism. Further important marks in the development of dramaturgical practice in China

---

33 Nikitin, Schlewitt and Brenk, "Vorwort," 11.
34 Cf. Nikitin, Schlewitt and Brenk, "Vowort," 7.

are Mao's *Talks at the Yanan Forum on Literature and Art* in May 1942, as well as the activities of Tian Han after the founding of the republic in 1949 and eventually the theatrical practice of the model operas (*yangbanxi*) in the Cultural Revolution. In all these cases, as with Lessing, dramaturgy can be understood as a *dispositif* that, after the collapse of the rules of art of the imperial era, attempts to redefine the relationship between art, war, revolution, and people. Shanghai theatre scholar William Sun also assumes the existence of a dramaturgy *avant la lettre* in China in his article "Official and Unofficial Dramaturgs: Dramaturgy in China." However, he dates its beginnings a little later, with the foundation of the state in October 1949:

> It [dramaturgy] was badly needed by the new regime eager to overhaul the entire theatre system. Without knowing the term "dramaturgy," or the exact meaning of the word, they usually set up an office, or a department called the Artistic Office or Office of Artistic Creation, into which they assigned playwrights, directors, and critics/editors.[35]

In this context, the activity of the playwright Tian Han, who headed the Bureau of Chinese Opera Improvement shortly after the founding of the People's Republic, is of particular importance. Mao commissioned Tian Han to reform the Chinese Opera. This project, which is enormous in significance and scope, made Tian's activity very influential. Sun describes him as China's chief dramaturg and compares his work with that of Goethe at the court of Weimar. However, during the Cultural Revolution, Tian Han was politically persecuted, and he died in prison in 1968. After the end of the Cultural Revolution, developments from the pre-revolutionary period were revived, and the decision-making authority then united in Tian Han was decentralized. The chief dramaturgy of China, formerly linked to his person,

> has been loosely taken over by various Chinese Communist Party (CCP) and government officials. Their work includes conceiving and announcing dramatic themes periodically according to the needs of the CCP and governments on different levels, oftentimes to coincide with specific anniversaries.[36]

Although Sun acknowledges the existence of such an "unofficial dramaturgical activity"[37] in China, he concludes that dramaturgy is still not an established profession in China, and he implies pretty much that it shouldn't be one, since the dramaturgical activity could still be carried out by the unofficial dramaturgs,

---

35 William Huizhu Sun, "Official and Unofficial Dramaturgs: Dramaturgy in China," in *The Routledge Companion to Dramaturgy*, ed. Magda Romanska (London: Routledge, 2015), 81.

36 Sun, "Official and Unofficial Dramaturgs: Dramaturgy in China," 82.

37 Sun, "Official and Unofficial Dramaturgs: Dramaturgy in China."

working mostly in state-administered organizations as "archivists, critics, play-wrights, directors, and/or administrators."[38]

Such a claim is what the training approach at the Dramaturgy Faculty in Bei-jing under Li Yinan's aegis contradicts. It is symptomatic that Sun, very early on in his article, claims that Lessing's Hamburg Dramaturgy is "no longer a relevant use"[39], whereas it is precisely Lessing's approach to dramaturgy as a questioning of power structures that underlies the work of the Beijing Dramaturgy Faculty.

Juchang as a Specific Mode of Postdramatic Theatre in China

As in Giessen, it was also true of the faculty in Beijing that the theatre training was intended for a theatre that did not yet exist, i.e., one that had to be significantly shaped by the (later) works of the students. In the field of theatre education, it was the Faculty of Dramaturgy and Applied Theatre at Beijing's Central Academy of Drama that was the first training institution in mainland China to include aes-thetic discourses and creative procedures around a postdramatic theatre practice in its curriculum, especially by relating to the tradition of the German documen-tary theatre. To understand the massive resonance that the postdramatic theatre eventually created in mainland China, I want to focus on the practice of the so-called *juchang* theatre-makers and their situatedness within the Chinese theatre history of the early 20th century, when spoken theatre (*huaju*) reached China via Japan.[40]

The already mentioned *Movement for a New Culture* (*Xin Wenhua Yundong*), supported by young intellectuals, saw in spoken theatre (*huaju*) a means of re-forming the old "feudal" culture, which it held partly responsible for China's lack of modernity. In 1918, the magazine of the *Movement for a New Culture* published an issue on theatre reform as well as on Ibsen, which shows how much the move-ment's focus was based on the aesthetics of Western realism. The movement's attacks were directed against the traditional *xiqu* opera—in the West also often referred to as "Chinese opera"—which they accused of being distant from life. In contrast, the movement ascribed to spoken theatre a potential for social renewal. The actors of the *Movement for a New Culture* overlapped in many ways with those of the so-called *May Fourth Movement* (*Wusi Yundong*),[41] which has been described (including by Mao himself) as the forerunner of the Communist Party

---

38 Sun, 84.

39 Sun, 82.

40 In 1907, the *Spring Willow Society*, founded in Japan by Chinese foreign students in 1906, staged the first spoken theatre play in Chinese theatre history in Tokyo: An adaptation of Harriet Beecher Stowe's *Uncle Tom's Cabin* entitled *The Black Slaves Sigh to Heaven (Heinu Yutian Lu)*.

41 This movement, which called for a radical modernization and democratization of China, arose from the protests of Chinese students against the transfer of German concession areas to Japan, which began on May 4, 1919.

of China (CPC). This intertwining of the two movements with the founding history of the CPC shows how important the form of realistic spoken theatre has been and continues to be for nation-building in China.

The distinction between spoken theatre (*huaju*) and the aforementioned *xiqu* opera was then institutionalized after 1949 by the founding of training schools and companies that kept the two practices separated. Realism of Western European provenance mixed with Soviet realism of the Stanislawski style was implemented as the educational norm for theatre education. Li Yinan's translation of *Postdramatisches Theater* has intervened in this aesthetic and ideological dominance of realistic spoken theatre. She expressed the difference between the words "drama" and "theatre," which is constitutive for the translation of Lehmann's text, with the words *xiju* and *juchang*. The term *xiju* represents the dramatic with its focus on text and literature, whereas *juchang* emphasizes, among other things, the reality of performance. The term *juchang* has been heavily criticized because, in its last consequence, as intended by Li, it aims to represent an understanding of theatricality as performativity that did not exist in the academic discourse on the theatre in China before Li's translation. In this context, it is important to emphasize that the term *juchang* was not invented by Li but is linked, on the one hand, to academic theatre discourse in the 1930s and 1940s in China, and on the other hand, to the self-descriptions of independent Chinese contemporary theatre-makers.

In defining *juchang*, Li builds extensively on statements by contemporary Chinese theatre artists. These artists use the term *juchang* for self-designation or to describe their theatrical work to distinguish themselves from *xiju*, which is connected with textuality and thus, due to a censorship practice that focuses mainly on text, with ideology and suppression. Among these artists are the founding figures and exponents of experimental theatre in China (Mou Sen, Wu Wenguang, Wen Hui, Zhao Chuan, and Zhang Xian) and the generation that followed them (Li Jianjun, Li Ning, and Wang Mengfan). Li emphasizes that the spatial dimension is crucial for the performance practice of these *juchang* artists. She highlights this spatial dimension through her translation of theatre with the word *juchang*, since the semantic field of the Chinese character "chang" is formed around the term "space." Space has always been a contested resource for *juchang* artists, as the majority of resources have been put at the service of the aesthetic practice of spoken theatre. As a result, the struggle for public space for performance has become a central theme of *juchang* theatre. Quite a few of the *juchang* artists have therefore founded their own studios on the outskirts of Beijing, for example, Wu Wenguang and Wen Hui's *Caochangdi Workstation/Living Dance Studio* (*Caochangdi Gongzuozhan/Shenghuo Wudao Gongzuoshi*) and Tian Gebing's *Paper Tiger Studio* (*Beijing Zhilaohu Xiju Gongzuoshi*),[42] or *Grass Stage* (*Caotaiban*) around Zhao Chuan, who developed theatre forms that make repeated brief in-

---

42 The workshops and studios of these groups no longer exist.

terventions in state-controlled space. In view of China's enormous size, the number of *juchang* theatre-makers is remarkably small, and they are mainly concentrated in the metropolises of Beijing and Shanghai. The catalog of the MCAM Museum in Shanghai, published in 2015 for the special exhibition on *30 Years of Experimental Theater in China*, lists 29 names of experimental theatre practitioners—and this includes Danny Yung from Hong Kong.[43]

Since *juchang* works are largely determined by their positioning beyond the official theatre landscape, it is appropriate to briefly sketch this official theatre landscape here to provide the background *against* which *juchang* theatre stands out in its specific modes of production.

The official Chinese theatre landscape is clearly marked by the state's influence. This influence takes two main forms: first, the form of censorship (*shencha*), which denotes the direct intervention of official authorities in creative work, and second, the mode of state-led commercialization. Shannon Steen gives a very good description of how censorship is situated within the Chinese theatre system. I quote her here in detail:

> Contrary to popular accounts in the international mediascape, censorship in China is at once more institutionally specific, inconsistently practiced, and deeply internalized by its artists than is easy to comprehend from the outside. Expressive controls are primarily content-driven (in other words, they tend to be exercised over certain topics, leaving formal experimentation largely open), and operate largely within state-sponsored arts organizations and training schools. Artists learn to avoid certain topics (the Tiananmen protests, Tibet, ethnic separatism, sexually explicit material, and so forth) while training for their prospective fields, with the result that they often self-censor when creating new work. In this way, the operation of censorship in China looks more like the forms of Gramscian soft power that we generally associate with liberal democracies than we might expect, and even the top-down organization of expressive control is more inconsistent than is often understood. The state censorship office will sometimes allow performances of shows that might fall foul of taboo topics, but that they think generate a useful discussion: They will sometimes, for example, send a representative on the closing night of a performance who, after the show, will declare the production out of bounds and closed—but only after the run has been completed, thus retaining the external impression of state control while also allowing distribution of nonexplicitly endorsed ideas.[44]

However, in recent works that deal with the Chinese theatrical landscape, as well as in the words of the independent theatre-makers themselves, the state influence in its second form is increasingly emphasized: namely the state-controlled commercialization of the theatre. To make this specific "connection of state, market

---

43 Qiu Zhijie and Wang Ziyue, eds., *Shiyanjuchang Sanshinian* [30 Years of Experimental Theatre] (Shanghai: Shanghai Mingyuan Contemporary Art Museum, 2015).

44 Shannon Steen, "World Factory: Theatre, Labor, and China's 'New Left'," *Theatre Survey* 58, no. 1 (2017): 28f.

and culture in China",[45] which began after the end of the Cultural Revolution (1966–76), nameable, the cultural journalist Mark Siemons uses the term "culture industry".[46] He argues that, in contrast to the rather pragmatic use of the term in English, the term culture industry, as the Communist Party of China uses it, takes on exactly the polemical meaning that Horkheimer and Adorno gave it, namely that of "a plan condensed into a seamless system."[47] The term culture industry was first used officially in 2001 in a five-year plan. Subsequently, research institutes for the national culture industry were established at Beijing University and Shanghai Jiaotong University. Since 2005, Shenzhen has hosted several culture industry fairs, and the eleventh five-year plan in 2006 gave the culture industry paradigm almost hegemonic status.[48] It calls for the "continued transformation of state cultural institutions into commercial enterprises,"[49] regardless of whether they are "film studios, television production facilities, theatres or intermediary organizations".[50] Siemons interprets the emergence of a Chinese culture industry as a necessary consequence of the erosion of central political concepts associated with the Cultural Revolution. The Cultural Revolution produced an ideological nominalism that made everyone who did not use the right words a victim of the political elite that was currently ruling. In particular, this nominalism eroded the term "people", which, due to its career in the Cultural Revolution, has lost its compelling nature and brought the party into a troubling situation, since it conceives of itself as the representative of the people. By implementing the concept of a "culture industry," the Party enabled itself to redesign what formerly was "the will of the people" as the will of culture consumers in the new millennium. That can be seen especially in statements like that of the former deputy minister of culture and vice president, Li Yuanchao: "It is popular culture that makes culture accessible to ordinary people and that really puts the right to consume culture in the hands of the people."[51]

Purely in terms of production, one could characterize the *juchang* theatre workers as trying to escape the influence of the culture industry described above. Many *juchang* works are therefore inevitably created as international co-productions. In the 1980s, international co-productions were still being made mainly within the framework of highly official bilateral cultural programs without the participation of *juchang* theatre professionals. Today's theatre cooperations are

---

45 Mark Siemons, "Über die chinesische Kulturindustrie," [On the Chinese Culture Industry] in *Zeitgenössisches Theater in China* [Contemporary Theatre in China], ed. Cao Kefei, Sabine Heymann and Christoph Lepschy, (Berlin: Alexander Verlag, 2017), 73. All translations by Kai Tuchmann.

46 Siemons, 62.

47 Siemons, 62.

48 Cf. Siemons, 71–73.

49 Siemons, 72.

50 Siemons, 72.

51 Siemons, 65.

highly dynamic compared to those of that earlier time and have been supplemented by various new formats. The residency programs of national cultural
institutes, cooperation between Chinese theatre-makers and international theatre festivals, or directly with municipal theatres or theatre academies and universities are only the most important phenomena showing how much cultural
exchange with China has changed. The diversification of formats has been accompanied by rapid growth in the number of collaborations. In terms of production,
the *juchang* works thus oscillate between the extremely limited performance opportunities granted by the Chinese culture industry and the international theatre
market, mainly European and Asian theatre festivals.

Bibliography

Balme, Christopher B. *The Theatrical Public Sphere*. Cambridge: Cambridge University
    Press, 2014.

Barthes, Roland. "The Reality Effect." In *The Rustle of Language*, 141–48.
    Berkeley: University of California Press, 1989.

Barthes, Roland. "February 17, 1979." In *The Preparation of the Novel: Lecture
    Courses and Seminars at the Collège De France, 1978–1979 and 1979–1980*, 70–
    77. New York: Columbia University Press, 2011.

Chen Xiaomei. "Performing the 'Red Classics.' From 'The East is Red' to 'The Road to
    Revival'." In Li; Zhang, *Red Legacies in China. Cultural Afterlives of the Communist
    Revolution,* 151–83. Leiden, Boston: Brill, 2016.

Deutsch-Schreiner, Evelyn. *Theaterdramaturgien von der Aufklärung bis zur Gegen-
    wart* [Theatrical Dramaturgies from the Enlightenment to the Presence]. Köln:
    Böhlau Verlag, 2016.

Kiefer, Jochen. "Re-Vision Dramaturgie." Inaugural lecture at the Zurich University of
    the Arts, February 21, 2019. Zurich.

Lehmann, Hans-Thies. *Postdramatisches Theater* [Postdramatic Theatre]. Frank-
    furt/Main: Verlag der Autoren, 1999.

Lehmann, Hans-Thies. *Houxiju Juchang* [Postdramatic Theatre]. Beijing: Beijing daxue
    chuban she [Beijing University Press], 2010.

Li Jie, and Enhua Zhang, eds. *Red Legacies in China: Cultural Afterlives of the Com-
    munist Revolution*. Leiden, Boston: Brill, 2016.

Li Jie. "Introduction: Discerning Red Legacies in China." In *Red Legacies in China.
    Cultural Afterlives of the Communist Revolution*, 1–22. Leiden, Boston: Brill, 2016.

Müller-Schöll, Nikolaus. "Polizeiliche und politische Dramaturgie." [Policing and
    Political Dramaturgy] In *Postdramaturgien* [Postdramaturgies]. Edited by Sandra
    Umathum and Jan Deck, 209–30. Berlin: Neofelis, 2020. Accessed October 4,
    2021.

Nikitin, Boris. "Der unzuverlässige Zeuge: Zwölf Behauptungen über das Dokumenta-
    rische." [The Unreliable Witness. Twelve Assertions about the Documentary] In
    Dokument, Fälschung, Wirklichkeit: Materialband zum Zeitgenössischen

Dokumentarischen Theater [Document, Fake, Reality. Materials of Contemporary Documentary Theatre]. Theater der Zeit Recherchen 110. Edited by Boris Nikitin, Carena Schlewitt and Tobias Brenk, 12–21. Berlin: Theater der Zeit, 2014.

Nikitin, Boris, Carena Schlewitt, and Tobias Brenk, eds. *Dokument, Fälschung, Wirklichkeit: Materialband zum Zeitgenössischen Dokumentarischen Theater* [Document, Fake, Reality. Materials of Contemporary Documentary Theatre]. Theater der Zeit Recherchen 110. Berlin: Theater der Zeit, 2014.

Nikitin, Boris, Carena Schlewitt, and Tobias Brenk. "Vorwort." [Preface] In *Dokument, Fälschung, Wirklichkeit: Materialband zum Zeitgenössischen Dokumentarischen Theater* [Document, Fake, Reality. Materials of Contemporary Documentary Theatre]. Theater der Zeit Recherchen 110. Edited by Boris Nikitin, Carena Schlewitt and Tobias Brenk, 7–11. Berlin: Theater der Zeit, 2014.

Piscator, Erwin. Das Politische Theater [Political Theatre]. Berlin: Henschelverlag, 1968.

Qiu Zhijie, and Wang Ziyue, eds. *Shiyanjuchang Sanshinian* [30 Years of Experimental Theatre]. Shanghai: Shanghai Mingyuan Contemporary Art Museum, 2015.

Rancière, Jacques. The Politics of Aesthetics: The Distribution of the Sensible. London: Continuum, 2011.

Siemons, Mark. "Über die chinesische Kulturindustrie." [On Chinese Cultural Industry] In Zeitgenössisches Theater in China [Contemporary Theatre in China]. Edited by Cao Kefei, Sabine Heymann and Christoph Lepschy. Originalausgabe, 60–75. Berlin: Alexander Verlag, 2017.

Steen, Shannon. "World Factory: Theatre, Labor, and China's 'New Left.'" Theatre Survey 58, no. 1 (2017): 24–47.

Sun, William Huizhu. "Official and Unofficial Dramaturgs: Dramaturgy in China." In *The Routledge Companion to Dramaturgy*. Edited by Magda Romanska, 81–86. London: Routledge, 2015.

Tobler, Andreas. "Kontingente Evidenzen: Über Möglichkeiten Dokumentarischen Theaters." [Contingent Evidence. On the Possibilities of Documentary Theatre] In *Dokument, Fälschung, Wirklichkeit: Materialband zum Zeitgenössischen Dokumentarischen Theater* [Document, Fake, Reality. Materials of Contemporary Documentary Theatre]. Theater der Zeit Recherchen 110. Edited by Boris Nikitin, Carena Schlewitt and Tobias Brenk, 147–63. Berlin: Theater der Zeit, 2014.

Walder, Andrew G., and Yang Su. "The Cultural Revolution in the Countryside: Scope, Timing and Human Impact." *The China Quarterly*, no. 173 (2003): 74–99.

Weiss, Peter. "The Material and the Models: Notes Towards a Definition of Documentary Theatre." *Theatre Quarterly*, no. 1 (1971): 41–43.

Wen Hui. "Female Memory Begins with the Body." In *The Body at Stake: Experiments in Chinese Contemporary Art and Theatre*. Edited by Jörg Huber and Zhao Chuan 131–34. Bielefeld: transcript, 2013.

Zhao Chuan, and Tao Qingmei. "Feldmanöver." [Field manoeuvre] Theater der Zeit, 2015/12 (2015): 32–40.

Rethinking Theatricality

A Conversation on Postdramatic Theatre and Chinese *Juchang*

Li Yinan, Boris Nikitin, Wang Mengfan, and Kai Tuchmann[1]

TUCHMANN: The book *Postdramatisches Theater*[2] by Hans-Thies Lehmann was published in 1999 and translated into Chinese in 2010.[3] Together with the translator of this seminal text, Prof. Li Yinan, and two outstanding theatre-makers working in China and the German-speaking theatre market, namely Wang Mengfan and Boris Nikitin, I want to discuss what kind of traces this text and the concept of postdramatic theatre have left in the European and Chinese theatre landscape. I am particularly interested in the controversial debates that have been and are still being conducted about it. A recapitulation of these controversies is especially relevant now, as the third edition of the Chinese translation is being prepared.

Perhaps we can first try to define the term. What is this "postdramatic theatre"? I will give you some keywords and invite you to add to this.

According to Hans-Thies Lehmann, postdramatic theatre is characterized by the fact that it favors the so-called theatrical axis over the inner-stage axis. The postdramatic theatre thus understands the act of communication between stage and auditorium as the central artistic material. This theatre is no longer primarily concerned with arranging a text invented by an author on stage. The focus on the process of communication is accompanied by a dramaturgical abandonment of the focus on drama/action/imitation that had previously existed in theatre. Instead of this triad, there is what one can describe an emphasis on the ceremonial. In terms of staging, this leads to a dehierarchization of the theatrical means: the performers' bodies, the light,

---

1   The conversation was held in German and Chinese. English translation by Pu Wenyan and Kai Tuchmann.

2   Hans-Thies Lehmann, *Postdramatisches Theater* [Postdramatic Theatre] (Frankfurt a.M.: Verlag der Autoren, 1999). English translation by Karen Jürs-Munby: Hans-Thies Lehmann, *Postdramatic Theatre* (New York: Routledge, 2006).

3   Hans-Thies Lehmann, *Houxiju Juchang* [Postdramatic Theatre] (Beijing: Beijing daxue chuban she [Beijing University Press], 2010).

the sound, the atmosphere stand on an equal footing with the text. Histori-cally, Lehmann locates the beginning of postdramatic theatre in the 1970s. He sees it as a reaction to the world as it was being changed by information tech-nologies.

Yinan, as a theatre scholar, would you like to supplement this first attempt at a definition and tell us why and how you translated this text?

LI: You are right. The postdramatic theatre pays special attention to the audi-ence's gaze. The mechanism of art is thus extended and becomes one of the social mechanisms. Literature/text descends from the top of the theatrical hierarchy to an equal position alongside other elements. This is partly a result of the development of aesthetics (in the sense of a "science of perception," which is the original meaning of the word) in the new media age. The postdra-matic theatre becomes rather an art of performativity instead of an art of representation. Lehmann not only provides us with a way of describing and analyzing new theatre but also gives the possibility of rethinking theatricality.

In the Chinese context, dramatic theatre used to be exotic, an intruder. The performative aspects of traditional Chinese theatre, on the other hand, were overlooked or despised, which led to a historical record full of ruptures, self-deprecation, and contradictions. Chinese scholars have been using terminol-ogy imported from 19th century Europe to describe and analyze theatre, which is not only inaccurate and insufficient but also led to a decline in the quality of Chinese theatre, which was only copying the Western "masters." Today, when global theatre cultures are getting to know each other much more deeply and are interweaving with each other in a more complicated way, introducing Lehmann's terminology (which is the opposite to the 19th century European understanding of theatre) seems necessary, even urgent.

TUCHMANN: In his work, Lehmann makes a strict distinction between the terms "drama" and "theatre." You translate these terms with "*xiju*" and "*juchang.*" What is the difference between the two concepts *xiju* (drama) and *juchang* (theatre) in the Chinese context? What is the relationship between them?

LI: Until now, Chinese scholars have had a very narrow understanding of theatre, namely as *huaju* (spoken drama), which was introduced into China from Eur-ope via Japan at the beginning of the 20th century with the experiments of the Spring Willow Society. On the other hand, Chinese traditional theatre has been excluded from the theoretical theatre discourse. The focus of Chinese Theatre Studies has lain upon the dramatic text, which is closely related to China's par-ticular way of modernizing by following the 19th century European model.

Another focus has existed almost from the very beginning of modern Chi-nese theatre but has not received widespread attention. In 1923, Song Chunfang first noticed the difference between the notions of "drama" and "theatre" when introducing Edward Gordon Craig's understanding of theatricality in *The actor and the Über-Marionette*[4] to China. During the 1930s and 1940s, Zhou Yibai and Dong Meikan also made efforts to differentiate two aspects in theatre studies—the dramatic and the theatrical – and laid particular stress upon theatricality as opposed to literature/textuality. They used various terms for the opposing pair of concepts – *wenxue* vs. *wutai* (literature vs. stage), *antou* vs. *changshang* (on the desk vs. *mise-en-scène*) as well as *wenxue* vs. *yanju* (literary text vs. performance). When translating *Postdramatisches Theater,* I preferred accuracy to interpretation (for example, interpretively translating "drama" as "literature" or "text" is, for me, inappropriate.) And I would rather use existing Chinese words, not create new ones. *Xiju* and *juchang* both have lived in the Chinese language for a long time. In *"Zhongguo juchang shi"*,[5] Zhou Yibai uses *juchang* as a term that corresponds almost exactly with what Lehmann means by "das Theater." In Hongkong and Taiwan, the term *juchang* is also used widely to translate "theatre."

Since the publication of my translation of Lehmann's book, it has encountered acclaim as well as denunciation. Criticism is concentrated on my choice of using the term *juchang* (rather than *xiju*) to translate "theatre." At one conference, I was even scolded for "blindly copying the trendy jargon of the ignorant Hong Kong and Taiwan scholars." This made me start my deeper studies of this particular term *juchang* more consciously. As I discovered, not only Zhou Yibai and the (for some Mainland scholars) "ignorant" Hongkong/Taiwan colleagues, but quite a few independent theatre-makers in Mainland China itself, such as Wen Hui, Wu Wenguang, Zhang Xian, and Tian Gebing have been using the term *juchang* to define what they do, while resolutely rejecting the more common term *xiju*, whose stress on text (which is closely related to ideology) means for them, oppression.

TUCHMANN: Mengfan, I would like to know from you, as a Chinese artist, whether and to what extent Lehmann's concept of postdramatic theatre has influenced you?

WANG: I don't think I understood the book at all. Later, I went to Germany to continue my studies in art history, and for some reason, I started making theatre. I began to understand the book after I did my first piece, *50/60-Old Ladies dance juchang (50/60-Ayimen De Wudao Juchang)* . So I cannot say that the book or this notion itself has influenced my creative work. But when I started creating, it gave me a standpoint to define my work. I began to understand where my work stands in the context of contemporary Western theatre and

4   Edward G. Craig, "The Actor and the Über-Marionette," *The Mask*, Vol.1 Nr.2. (1908).
5   Zhou Yibai, *Zhongguo Juchang Shi [A History of Chinese Theaters]* (Shanghai: Shangwu yinshuguan, 1933).

in history. I also started thinking about what theatre I'll make in contemporary Chinese theatre in the future.

TUCHMANN: Yinan, you say that this term *"juchang"* is, above all, a term used by Chinese artists who, as independent theatre-makers, stand outside the system to talk about their work. Can you explain to us: What is the official system, the Chinese theatre system, to which *juchang* is in opposition? And how exactly does it enter into this opposition? Who are these artists?

LI: As I said, the controversy the book aroused seemed to be about the translation of the term "theatre." However, as time went by, I realized it was not so. It was because of the notion of theatricality, in German "Theatralität". I translated it into *juchangxing* (theatricality), while the mainstream theatre study has always translated it as *xijuxing* (dramaticism). Tan Peisheng wrote a book in 1981, *"Taolun juxing"* (Discussing dramaticism), which is still part of the canon at The Central Academy of Drama. He translated theatricality into *xijuxing* (dramaticism). However, what independent theatre-makers like Mengfan do does not conform to the principle of dramaticism.

You might ask what this dramaticism is. I believe most of you here are active in theatre circles; you are probably not unfamiliar with the term. The book Tan wrote drew mainly on three Western theorists, all from the 18th and 19th centuries. One is Schlegel; one is Baker, the founder of the School of Drama at Yale University, from around the end of the 19th century and the beginning of the 20th century. The third is Archer, who wrote *Play-Making*.[6] All three writers focus on drama, especially Baker, who talked about how to write the particular form of well-made plays. These theories are all about dramaticism, and they are identical to what Lehmann calls the dramatic theatre of Europe in the 19th century. Back then, the characteristics of drama were identical with the characteristics of theatre because the dramatic theatre was a very popular art form at that time. Later in the 20th century, though, some features of theatre became different from those of dramatic literature. The characteristics of theatre received greater emphasis. From this perspective, theatricality stands opposed to dramatic literature. With the growing emphasis on performance in new theatre works, the characteristics of theatre are changing. However, in what are considered "theatrical circles" in China, people are still making plays according to the principle of well-made plays in the 18th and 19th centuries. *Xiju* is an apt translation for this. Lehmann and I both think that it's a good equivalent for "drama." And at the center of dramaticism is actually what Kai mentioned: dramatic action. Dramatic action is emphasized to prevent the audience from being bored, to arouse their interest. This is still the principle of

---

6   William Archer, *Play-Making. A Manual of Craftsmanship* (Boston: Small, Maynard and Company, 1912).

making drama, but not of theatre works like Mengfan's at all. This is one reason this book is looked upon with skepticism in China.

TUCHMANN: Boris, could you describe the effect of the term and the text *Post-dramatisches Theater* on your work? And more generally, how would you describe the influence that this term has had on the German-speaking theatre scene?

NIKITIN: I was born and grew up in postdramatic theatre, so to speak, because I studied at the Institute for Applied Theatre Studies, which was more or less co-founded and decisively influenced by Hans-Thies Lehmann. In this context, it is very important to note that, in Giessen, the concept of postdramatic theatre is not only reflected in what happens on stage but is fundamentally part of the structure of the training and development of this institute. This is manifested above all in the fact that, in contrast to almost every other theatre school in Germany, if you study at Giessen, your training is not compartmentalized by specialization: Some study directing, others study acting, others study stage design, and others study lighting design; but rather: Everybody does everything. The theatre is understood there as a multimedia art discipline, where everyone should be informed about all the different means of artistic expression. One consequence of this, however, is that there are no real actors or no people who are trained for this purpose. That was a crucial premise in the founding of the institute: A theatre without the hegemony of the actor or of the canonical dramatic text.

In other words, one had to solve a problem first: Who do you now work with on stage and what should happen there? What is the alternative to the classically trained actors and actresses who have a trained speaking technique, who have learned to use different acting techniques to portray characters and not be themselves? The solution, of course, was not to let amateurs play Shakespeare, but rather to look for completely different forms of text and content that could be performed by people who are not amateurs. In other words, it was a question of a new constellation: of people on the stage, content, and the space in which this takes place. This led directly to the development of forms of documentary theatre or performative theatre. Here, people are on stage who no longer represent a character but who go on stage as themselves and negotiate themselves, their biography, their body.

TUCHMANN: There is this famous sentence by the theatre critic Gerhard Stadelmaier, who speaks of Giessen as a site of disaster for German theatre. Nowadays, the dramaturg Bernd Stegemann is strongly critical of postdramatic aesthetics, whose documentary variants he accuses of serving the ideology of capitalism by uncritically reproducing its surfaces. Both examples indicate that the idea of the postdramatic has always been—and probably still is—very controversial. From this perspective, would you like to talk again about the influence of postdramatic theatre on the German-speaking theatre scene?

NIKITIN: I would say that Lehmann did not, of course, invent the postdramatic theatre with *Postdramatisches Theater*, but he described it and made certain phenomena understandable that had begun to be effective since the 1970s. It also has a great deal to do with emancipatory movements that have impacted the theatre and strengthened the independent scene. After the appearance of *Postdramatisches Theater*, which is part of this development, especially from the 2000s to the present day, there was an extreme expansion and strengthening of the independent scene in Germany. Even though there have been repeated attempts to neutralize them, I believe there are huge differences in production methods and aesthetics between theatre and dance productions in the independent scene and the municipal theatre.

TUCHMANN: That's quite exciting; it means that, for the German context, you would say that this publication is something like the grammar of the independent scene. A point that follows almost seamlessly from what Yinan said about the term *juchang* in China. Mengfan has brought along short video clips documenting her *juchang* work: Excerpts from her works 50/60-Old Ladies dance *juchang* and The Divine Sewing Machine (Shensheng Fengrenji). Maybe you will now show us these excerpts and tell us a bit about these projects.

https://tinyurl.com/Wang-50-60

https://tinyurl.com/Wang-Sewing-Machine

WANG: As you can see, I've always chosen to work with unprofessional actors. Both pieces start from my focus on people's bodies, specifically Chinese people's bodies, how they are shaped under the socialist ideology and aesthetics, and how they speak. I think when they are presented as a group, as you see here, a group of square dance aunties or a group of kids—when they are presented as a group, something hidden will surface, something physical perhaps. Something else the two pieces have in common is a relationship with performativity. *50/60-Old Ladies dance juchang* is about square dancing, while *The Divine Sewing Machine* is about *speech intonation* (which is the preferred method of elementary education in China). The second piece may not seem to refer to speech intonation, but in the beginning, I started working out of interest in the way kids speak. So what we are trying to do in theatre is to create a different body from the body of our daily lives. Kai asked me earlier about making theatre in China and our relationship with the academies. After show-ing this piece, the question I most often get is: "What does this mean? Can you sum up in one sentence what you are trying to express?" I think this is a com-mon question the ordinary Chinese audience has, and this is related to drama as it is taught at the academies. They need a work to have a plot so that they can understand it. Quite on the contrary, my work has no story or plot what-soever. What the kids say on stage, as you might have heard a little in the video, has no meaning, and delivers no information. By presenting such a piece in the Chinese theatre, I mean to pose a question to the audience, that without anything to grasp, how do we read the bodies themselves, and why do we look at such bodies?

NIKITIN: I think it's very similar in Germany and Switzerland. A far greater diver-sity of people is visible on stage: people with diseases, people with disabilities, and migration backgrounds. Representation has been broken up as a result, and this is a very central concern of the developments that Lehmann describes as postdramatic. These developments have only been enabled by breaking up the drama, because the drama has been synonymous with the canon. The canon is a historical, literary canon that has only made available a certain repertoire of roles with an apparent division of race, gender, and gender hier-archies and an evident typecasting: Who plays Romeo, who plays Juliet? Who plays Lady Macbeth and who plays Macbeth? The guidelines were very clear as to who was represented on stage at all. So you first had to thwart the drama to make room for other forms.

Just one more short thing that is of concern to me: When you postulate things like "postdramatic theatre," it often has the character of: "This is the new theatre now and what was before it is bad!" I think it is crucial to point out that it is not about destroying dramatic theatre. It's about expanding the theatre as a space of possibility. It is not per se about completely displacing the old. That won't work because then you end up provoking reaction, and that's what Bernd Stegemann is. Many traditionalists feel very strongly threat-ened. Then I always say: Don't panic! It's not about destroying dramatic theatre but about expanding it.

TUCHMANN: Now Boris has just made the point that there is a decidedly political dimension in postdramatic theatre; for example, documentary procedures give people a stage who are otherwise not represented in the dominant public discourse; the aesthetics of postdramatic theatre thus quasi creates a new public sphere around these people. How would you see this point for China? Are there correspondences?

LI: I think that promoting theatre without dismissing drama is an important prin-ciple of postdramatic theatre. Boris said this well. Bringing up the postdramatic theatre is actually expanding theatrical art. Theatre is inclusive. In China, the concept of the theatre arts is more general. The kind of non-dramatic theatre that Mengfan does, makes up less than five percent of all performances in China. These works are more often shown in the relatively marginal, less grand theatre spaces. They won't be shown, for example, in the National Theatre. They are put on in the smaller theatres, even in specific sites, in the irregular spaces, and receive no governmental financial support. So really, these theatre theorists are saying that drama is now in crisis, that Chinese drama today is not good, not well-written, and young people like Mengfan are to blame, that their existence poses a threat to drama? I don't think such a threat exists. Mengfan's existence threatens no one. But allowing them to live is a great thing. And I think allowing young creators like Mengfan to exist is one very political aspect of postdramatic theatre. Not that what they do is political in the sense of propaganda slogans, but to allow their existence to supplement or co-exist with the dramatic canon, this is very political.

WANG: Professor Li introduced to us the political aspect in this sense. I'll talk about another layer – the political element of presenting unprofessional ordinary people in the theatre. When I was making the piece about square dance aunties, some say that they are affected by, as we know, stuff like *zhongzi wu* (the dance of loyalty) from the Cultural Revolution, which is undoubtedly seared on this generation. For me, however, the political meaning of this work is not so simple. These people, who have no claim to any space in the Chinese cities, can, for an instant, claim the public space of the theatre, where they present their actual bodies and express what they wish to say. This, for me, is a political expression. And the kids. I've realized that kids are deemed inferior animals in Chinese education, whose education consists of sermons and who are not supposed to think for themselves. I wanted to discuss this. In the process of working together with these children, I somehow found myself to be the student, learning from them. And I wanted to share this kind of experience with others. The groups of people with no voice, no freedom or space to express themselves gain the right to speak in such a public space as theatre. This, for me, is political.

TUCHMANN: Mengfan, what kind of audience does your theatre attract? And, more generally: Who is the *juchang* audience? Especially if this theatre has such a political dimension, what's the difference to the audience of the so-called official theatre?

WANG: As for my expectation of the audience, who I want them to be? Well, I want them to be Chinese. This is the first thing. I think my plays are not made for foreigners. They are made for Chinese people. This is the general expectation. And this play, it's true, is very difficult to describe in the creative environment today. After all, even Lehmann used a whole book to describe the postdramatic theatre. So, I often encounter questions during promotion: what is this that I've made. Ultimately our audience is quite varied. Since I'm working with ordinary people, we first get a whole bunch of relatives. I think this is a great thing, though I didn't expect it, we can have more discussion with people who don't usually show up in theatres. How do they think of an art form that has nothing to do with their lives? They might not even know what dramatic the-atre is. They probably never go to the theatre. I find this very interesting—and how do kids understand it? Apart from this, the audience is more like people who pay attention to independent theatres and marginal artists, who are long-time small-theatre-goers. But we can hardly reach the audience that routinely visits, say, Beijing People's Art Theatre. We can't even pass any message to them.

TUCHMANN: Then I would now ask the last question before we open the conver-sation to the auditorium. This last question has to do with the future. At the beginning of our discussion, I mentioned that Lehmann dates the beginning of postdramatic theatre to the 1970s and that he sees it as an answer to the chal-lenges of an emerging information society. Well, the information society and the mechanization of our lives have not stopped. We live in a world where a handful of tech companies colonize everyday life, the public sphere, and poli-tics. We are meeting here in a state where the so-called social credit system will soon be introduced, i.e., in a state that produces its inhabitants as digital subjects in an unprecedented system. What could be the potential of postdra-matic theatre there? Precisely if one thinks of its origins as a form of, I don't want to say criticism, but as a form of behavior in the face of a profound change in the media.

LI: I think in the West, a trend is beginning to show at the start of the 21st century, as mainstream theatre is opening up to creators of the postdramatic theatre. Rimini Protokoll, for example, has staged works in some huge theatres. Hans-Werner Kroesinger, who graduated from Giessen, has received an invitation to the Berliner Theatertreffen. In China, the trend is similar. At first, the inde-pendent artists outside the system and "theatrical circles" within the system were totally incompatible. For example, *Caochangdi* was, in the beginning, a center of independent theatre arts. The hosts, or owners of the place, Wu Wenguang and Wen Hui, were very opposed to the drama establishment. So theatre and drama became two incompatible worlds. In the recent four or five years, however, as far as I've observed, many mainstream theatre festivals have started to welcome works by artists like Mengfan. For example, the *Divine Sewing Machine* was shown at the Beijing Fringe Festival. Festivals like the Wuzhen Drama Festival, and the Nanluoguxiang Drama Arts Festival—festivals with "drama" in their name—are opening doors to the new theatre. Another important reason is the gentrification of cities. As rents go up, theatre artists like Mengfan have to find opportunities to stage their works in ordinary spaces. It is this process that brings drama and theatre together. The old generation welcomes the new, and the new reaches out to the old. So it's a gradually mixing world. This is an optimistic trend that I've seen.

NIKITIN: I would like to point out another aspect. I would say that the strength of the theatrical and perhaps postdramatic theatre is actually the theatre space. The theatre space has the special characteristic that it is a space in which we gather as individuals who at the same time form a community, without necessarily sharing the same views. It is a space in which—and this is very important for postdramatic theatre—dissent is possible. It has something to do with co-presence, that we are together in a space in which this dividing line between stage and audience is present and in which we have to negotiate this dividing line permanently. In contrast to digital space, which is a space simulation, the theatre space is physical and sensual. Therefore, it is a space of vulnerability, of possibility, a space of the alternatives, which fundamentally means: of disagreement. I can be in a space together with others who, at the same time, I can be in disagreement with. That's what makes this space political. That's what its modernity consists of today.

WANG: Although I've always shown my works in theatres, I've still been thinking about this question—how to think in a theatrical way? If we can be clear on this question, we don't have to restrict ourselves to the space of theatres or even the form of theatre. What I wish to share more with people is this way of thinking: how to think about all kinds of things theatrically, and not only artistically. This is my thought about the future.

TUCHMANN: Let us now direct our gaze into the auditorium and wait for questions, comments, or other reactions![7]

AUDIENCE MEMBER A: Hello, I'm a beginner at theatre and have two questions. The first is for director Nikitin. I wonder about the role of identification in postdramatic theatre. Can I understand it this way—just like an audience of traditional drama, we watch a postdramatic play, and because we are moved, we start to think. First, we are passive, and then we become active. Is it a process like this?

NIKITIN: The audience doesn't always have to be passive. I have not dealt with this in my practice, but in the varied approaches of the postdramatic theatre, some artists have already completely broken the principle of a passive audience. Some immersive plays, for example, totally wipe out the clear division between the stage and the audience. Some present their works in public

---

7   This is a selection of audience questions.

spaces. There are many experiments. Some, for example, give the audience a set of headphones through which you hear a performative text. Then you walk across the city and participate in composing a new text. There are a lot of possibilities.

Personally and artistically, I prefer to highlight and use that line between the stage and the audience and to play with the difference it creates. I very often play with the role of the spectators, their position, their expectations. It's crucial for me.

Anyway, in my eyes, the audience is never passive. The gaze or the seeing of the audience is a frame. And every kind of seeing is active, never passive. And clearly, the presence of the audience is active. It changes everything. A spectator who is sleeping is quite an active event in a performance.

AUDIENCE MEMBER A: The second question is for director Wang Mengfan. The director has the job of delivering a message. But what do you do if the audience fails to understand the message? It might be its problem if they don't understand. But, I want to ask, the work you do, when you are rehearsing, the actors, kids, aunties, do they understand what you want them to do? Or do you just ask them to play and perform according to your instructions?

WANG: We work collectively. I pose questions for them, or we accomplish missions together. In this process, I accumulate materials, some of which end up on stage. But what appears explicitly on stage is for me to decide.

AUDIENCE MEMBER A: Sorry, but I suddenly have an idea, as a beginner. If I, say, find two strangers, let them sit on stage and start drinking. With drinking, they get familiar. They start chatting. So, in the end, I think, perhaps it shows the strangeness among people and how they talk after letting down their guard, getting drunk even. This, of course, cannot compare with your work. But I want to know what the difference is.

WANG: Nikitin has talked a lot about the problem of whether we need professional actors at all. Your question is similar to this, right? What's the division between creation and non-creation?

AUDIENCE MEMBER A: I mean could I stage this kind of situation and call it art?

NIKITIN: A conversation? Sure, you just have to frame it well as an artistic work and somehow organize an audience to watch it, then it could work well as a theatre product. And I would always be careful about thinking of postdramatic theatre or performance as easy, that it's just about putting something authentic on stage without directing it, and then it automatically becomes postdramatic theatre. There's always the possibility that it just becomes a postdramatic something else. Of course, it still has a lot to do with staging, with work, with forms, with dedication, and the investment of time and of one's own vulnerability.

AUDIENCE MEMBER B: I have a question for Professor Li. I'm reading *Houxiju juchang*[8] (Postdramatic Theatre) and have read only a small part so far. In the translator's foreword, you wrote why traditional Chinese opera is not well known to the present Chinese audience. You say it's because the "*chang, nian, zuo, da*" (singing, dialogue, acting, and acrobatics) are theatrical, and the audience lacks the general cognition to understand this. I would like to know more about this subject.

LI: In fact, this is not only my opinion but Lehmann's as well. He thinks his book *Postdramatisches Theater* rightly describes the Chinese traditional theatre, which we call traditional opera. In the beginning, our Academy of Drama didn't think it was drama at all and only included it in recent years. This bias is related to wholesale Westernization during the May Fourth Movement. When drama was introduced from the West at the beginning of the 20th century, people thought it was a superior art form. This causes a massive gap in our own theatre culture. It's Lehmann's book, however, that tries to raise our attention to our own tradition. Of course, there are stories and characters in our traditional opera that are the same as in drama. But in the 20th century, we moved our emphasis almost entirely to storytelling and characterization. Even the famous Opera performer Mei Lanfang said that the emotions he expressed on stage were genuine. He became more and more loyal to the genuineness and building of real characters, which were ideas from drama.

AUDIENCE MEMBER C: My question is not so theoretical. I want to ask one of the theatre-makers here, do you know clearly from the beginning what you are doing, or not so clearly, but rather make decisions out of intuition? I think this is a question faced by artists in all art forms. Thank you.

NIKITIN: It depends. When I do a theatre project, I often have an idea; I have a hunch. I often have the idea of an effect. And then, of course, it's the process of artistic work, this remaining in a space, in a time, in which you influence the raw material, in which you try to bring it into a form, during which the understanding of what you're dealing with is then sharpened: and I think that's also what artistic work is. I refuse to say: "No, I never know the answer! It's just a question." Sometimes I have an answer, but I don't know how to formulate it, and that's the work.

---

8   Lehmann, Houxiju juchang

Bibliography

Archer, William. *Play-Making. A Manual of Craftsmanship*. Boston: Small, Maynard and Company, 1912.

Craig, Edward Gordon. "The Actor and the Über-Marionette." *The Mask*, Vol.1 Nr.2. (1908): 3–16.

Lehmann, Hans-Thies. *Postdramatisches Theater* [Postdramatic Theatre]. Frankfurt/ Main: Verlag der Autoren, 1999.

Lehmann, Hans-Thies. *Postdramatic Theatre*. New York: Routledge, 2006.

Lehmann, Hans-Thies. *Houxiju Juchang* [Postdramatic Theatre]. Beijing: Beijing daxue chuban she [Beijing University Press], 2010.

Zhou Yibai. *Zhongguo Juchang Shi* [A History of Chinese Theaters]. Shanghai: Shangwu yinshuguan, 1933.

Hans-Thies Lehmann's Postdramatic Theatre and the New Aesthetics of *Juchang*[1]

Li Yinan

Translated by Kai Tuchmann and Jo Riley

I first encountered the book *Postdramatisches Theater* (*Postdramatic Theatre*) by Hans-Thies Lehmann in 2000.[2] Back then, I was studying for a master's degree in Theatre Studies, and had only recently moved from the US to Germany. There I saw some theatre performances of a kind I had never seen before. Reading this book resolved much of the confusion I had felt when I first saw these new forms of theatre. Lehmann distinguishes between "theatre" and "drama." In order to describe the very recent phenomenon of postdramatic theatre, he divides the whole development of theatre into three periods: predramatic theatre, dramatic theatre, and postdramatic theatre. In defining these distinct periods, Lehmann points to a major shift in theatre that occurred after the 1960s, which he implicitly expects to become a driving force in its further development. I thought that this work of theory would be a great help for Chinese theatre scholars and theatre-makers, so I decided to translate it into Chinese.

The process of translation, which took about four years, was full of hardships, but also delights. Professor Lehmann is a theatre scholar, but to describe and analyze the new form of theatre, he applies terms from literature, linguistics, philosophy, psychology, and even from physics, biology and other fields. The translation of some words, such as *juchang* ("performance art"), *zhanyan* ("performativity"), *cunxian* ("presence"), and others, presented me with considerable challenges, and I repeatedly had to reconsider my translation practice. A particular difficulty was that the theatrical phenomena of the 1980s and 1990s that

---

1   This essay is a revision of a text that was first published under the same title in: Li Yinan, *Juchang Performance in Contemporary Chinese Society (1980–2020)*, Münchner Universitätsschriften, Theaterwissenschaft 34 (München: utzverlag, 2020).

2   Hans-Thies Lehmann, *Postdramatisches Theater* [Postdramatic Theatre] (Frankfurt/Main: Verlag der Autoren, 1999). English translation by Karen Jürs-Munby: Hans-Thies Lehmann, *Postdramatic Theatre* (New York: Routledge, 2006).

Lehmann described in his book were still unknown in China, which meant that no corresponding Chinese terms existed. I had to use literal translation and refer to other scholars' perspectives and translations. Sometimes I even had to construct a new word by expanding on the meaning of a Chinese character. For example, expanding on the context of the character *chang* (space), I constructed *juchang* to convey the term "performance art"; from *zhanshi* (presentation) and *yanchu* (show), I constructed *zhanyan* to mean "performativity," which follows Shen Lin's literal translation practice from the 1990s. Expanding on the context of the characters *cunzai* (existence) and *xianzai/xianchang* (now/on the spot), I constructed the word *cunxian* to convey the word "presence."

Since Lehmann's book came out in China, it has become the target of concentrated attacks by scholars and the Chinese theatre world. Mainly the accusations are that Lehmann's postdramatic theatre is a kind of formalism. The criticism levelled at Lehmann's postdramatic theatre in China was not based on the fact that the examples he analyzed were aesthetically incompatible with Chinese taste, but because his theory attacked the basic foundations of *huaju* (spoken drama), *xianshizhuyi* (realism) and *xijuxing* (dramaticism).

Western drama was introduced to China via Japan at the end of the 19th and the beginning of the 20th century. This imported form was called *huaju,* and it was based on text and plot. Under the specific historical conditions of the time, the Chinese reformers regarded Western naturalistic *huaju* drama (bourgeois plays from France in particular, and from all over Europe in general) as something that could be opposed to traditional Chinese opera (*xiqu*). The reformers thought of *huaju* as something advanced, something that represented the ideas of Western Enlightenment and the West's wealth and technology. They felt *huaju* could become a weapon for resisting feudal autocracy. In addition, during the Communist revolution, the creative principles of Russian socialist realism were introduced to China. They became an important factor in revolutionary propaganda. After 1949, the new Chinese government drastically reformed *xiqu* and established a nationwide opera movement, while also creating, with the help of local governments and the army, a large number of *huaju* troupes that would instrumentalize realistic drama to create a totalitarian perspective on reality and history by propagating the policies of the new regime. At the heart of this understanding of dramatic arts was the principle "take from life to elevate life." This creative principle matched Confucian morals, which upheld that writings are for conveying truth. Confucianism was an important cultural tool for the consolidation of the new regime.

During the Cultural Revolution, literary and artistic creation was extremely limited because government controls were constantly drawn tighter. There were only eight model operas performed in the whole country. Although their stylistic form had changed, the creative principles they followed were still socialist-realist ones, which demanded that playwrights apply their skills to express content and present perfect heroes on stage. After the Cultural Revolution ended in 1976, there was a rise in dramatic production: political satires and critical reassessment of realistic forms thrived for a few years. But this wave very quickly fell prey to the economic reforms of the time. China's drama academies, embedded in a national system, faced structural challenges; and they had to seek a way to survive between commercial needs and national propaganda tasks.

Since the 1980s, under the impact of television and the internet, the once-popular dramas have lost mass appeal; at the same time, they have slipped under the radar of the national propaganda organs. Although *huaju* and *xiqu* have long since lost their important position in the cultural lives and minds of Chinese people, the creative principles of dramatic realism have not changed at all. In the drama academies, these principles are still widely taught, alongside the principle of *xijuxing* (dramaticism). Under the impact of these principles, form and content are strictly separated from each other. The purpose of form is to express content. This creative rule is not only applied in mainstream national propaganda drama but also in the commercial context of comedies and melodramas. In recent years, following the crisis in the system of mainstream drama, the voices that criticize the principles of classical dramatic creation have become louder and louder. But in the Chinese theatre world, the crisis in drama has not been profoundly examined in the manner of Szondi, who analyzed the crisis in European drama.[3] It is commonly asserted that the failure in playwriting is the main source of this crisis.

This is the context in which my translation of Lehmann's *Postdramatisches Theater* landed in China in 2010. While it caused a lot of discomfort and aggression within the mainstream world of drama, at the same time, it won great interest among some creative practitioners. Li Jianjun,[4] an independent director of the *New Youth Theatre Group (Xin Qingnian Jutuan)*, said:

> This book had quite an impact on me. It sketched the map of the postdramatic. I began to think about Western contemporary drama according to this postdramatic map. This process of thinking helped me to find my own creative methods.[5]

These sentiments are echoed by others. Li Ning[6] comments:

---

3   See Peter Szondi, *Theorie des Modernen Dramas* (Frankfurt/Main: Suhrkamp, 1963), (Peter Szondi, *Theory of the Modern Drama. A Critical Edition* [Minneapolis: University of Minnesota Press, 1987]).

4   Li Jianjun (born in 1972 in Jingchuan) is a Chinese director who studied Stage Design at Beijing's Central Academy of Drama. After three years working at *China Youth Art Theatre (Zhongguo Qingnian Yishu Jutuan)*, he began to work independently in 2007. He is the founder of the *New Youth Theatre Group (Xin Qingnian Jutuan)*.

5   All quotes from artists reproduced in this text are from unpublished WeChat interviews Li originally undertook for her book *Juchang Performance in Contemporary Chinese Society (1980-2020)*.

6   Li Ning (born 1972) is the founder of the physical arts collective *J-town Physical Guerrillas (Lingyun Yan Zhiti Youjidui)*, which has been producing *juchang* performances since 1997. He studied sculpture at Shandong Art School and modern dance and performance with the

Before reading *Houxiju juchang [Postdramatic Theatre]*, I had no sense of belonging. The biggest feeling after reading was: For the first time, I could really determine my own position, it was like opening the Baidu map on the App and recognizing one's own position.

Wen Hui[7] said:

I read this book around 2012 in mainland China and it is one of the rare ones about contemporary theatre. I remember that this book excited me and it felt really fresh. I bought a copy for a friend in Hong Kong as well.

Wang Mengfan[8] said:

I read this book for the first time in the Winter of 2011 after attending Li Yinan's class on Western contemporary theatre arts at the Central Academy of Drama in Beijing. But I only understood fully what this book is about after I started my own creative productions. I think that the emergence of this book provides European and domestic practitioners with a name for our own productions; or to put it in another way, it allowed me to understand more clearly my own productions in relation to the Western theatre.

The concept of *juchang* is my invention, arising from my translation of *Post-dramatisches Theater,* by Hans-Thies Lehmann.[9] It takes its point of departure from the meaning of the Chinese character *chang* (space). I use this term to describe something that is not a linear and narrative-based *xijuxing* (dramaticism), but rather to emphasize the performative and spatial dimension of the performance creation. In this understanding, *chang* does not refer to physical space alone, but it points to the organism that is created through the mutual interaction between the performers and the audience. This emphasis on the Chinese character *chang* represents a new aesthetics that declares war on the concepts of text, pro-

---

renowned choreographer Jin Xing.

7   For information on Wen Hui please see the *Introduction* and *Biographies* in this volume.
8   For information on Wang Mengfan please see the *Biographies* in this volume.
9   Li Yinan re-established the term *juchang* in the course of her translation of Hans-Thies Lehmann's *Postdramatisches Theater*. In 2010, when she translated the book title and term as "*Houxiju Juchang,*" the word *juchang*, which was unfamiliar in mainland China's theatrical discourse at the time, served primarily as an opposing concept to the established concept of drama, *xiju*. The concept of *juchang* thus had the purpose of pointing to the dimension of theatricality/perfromativity. For the conceptualization of this term, Li Yinan was able to draw on both the theatrical discourse of China before the foundation of the People's Republic in 1949 and the self-designation of independent Chinese theatre-makers since the 1980s, who refer to their work as *juchang*, in contrast to *xiju*. See also the panel discussion "Rethinking Theatricality. Hans-Thies Lehmann's Postdramatic Theatre and Chinese *Juchang*" in this volume.

fessionalism, dramatic nature, linear narratives and logos. This term has also been used by Chinese independent theatre-makers to describe their own works. Choreographer and author Tian Gebing,[10] founder of the *Paper Tiger Theatre Studio Beijing* (*Beijing Zhilaohu Xiju Gongzuoshi*), commented:

> The Paper Tigers have used this word juchang since the 1990s. Xiju is a concept that is driven by assumptions of text and literature, but the term juchang emphasizes the spatial and live elements. The Paper Tiger Theatre Studio was founded in order to oppose literalization; that's why we use the term juchang to describe our practice.

Wang Mengfan adds:

> My personal aesthetics and creative methods are deeply influenced by the German dance theatre tradition, but this statement alone is not so important, because I do not work together with professional dancers and actors, but with ordinary people—with groups whose social identity is not classified into one category. Under the current domestic discourse and practice, it is not important to discuss if something is dance or *juchang*, but to pose the question: how should we present and perceive the bodies of these people, and why should we watch them at all? In the theatre, their bodies are much more linked to their actions than to their language. This is why I would prefer my work to be described as *juchang* instead of *xiju*.

A preference for the term *juchang* over the word *xiju* for defining one's own performance work is connected to the position of being outside the mainstream drama system that owns all the discursive power. Li Ning comments:

> I uphold a strong rejection of the term *xiju*, and perhaps this is because when I was a child, I lived in a military compound and when the cultural workers' groups came to perform *huaju*, I was never allowed to enter the auditorium. Afterward, as I started to become involved in performing and creating, some people told me: Your works are the opposite of *xiju* drama, and I started to notice it too, and then there came a time when I consciously affirmed it.

Zhang Xian,[11] one of China's earliest experimental theatre-makers, agrees:

> I call almost all of my works *juchang*, including many of the rebellious interview texts that are called Speech-Action-Theatre. I subsume my non-artist, life-based creation projects under the term *juchang*, too.

---

10 Tian Gebing (born 1963 in Xian) is a Chinese director, choreographer and author, who graduated in 1991 from the Central Academy of Drama in Beijing. In 1997, he founded his own company *Paper Tiger Theatre Studio Beijing (Beijing Zhilaohu Xiju Gongzuoshi)*.

11 Zhang Xian (born 1955 in Shanghai) is a playwright and director. He is considered to be one of China's earliest experimental theatre-makers. In 2013 he was visiting professor at the University of Giessen.

Wen Hui says: "We should call our *Living Dance Studio* works *juchang*, they are definitely not *xiju*."

In the beginning, the new *juchang* aesthetic was related to the difficult position of being outside the official theatre system. Due to a lack of funding, the *juchang* practitioners had to use unconventional spaces outside city centers: tent theatre was performed in temporarily erected structures; Beijing's *Caochangdi Workstation* operated beyond the Fifth Ring Road and performed in their own spaces; Shanghai's *Grass Stage* performed in any possible space (auditoriums, hotel lobbies, art museums, schools, etc). Li Ning performed in an unfinished building on the outskirts of the city of Jinan; Zhang Xian extended the definition of *juchang* by calling all forms of public intervention *juchang*. He included interviews, online texts and flash mobs because his scripts had no chance whatsoever of being performed. The production of *juchang* became a way for theatre-makers outside the system to seize public space.

The independent theatre practice of *juchang* probably emerged in the 1980s at the latest. In this post-Cultural Revolution era, the first *juchang* experiments were led by young artists. The most representative artist within this context is Mou Sen and his *Frog Experimental Theatre Company (Wa Shiyan Jutuan)*.[12] Mou Sen explained:

> My productions in the 1990s such as *The Other Side (Bi An)*, *Zero Archives (Ling Dangan)*, *Related to AIDS (Yu Aizi Youguan)*, *Red Herring (Hong Feiyu)*, and others should all be understood as *juchang* practices.

Yi Liming, who often collaborated with Mou as a scenographer, also stated:

> Much of my work back then was very close to the essence of *juchang*, for example, my collaboration with Mou Sen on *Zero Archives*, and *Related to AIDS*, and others.

The performance space of *The Other Side* was a small classroom in the performance department of the Beijing Film Academy. *Related to AIDS* was performed in the Yuanen Temple Theatre, which was under construction at the time, and Yi Liming wanted to change the traditional form of theatre space. During the performance, he had thirteen migrant workers build a wall around the crowd in the performance space, thus emphasizing that performers and observers were sharing the same space at the same time. In these works, the emphasis on space and the stress on and application of the concept of *chang* are obvious.

After 2000, the *Living Dance Studio/Caochangdi Workstation (Shenghuo Wudao Gongzuoshi /Caochangdi Gongzuozhan)* became one of the first independ-

---

12 Mou Sen (born in 1963) graduated from the literature faculty of the Pedagogical University Beijing. In the 1980s he founded his company *Frog Experiment Group (Wa Shiyan Jutuan)*.

ent Chinese centers for producing *juchang*. Wen Hui and Wu Wenguang,[13] inspired by having performed in several of Mou Sen's performances, opened up their private living space and turned it into a performance space. They then brought practitioners from all over China together. One such group of practitioners established a commune with shared living facilities. They ate together, rehearsed together, and thus formed the active *juchang* ensemble at *Caochangdi*. This space extended artistic creation into the spaces of everyday life, and the ensemble was united by a sense of family. This specific mix of familial behavior and public life, which is closely related to the concept of *chang*, strongly opposed the control of public space by the authorities as well as the powerful system of *xiju* that dominated cultural life. In 2007, I collaborated as a dramaturg with *Caochangdi Workstation's* Young Choreographer Project and also introduced the fundamental concepts of postdramatic theatre to China by giving lectures. Since then, I have discovered the important nature of the *juchang* concept. In his documentary film workshop, Wu Wenguang gave the participants two topics: A self-portrait and public space. Recording with a video camera is a means to amplify observing. If observing is the essence of *juchang* art, then people who are powerless in their normal life can gain the initiative by observing daily life and thus turning it into theatre. I still remember how one participant of the Choreographer Project videoed on a public bus. Many years later, this student, Li Jianjun, created a piece of work called "*25.3km*", which turned the bus into a performance space.

Suffering from the pressure of sharply rising rents, many *juchang* practitioners were forced to give up their performance venues. In 2014, the *Caochangdi Workstation* was destroyed by the power of capitalism and fell prey to the dynamics of urbanization and gentrification in Beijing. Wu and Wen lost their studio space. Since then, *juchang* practitioners have had to compete for performance spaces in the cracks between the state and the commercial market. In the National Cultural Centre of Beijing, the *juchang* artists have no choice but to search for a tiny space of their own. Some venues that have the spatial capacity for performance, such as the Nanluoguxiang Theatre Festival, Wuzhen Theatre Festival, and the Beijing Youth Theatre Festival, have expressed a more open attitude towards the *juchang* artists.

After the publication of my Chinese translation of *Postdramatisches Theater*, Professor Lehmann took up an opportunity to visit China and gave direct and powerful support to independent Chinese *juchang* artists. In Wuzhen, he saw works by Li Jianjun and Li Ning. He was very appreciative and encouraging and was instrumental in helping these once marginal theatre-producers to gain a place within the Chinese mainstream theatre industry. This year, Professor Leh-

---

13 Wu Wenguang (born 1956 in Yunnan province) studied literature theory at University of Yunnan. He worked for Chinese State Television to fund his production of independent documentary films. From 1994 until 2014 he collaborated with the dancer Wen Hui, with whom he set up the *Living Dance Studio/Caochangdi Workstation*.

mann also served as an academic advisor to the Laiwu Factory Theatre Festival. Chen Tian, a young scholar at Nanjing University, responds to the baseless criticism by mainstream drama practitioners with which postdramatic theatre and China's new *juchang* artists were confronted:

> If so many mainstream national drama ensembles, who enjoy national financial support, are not able to prosper commercially in the drama market, why shouldn't a minority of non-mainstream and financially oppressed artists attempt to play a bigger role? If we do not start to spread the theory of postdramatic theatre, how can we ever harvest a prosperous mainstream drama?[14]

The year 2019 marked 20 years since the publication of *Postdramatisches Theater*. Since it has been in print, the theatre community in the West has discussed it in a very intense way. Some scholars have doubted the argument expressed in the book that theatre will continue to develop in a non-expressive, non-mimetic direction. I believe that the context of postdramatic theatre in China is quite different from that in the West. Contemporary China is characterized by the pressure on space for independent art practitioners, and also the phenomenon of aphasia is increasingly severe. From a broader perspective, once-colonized Asia is looking for a way to find its own voice and find a place within a world still largely dominated by concepts derived from Western Enlightenment. In the struggle for public space, postdramatic theatre can provide us with many useful insights.

Bibliography

Chen Tian. "Yingguo Guojia Juyuan Xianchang Yu Xiju Juchang De Weiji—Jian Yu Fei Chunfang Jiaoshou Shangque." [The National Theatre Scene and the Crisis of Dramatic Theatre in the UK—A Debate on Professor Fei Chunfang] *Xiju Yingshi Pinglun*, no. 2 (2018).

Lehmann, Hans-Thies. *Postdramatisches Theater* [Postdramatic Theatre]. Frankfurt/Main: Verlag der Autoren, 1999.

Lehmann, Hans-Thies. *Postdramatic Theatre*. New York: Routledge, 2006.

Li Yinan. *Juchang Performance in Contemporary Chinese Society (1980-2020)*. Münchner Universitätsschriften, Theaterwissenschaft 34. München: utzverlag, 2020.

Szondi, Peter. *Theorie des modernen Dramas*. Frankfurt/Main: Suhrkamp, 1963.

Szondi, Peter. *Theory of the Modern Drama. A Critical Edition*. Minneapolis: University of Minnesota Press, 1987.

---

14 Chen Tian, "Yingguo guojia juyuan xianchang yu xiju juchang de weiji—jian yu fei chunfang jiaoshou shangque" [The National Theatre Scene and the Crisis of Dramatic Theatre in the UK—A Debate on Professor Fei Chunfang] *Xiju Yingshi Pinglun*, no. 2 (2018).

II
POSTDRAMATIC RESONANCE
IN THEATRE PRACTICES

There Is No Empty Space on Earth

Zhao Chuan

Two years ago, I worked with the Korean director Lee Kyung-Sung. We were doing a workshop in Seoul, together with a Japanese director. I have the habit of starting workshops, my own *Grass Stage* included, with self-introductions. It doesn't have to be long, just so that we have a basic understanding of one another on this first encounter. The three of us were collaborating with a Korean theatre troupe called Yohangza, a big theatre company in Korea. They have 70 to 80 actors. However, those actors are not salaried employees. When they have a new play, suitable actors are chosen, and they get paid for the project. Senior actors enjoy greater stability, economically speaking, since they are chosen more often. However, in the first few years, a new member fresh from the theatre academy might not have many tasks throughout a year. So many of them still need other jobs to make a living, unless they come from a wealthy family.

When we sat together for self-introductions, they started by introducing their occupation: "I'm an actor." Some earn a living by working at McDonald's, some by manual labor, babysitting, and all sorts. But they don't see their occupation as a McDonald's staff or a worker. They all said that they were actors, although none of them actually lived from acting.

In *Grass Stage*, even now, most of us will never say: "I'm an artist" or: "I'm an actor." They tell you the job that they make a living with. So we have teachers, photographers, and people working in all kinds of occupations. The job comes first in the introduction. I find this very interesting. I discussed it with the Korean actors. The first reason might be *reality*, which I will talk about later. I think what Kai Tuchmann does in his dramaturgy and documentary theatre has a lot to do with the question of reality. The thing about reality is that it is there, but somehow, it's not very certain. So when you assert that you are an actor, it is, to some extent, true. But there can be deviations, because this identity might not explain you or introduce you very well. So what is real? When we work together, it is all about the question of how people connect. In the first place, we are different human beings. And we realize the differences. We recognize how we are connected in our real social relationships. Only then comes the question of how we work together as theatre-makers, which is easier. The first question is more difficult. A theatre troupe often seems united, powerful, and organized. But all problems surrounding people in the real world still exist in the world of theatre and the creative arts. In the end, it all comes back to the problem of people.

I've been making theatre for more than ten years. When people ask me what I do, I reply that I make theatre. The truth is, all these years, I haven't found an entrance to proper theatres or to a drama academy. Thanks to Kai, I've come to a drama academy today to hold a lecture for the first time. So let's talk about the issue of entering spaces. I don't know if you've read the book *The Empty Space* by Peter Brook. It was quite a hit and sold very well after publication. Young people fond of culture and the arts love to refer to its definition of theatre, which states that theatre is something that happens when one person watches another, who is walking across a space, and so on. But from the beginning, I had some suspicions. His claim was very different from my notion of theatre. A theatre space is not empty; just like this room: it's not empty. There are traces. Look at the walls. There were many props when we entered the room this morning, and we removed them from the room. Even if we all leave the room until our next entrance, it's still not empty. It does not only exist because you walk in. It is already there. This room, together with the new, somewhat vacant campus which sits in Changping that I walked across this morning—all this space, it is not empty. There are many things, lively things happening in the space.

Generally speaking, in the environment of China, to enter a theatre, you will need a ticket. Tickets for shows in Shanghai, Beijing, and Tianjin cost about the same. In the last few weeks, we participated in China's biggest theatre festival in Wuzhen, where a ticket is more expensive, and transportation and accommodation costs have to be paid in addition. This kind of expense is no big deal for our country's middle class. They can afford it. But how many of the population can afford these theatre tickets? My point is, you need to be economically qualified to go to the theatre. I don't think more than ten percent of the citizens in our country are willing to spend money on an evening in the theatre. Right? Also, one doesn't show up at the theatre for no reason. It's not like having a meal. One needs to be intellectually qualified, educated, and cultivated, or hoping to become cultivated and investing in it. Think about it this way: Theatre is the top layer of a cake. It's the cream. These are what we call grand theatres or city theatres today. So it's not an empty space. It has various intricate tensional relationships with the society, culturally and economically.

There is no empty space on earth, not with our ever-growing human desires and overlaying histories. So—this is very important—when we talk about theatre and drama, we should talk about our relationship with the space when we walk in and about what this space means.

When we sit here today, a power relationship exists in this space. You have left this generous space for me and have crowded in the corner around the front door, because I am the invited teacher. The space is reserved for me. It would obviously violate the common power relationship if you would push me into the corner. When we talk about theatre, we shall recognize these aspects and we should be sensitive about them.

I know you have politics classes; do you also need to learn party history? Drama played a big role in our politics and culture in the past. The Anti-Rightest Campaign in the 1950s started from criticism of a play called *Hai Rui Dismissed from Office* (*Hai Rui Ba Guan*). Many political movements before and after were connected with plays in those years. Because earlier than that, many leftist cultured youths were making theatre, went to Yanan later on, and became important cultural officials when the Communists came to power after 1949. In contrast to literature, theatre is much more practical and spatial. So the theatre space has never been simple.

In the ideology back then, the theatre stage had to serve workers, peasants, and soldiers. For instance, if I had wanted to study acting, I wouldn't have succeeded. I don't look good. According to the 1970s standard, I am too slim. The workers, peasants, and soldiers should be strong and loud, have a square face, and look powerful on stage. But do actual workers, peasants, and soldiers look like this? They have all kinds of looks and maybe are not pretty. Today—when you walk on the campus of the theatre academy in Shanghai—everywhere you look, the boys are handsome, and the girls are always very beautiful. They will be in television, commercials, movies in the very near future. The ultimate goal is to sell. So all these pretty looks are eventually for sale. Far from the old workers, peasants, and soldiers, we have left the ideological space for the commercial space.

So there is no empty space.

An anecdote: Eugenio Barba was the honorary president of a Chinese theatre festival. The artistic director of this festival, who thought of himself as a qualified master, wished to organize a conversation between master and master. Barba's assistant once came to a performance by *Grass Stage*, liked it very much, and became a friend of ours. He told me about this conversation between the two "masters." When the two men sat down, Barba asks the other master: "We make theatre because of an interior lack of something. What is yours?" The other master was lost for words and beat around the bush. So this other master was somewhat looked down upon since he couldn't even answer this fundamental question—what do you lack? So I want to ask you. You come here to study theatre, do you lack anything? Does what you study and what you do have anything to do with your lack or your deficiency? (Student: I think I lack life.) You lack life. You think you are not living. Anyone else? (Student: Time.) You lack time. You come here to study theatre-making. Has this question never occurred to you even you're not a master? (Student: self-cognition) Self-cognition. (Student: Connection with the world) Connection with the world. Good. No hurry. Take your time to think about it. This is a master-level question. Think as if this senior master in his seventies sits opposite you and poses this question to you. I think it's a question of some weight. You can save it for later. I'll give you my answer. I began thinking about it after hearing this story.

I never studied in a theatre academy. As I told you at the beginning of this lecture, I haven't found the door to theatre and its academies. When I was young, I went to the Fine Arts School, which is affiliated with the Shanghai Academy of Fine Arts. I studied painting. I also spent over ten years on literature, writing fiction and movie scripts. More than ten years ago, almost by accident, I made my first play. I found it very interesting and since then have worked in theatre for almost 15 years. So, to answer this master question, I began wondering why. I think in the very beginning, the reason I made theatre was due to dissatisfaction. There was a lack of reality, a deficiency of truth where I lived. I grew up in Shanghai and also spent over ten years overseas, but I'm not specifically referring to one place when I talk about the lack of truth. So for me, the theatre became a way to the real. Last century, we believed workers, peasants, and soldiers should look like that on stage, because we believed that was true. When the five or six Korean young people sat together with me, introducing themselves as actors, they were not trying to deceive me. They only said what they believed to be true. But what I expect, or what I seek, is another form of truth, which I think is more real than what they told me.

In the 1970s, the famous Italian leftist filmmaker Michelangelo Antonioni was invited by Premier Zhou Enlai to come to China and make a documentary film that is called *Chung Kuo Cina 1972*. Today it's very precious since we don't have many documentaries about the seventies in China—plain scenes of people in Beijing, Shanghai, of the social life back then. But after the film was done, a political movement raged across the country, in which it was condemned to nothing. We didn't see it then; the screening was not allowed in China, but it was shown in Europe. The environment shown in the film is not the modernized version as in propaganda; it also shows the ragged clothes. The criticism was led by the government, and there were debates in Europe, too. One passage in Susan Sontag's *On Photography* discussed this film. She took the side of Antonioni, making many criticisms of the Chinese. My argument is: what is the reality of people? If you go into a village and ask to take a picture of an old granny, she will refuse, saying that she's not tidy. She needs to clean herself up, dress up in her best attire and sit before the camera with a smile because she thinks that is her true self, although she usually might look menacing. A casual photo of her is untrue, or in another aspect, not pretty. Pretty is one kind of truth we are after, like the good look of workers, peasants, and soldiers we pursued on stage.

There is another experience of mine: I went to Kinshasa, Congo. People there refused to be photographed, especially by foreigners. You raise your camera, no matter how far, someone will instantly come and demand you to stop. My intention was to photograph everything interesting as it was my first time in Africa. I was confused in the beginning but understood later on. They thought their daily life was dirty and indecent. They felt harmed by being photographed. The other reason is that they thought the foreigners were taking the photographs to sell. That is unfair for them. So, the truth is not as simple as Ms. Sontag or Mr. Antonioni thinks. There is something else in it—dignity.

In an era in which visibility is almost the only belief, this is somewhat difficult to understand. The real seems to be based on what is exposed to our eyes, but it is not completely identical with what is right before our eyes. The truth is a complex process of exploration, and the real includes our inner world, thus forming a more complex reality—that is, our existence. Therefore, the real is not only about what has happened, but also about the future. Our existence has a future. It is for the sake of existence that we have to fight forgetting.

I have no intention here to judge what is right or wrong with what I mentioned above. Just that there is a doubt, and I think these doubts are part of the real that I seek in my theatre-making.

I now want to present something from my own practice and talk about how it connects to this topic. Kai has already introduced you to my group or my collaborators. We are called *Grass Stage* (*Caotaiban*). We started in 2005 and met weekly for discussion, reading, theatre workshops, and small seminars. During these discussions, we formed something, a consensus about how to make theatre. We worked a lot in a place in Shanghai called the Downstream Garage (*Xiahe Micang*). Some of you might have heard about it. It's gone now. It existed for nine years and played an important role in supporting independent, experimental, and rather marginal theatre-making. We were based in the Downstream Garage and made theatre pieces. Then a question occurred to me. If we go on staying here, would it be too safe? Of course, academies and universities are also very safe places. Well maybe not—with all the CCTV cameras indicating it's not that safe. Back then, we felt safe. And I thought this was a problem. Safety cuts us off from the outside world. How do we find something unsafe? How do we explore our connection with the space? So we decided to leave the space where we met every week. We decided to enter communities, get in touch with different people, and bring our theatre to many different places, to see whether our so-called artistic creation could endure the sunshine and the crowd. We went on and started the project *Field Maneuvers* (*Lalian*) in 2009. Kai may have shown you some documentary footage of it. We produce one or two new plays and tour with them for one month. We take trains only, not airplanes from one city to the next. We stop, we put on the show, we leave. One tour covers 5000–8000 kilometers, 5–7 cities. We arrive at one place, put on 1–3 performances, and move on to the next place. We've done this five times since 2009. In this way, we've been to many new places. The plays were experimental and thematic small theatre pieces. We've been to Xining, Yinchuan, Neimenggu, Guiyang, and other second- and third-tier cities. All this is connected to the notion of tension in the space.

I have a question to ask. Who can tell me what politics is? After all these years of politics class. [Student Feng Taojing: human relations.] Excellent. This is also my understanding. Politics is how people connect. A suggestion or a proposal about how people should connect is a political idea. To implement it is political action.

In 2014, we made a play collectively called *World Factory* (*Shijie Gongchang*). The original version of the play took around four years of research. During those years, I spent one or two months on research every year. I traveled to different regions and countries and met a lot of people: from scholars and workers in leading-edge industries to factory owners and entrepreneurs to understand industry, industrialization, and the current conditions of workers and the factories. When these people from different social backgrounds, occupations, identities, and ages join in creation, how do we cooperate?

In the beginning, I had this belief that after a long, long time, we would come up with a unifying idea on which to build a play. Basically, it's the strategy this country adopts: to unify thoughts. If there is a good idea, at least when they think it is, our thinking need to be unified under it. Only when thoughts are unified can things be done. But when I began, I quickly realized that what's more interesting and important than a unifying concept are the different opinions that people have. These differences form one of the foundations of drama and theatre: conflict. People think differently. But how do people connect when they think differently? And how does the difference transform into a clue, into a force of the play? This seems to have become my main aim in work. Not to unify ideas but to let different opinions be, grow, and connect.

Reflecting on this, I will introduce the basic working method we have used for more than ten years since 2005. In the beginning, we believed in collective creation. We started working collectively with our first production, *38th Parallel Still Play* (*38xian Youxi*),[1] which lasted one to two years. In collective creation, we gather and discuss the issue again and again. From the discussion, we extract valuable materials and transform them into something suitable for the stage through workshops. Then we weave the materials together.

This is our method of collective creation. We did this for almost three years. In the process of collaborative creation, a problem gradually appeared. When 90 percent of the twenty people here in the room raise their hands in favor of something, it's also what people on the street will mostly agree on. The opinions that are too marginal, too radical, or too conservative are wiped away. What's left is the chaos in the middle, the mainstream. So the outcome of this collective creation is too soft. This seemed to us to be a problem. So after a year or two, I thought about changing this process. I realized that each individual had great initiative and creativity. How can we sharpen this creativity instead of blunting it in endless discussions? So on the basis of collective creation, we started individual creation—solo performance. You have an idea, then the rest of our collective helps to push forward your idea.

The Japanese theatre maker Daizo Sakurai also makes tent theatre in Beijing. Daizo has this method called "self-rehearsing." What we do sounds similar but is

---

1   38th Parallel: The Military Demarcation Line (MDL) is the land border or demarcation line between North Korea and South Korea. The DMZ runs near the 38th parallel, hence the name. "Line 38" later refers to a forbidden line, for example, on the classroom table between two students.

in fact very different. In his method, the director works with you, one on one, for two or three days. The process is very private. The purpose is to incite something in the performer. By contrast, our individual creation is formed between the performer and the rest of the troupe. We use collective discussion as a basis on which we interact. But by the end, performing a solo piece is physical and personal. You need to accomplish it by yourself.

We started from collective creation. Years later, we promoted solo performance for personal development. And how do individual elements become a play and end up on the stage? This is mainly my job. My job is to reintegrate the results of collective creation and individual performances. Usually, after the first phase of creation, I have one or two weeks to form all materials into a script. Something might be developed, something reduced, something pushed further. For the final script, the question is: How to create a connection among different opinions on the same subject from different people? Me and you, we can have very contrasting views on the same issue. So what is the connection on stage under a common narrative? How to present the connection, the inner tension of different opinions to the audience? How to form the play out of the differences? So we came from collective creation to individual creation and now to what I call the comprehensive method. The status of the power relationship is clear and known by all in *Grass Stage*. It is collective creation, as a foundation, plus individuals, plus Zhao Chuan. There are three parts. And they integrate to accomplish our goal.

Have I made it clear? Any questions?

[Student Xu Li: So the collective creation incites the individuals who make their performances. Then you filter the materials and form a play on stage. Can I understand it this way?]

Not entirely. For example, most of you are the only child in the family, right? Suppose we want to tell a story about the "only child." We discuss, which forms a foundation, meaning we understand one another's view on the subject. And you return to your own view. What you present on stage is your view. This is what we called individual creation. As for my part, I don't mainly do "filtering," but connecting. You express your thought on the same subject differently than someone else; how do these ideas connect? Individuals work on their opinions, but what's shown on stage is "we." When "I" becomes "we," the context is the whole society. This is my hope. "I" is not isolated. There is always a tension between "I" and "we".

In the first couple of years of *Grass Stage*, we used many physical techniques. In the first version of *World Factory*, for example, the actors worked hard on stage, creating great tension and force. In 2006 we came to Beijing and staged the play *Madmen's Stories* (*Kuangren Gushi*) in the small theatre of National Theatre Company. Tao Qingmei, a good friend of ours, came to see the show. She asked me: "Could you let them move less on stage? They move so much that it's hard to hear what they say." Actually, at that time, it was impossible for the actors to move less.

I could put it this way—they were excited. It's a sudden acquisition of power and a release. Most of our participants might have never thought, a few years ago, that they could be acting on stage one day, loudly speaking their thoughts and stretching out their bodies to let others realize their existence. They could not imagine it a few years earlier because they had no professional training. Some people weren't even interested in acting. But they had other interests and focuses, which led them to *Grass Stage* and onto the stage. So when they finally enter the stage, the force is spectacular.

People often, especially in academies like this, discuss the acting in a play, whether it's good acting or not. I mentioned Eugenio Barba, the European master. I had the honor of being invited to see his workshop at Shanghai Theatre Academy. He is renowned for his cross-cultural performance studies with an anthropological approach. He wrote books about how acting works, how an actor gains energy by simply standing on the stage, where the energy comes from, how the body should move to attain the strongest existence and tension. His workshop was related to this. He had invited two Brazilian performers specializing in Brazilian folk dance, one Chinese Yu Opera performer, and a dancer of Bali traditional dancing from Indonesia. The performers dressed up in traditional costumes and danced, one by one. After the performances, he commented "very beautiful" and asked if we all agree. These traditional arts, of course, contain both dancing and singing, so there was a libretto in every performance. First, they were asked to leave out the libretto by Barba. Then to leave out the costumes. They danced again with casual clothes on and no singing. He asked again: "Do you think they're beautiful? I still think they are," he answered himself.

He wished to establish some basic rules about physical movements in performances. He explained that it's this or that way of moving that makes acting work. I quite understand this approach—but there's a big problem here. When he introduced the performer as a Peking Opera actress, the performer (also a teacher in traditional opera) corrected that what she performs is not Peking Opera, but Yu Opera. Barba said to all of us: "Well, it doesn't matter, they're the same!" In our traditional opera, stories are told in the libretto. This says something about why people put it on stage in the first place. Maybe for rituals, maybe to educate. It gradually evolved into the performance it is now. The costumes are identities. *Sheng, Dan, Jing, Mo, Chou.* These roles roughly suggest the genders and social status. A man can be a general, a king or a servant, a clown, all with different costumes. When we take out the historical context and identities—you can't say you understand it without all these. I think it's impossible and rather rude. How can you understand the performance when you don't even care whether the character is male or female? It doesn't work, in my opinion. Acting, what we do on stage, is about the people. We discussed dignity and reality.

I had this substantial doubt, or even criticism about the master Barba, how he cut out all the contexts and claimed to understand the performance. I told you what our participants at *Grass Stage* thought of their occupations when they introduced themselves. None of them came to *Grass Stage* to learn acting, but most

of them start practicing and studying acting in *Grass Stage*. Their stage experiences begin here. Is this a paradox? In standard acting classes in theatre
academies, actors are asked to "empty themselves," right? We hope the freshmen
can learn, through exercises, to empty themselves and open up their bodies. Then,
you are brand new; you are a fairy. Who you are doesn't really matter. You'd better not be yourself. Actors are empty vessels. The director can, at any time, pour
in something new. The academies teach them, in the Stanislavsky system, for example, to attain an inner self through inner experiences. Within the Stanislavsky
system are many acting techniques that help to fulfill the director's requirements.
The directors also learn the techniques to know how to let the magic happen.

Grass Stage is the opposite of this practice. I hope all participants are very
clear about who they are. I hope they build a connection between the issue and
themselves during the discussion, but not between the issue and their roles.
Whether you live in Changping or Beijing, what is your connection to the issue?
Who are you? Who are they? What are the social relationships among you? We
always have this premise. The participants come to *Grass Stage* to make theatre,
and they always have different motives, as small as doubts about themselves,
about daily life, as big as questions about society and history. The study of acting
goes along with queries into these issues and the expansion of vision. So acting
comes from subjectivity and doubts, comes from the motives of queries. It's very
hypocritical how we keep telling actors to build a strong inner self while not caring about their true inner selves at all. The actual inner self lies only in the actor
as a person.

The word "lively" is often used to praise an excellent imitation. "Lively", however, should not be an adjective but an action. It means inner vitality. Acting
comes from subjectivity and is a result of the motives of your queries. It is not
about merely displaying yourself. This is why I like to learn acting from performance art. In performance art, everything is about exploring an issue, not
performing a performance. Why do we make theatre? Not to show others our ca-
pabilities of acting, but because we have issues to discuss. This year I've found
another approach to acting—other than performance art: acrobatics. I met this
gentleman artist named Ueli Hirzel in Europe two years ago. This summer, he, Kai,
and I were in France together and watched some performances. Through acrobatics, I gained a further understanding of acting: It is the actor's challenge and
adventure. Every single performance is a challenge, an adventure. Nothing is easy
or simple. The energy and vitality on stage is spectacular. In 2015 and 2016, we
continued to work on a new version of *World Factory*. It seemed more polished
but less edgy. We have changed inside. We went deeper into the issue, worked
together, and had similar experiences. As a result, however, our attitudes converged. For years, the workers' brutal living surroundings have impacted me and
the other constant participants. Presentations of *World Factory* have uncon-
sciously transformed into giving voice to the workers. We've also changed from
come-and-go researchers to close friends in the worker communities and have
been involved in other worker campaigns elsewhere. Inside, outside, acting, prac-

ticing, these interweaving elements are changing. In this sense, for some people, life and art synchronize.

In short, the acting exercises and the creation process of *Grass Stage* are about connecting ourselves to what we wish to discuss. In *Grass Stage*, life, earlier and current work experiences, physical characteristics, behavior, and habits are all essential materials. I call it "theatre from people" (*yinren chengxi*). Above all, it's based on a general respect for humans. Only then can one make deep intellectual inquiries and convey one's opinions. A quick example: One participant with whom we've worked for three or four years has been a policeman for about twenty years. I don't know what led him to *Grass Stage*. He loves acting. He said he wanted to study dramatic literature here at the Central Academy of Drama but failed the exam. Then he was assigned to a police school, where he stayed. So he was a student fond of acting in the police school. He had a very different eye than others. The professional eye of a twenty-year-long policeman. Cold and fierce. He participated in several plays with us, and it was very interesting. He is a drama himself. He's afraid of height and many other things, fire, water. But he looks very strong with fierce eyes. My job is to incite everyone's sensitivity and mobility to learn, dig, discuss or reflect upon themselves, understand and imagine, and, most importantly, seek the connection between the issue and oneself and face it truthfully. So that acting is not about knowledge anymore. Participants are subjects of action. If we think of acting as a metaphor, it might refer to how one wishes to clarify one's relationship with the world.

The theatre that I believe in is not constituted on aesthetics but rather on ethics, which includes the goodness of the body. This goodness emerges on the path of our existence. Such an aesthetics of ethics realizes itself through practice, through an infinite approximation towards good deeds. It can never be just a copy of good values. The Good is not reproducible.

My theatre is a theatre activity with the least amount of accessible resources in today's city life. In this almost *poor theatre*, we take the liberty to use the body, text or image, and so on, wishing to open a brand-new space to communicate ideas. For more than ten years, I have worked on this margin that has been growing under the oppression of Chinese mainstream theatre and acting techniques. Its aesthetics, therefore, are constantly returning to the most basic human needs.

WORLD FACTORY

Zhao Chuan and Grass Stage

COMPOSED BY THE FOLLOWING GRASS STAGE MEMBERS: Wu Meng, Yu Kai, Wang Yifei, Wu Jiamin, Yu Lingna, Zhao Chuan, Yuan Jian, Christopher Connery, Xu Duo, Qin Ran, Liu Nian, Lü Lü, Wen Haishao, Chen Jingjie, Ding Bo, Jia Ying, Wang Ren, Li Ziyi, and Li Mengxi.

https://tinyurl.com/Zhao-World-Factory

ENGLISH TRANSLATION FROM THE CHINESE Lennet Daigle and Christopher Connery

TRANSLATION RIGHTS Grass Stage and Christopher Connery

WITH (in order of appearance)

STREET MUSICIAN, XU DUO – Xu Duo/Li Ziyi

MASKED CLOWN, WORKER C, HR MANAGER, CROWD MEMBER – Yu Lingna

PSYCHOLOGIST, PASSERBY, ENVIRONMENTAL EXPERT, WORKER A, CROWD MEMBER – Lü Lü

PERSON IN SMOG, NEW INDUSTRIALIST, CROWD MEMBER, YU KAI – Yu Kai

PERSON IN SMOG, WORKER B, YOUNG MAN, LEFT-BEHIND CHILD – Wu Jiamin

PERSON IN SMOG, FEMALE WORKER, CROWD MEMBER – Wu Meng

ASSEMBLY LINE WORKER A – Christopher Connery

ASSEMBLY LINE WORKER B – Jia Ying

DIRECTOR, WORKER D, CROWD MEMBER, WANG YI – Ding Bo

FINAL COMPOSITION, STAGING, AND ORGANIZATION – Zhao Chuan

PREMIERE June 5, 2014, at the Xi'an Academy of Fine Arts, China
PERFORMANCE RIGHTS Zhao Chuan and Grass Stage

1. Introduction: Eight Easy Steps

Audience enters. Street musician sits at a table in front of the stage playing the guitar and singing "In Love with the World" to the audience.

STREET MUSICIAN: (sings)
    Qi duo le, Qi duo le,
    Have a look at this world.
    This world is so lovely,
    I want to make love to it.

    How lovely, how lovely,
    How lovely is this fine world?
    Like goods on display in the store window,
    You can look but you cannot touch.

    Why is this? Why is this?
    Someone left this world in despair.
    Have we given up on the world?
    Or has the world betrayed us?

    Be patient! Be patient!
    We've been patient all these years.
    But we have no time to grieve,
    For we're making love with this world.

    Ai, we love you so very much,
    Although you say you love us too.
    But all you ever bring is harm;
    You take everything we have made
    And cruelly make it yours.
    But still but still.
    We keep on firmly loving you.
    Because we want, we want to conquer you.

    Ai, we still love you fiercely.
    Because we want, we want to conquer you.

    Making love, making love,
    We have paid so very dearly.
    And you are so heartless,
    But we still want to conquer you.
    You are so heartless,
    But we still want to conquer you.

Hei, you cruel-hearted beast;
Let's wait and see!

Fall in Love with the World. Lyrics/Music: Xu Duo.

The masked clown enters with two toy figures at her waist, holding a stack of paper and a pair of scissors. She flitteringly climbs onto the stage and dismissively tries to shoo the musician away. She spreads out the paper on a stool, uses the figure at her waist to trace shapes on the paper, then cuts out a number of male and female forms. She clips the cutouts to a string and stretches it out, humming and dancing. Finally, she forces the street musician off the stage. The masked clown dances, now joyfully, now sadly, with exaggerated gestures. She dances for a while then stops.

MASKED CLOWN: Why hasn't the performance started? Where are the actors? Where is the World Factory? (*stops, looks around*) How lame—How about (*suddenly excited*) I act out a scene called "Healthy and Wealthy in Eight Easy Steps" for your amusement.[1] Wealthy and healthy, 8, 8, 8, 8, 8, making the leap to wealth! (*stops, looks around*). Now what I really need is an assistant. (*looks at the audience*). Ahh, isn't that Professor Lü—I hear you are a psychologist, can you come give me a hand? Come on!

The psychologist excitedly jumps up on stage and greets the audience.

MASKED CLOWN: Professor Lü, welcome. Last time I saw you, you were in pyramid sales (*he helps the Masked Clown by holding one end of the string*). So tell us, in a factory with ten thousand workers, why do some commit suicide while others do not? What kind of person commits suicide?

PSYCHOLOGIST: Well, that's a very good question, and you've come to the right person. In psychology we use the special term "psychological resilience," which refers to a person's ability to deal with setbacks. Some of the young people who work in factories are raised by loving parents, they are physically healthy, and they have broad knowledge of the world. So when they encounter some difficulty. they are able to put it behind them and move on. Other people do not get enough love from their parents, and they're physically and emotionally unwell, so when something bad happens they just can't take it and throw themselves off a building. HaHaHa –

MASKED CLOWN: Professor Lü, could you take a look at these people and tell us which ones seem to be lacking in psychological resilience?

---

1   Healthy and wealthy is a pun on the Chinese word for Foxconn, the company noted for employee suicides.

PSYCHOLOGIST: Well this one for instance (*pointing to a blue paper person hanging crooked*) can't even stand up straight. The psychological resilience in this case is most assuredly weak.

Masked clown takes the scissors and cuts, and the paper figure falls to the ground.

MASKED CLOWN: (*excitedly*) HaHa! Who else? Who else?

PSYCHOLOGIST: This one works day and night; 14 hour shifts, six days a week. Can't handle it. He's a jumper –

Masked Clown cuts him down.

MASKED CLOWN: HaHa! Professor Lü, who else?

PSYCHOLOGIST: Look at this girl, thin as a rail. She can deal with the overtime, but not heartbreak. Lost love sends her straight over the edge.

Psychologist takes the scissors and cuts her off at the head, and the headless paper figure floats to the floor.

MASKED CLOWN: Professor Lü! What a heartless guy you are! No compassion for the fairer sex. Is there anyone else?

PSYCHOLOGIST: Take a look at this honest lad (*points to a blue figure*), what a sad case. He worked a whole year and when New Year's came, he didn't get paid. His boss ran off with his mistress and the money, HaHaHa (*gleefully cuts him down*).

MASKED CLOWN: (*Pointing to another blue paper figure*) How about this one?

PSYCHOLOGIST: HaHa! He worked at a factory for several decades, took his overtime in stride and got his pay. No heartbreaks either. But he did run into the glass ceiling, and with no hope for promotion, he jumped too (*cuts another down*).

MASKED CLOWN: Looks like they've all jumped. There's one left though, what about him?

PSYCHOLOGIST: HaHa! One left. I'm not sure what's going on with him, but he's got to die, regardless (*cuts down the last blue figure*).

The masked clown and the psychologist cut down all the remaining paper figures and watch them float to the floor, occasionally yelling "Jump! Jump!" and laughing.

Their actions are nervous, excited, exaggerated. When all the paper figures have fallen, the masked man looks at the empty rope and sighs.

MASKED CLOWN: Ai... you poor things.

PSYCHOLOGIST: Yes (*looking at the floor*), look at this: heads cracked open, brains splattered, missing arms and legs... Ai, the best years of their lives and they're willing to die like this, long before their time, throwing it all away like a pile of chicken feathers. 'Death lies on them like an untimely frost upon the sweetest flower of the field'. Well, it seems like in this day and age, you're either brave enough to stare death in the face, or so weak that you starve to death. You have to risk it all to win.

MASKED CLOWN: (*suddenly excited again, speaking to the audience*) That's right! Thank you, all of you! Thanks to the tech team! Thank you GDP! Thank you MoFo! Thanks to our corporate sponsors! And many thanks to all you consumers! Cheer up everyone! Hahahaha! (*points backstage*) Look! The actors are coming, let's go...

2. In the Smog

Several people come onstage. Some sit at tables in front of the stage, turn on the stage lights and busy themselves with their work. Others pull out a large drop cloth resembling a cinema screen. Darkness.

A projected image of a line of small boxes resembling factories, chimneys smoking. Behind the boxes is a group of elegantly dressed people vigorously sucking fluid from the boxes. The harder they suck the more smoke emerges from the chimneys. The smoke gradually obscures the people's faces, and the words "World Factory" appear on the screen.
The screen descends. Dim light.

The drop cloth now covers people's heads, wrapping around their faces like a haze. People get in each other's way as they try to go about their daily lives in the smog...

PEOPLE IN THE SMOG: Towers rise from the earth, cars clog the streets; it's hard to tell if spring is still spring, to distinguish a person from a dog, to see Mao's face on a banknote. Who blackened the rivers? Who greyed the skies? Who trashed our lives?

A fashionably dressed man clutching handfuls of shopping bags arrives by motorcycle. He is caught up in the smog and struggles to free himself, only to be caught up again and again...

PASSERBY: (*yelling*) Who did this? Who did this? Who did this to me? (*shouting until he's exhausted*)

The man sinks into the smog.

3. The Workers' March through History

The new industrialist stumbles out of the haze. Light.
She brushes off her clothes and hair and walks forward to look at the assembly line.

NEW INDUSTRIALIST: Who was it just now talking about "working endless over-time, 14 hours a day, six days a week..." I was a laborer too at one time, but now I own my own factory, and we develop new technology to take care of industrial waste. (*pauses*) A few years ago I went abroad to learn about labor protection and stopped in Manchester, a city that played an important role in the early industrial revolution...

A deafening sound comes from the machinery on the assembly line and gradually fades.

NEW INDUSTRIALIST: You can just imagine Manchester at the time, full of cotton, spindles and cloth... the steam engine had just been invented, passengers awaited the world's first trains at the world's first train stations, and the world's first industrialists were hard at work. It was also here that the world's first proletarians appeared—and the world's first capitalists too, they all came from these very streets and houses.

An image is projected: whirling machinery inside Quarry Bank Mill.

NEW INDUSTRIALIST: The Quarry Bank cotton mill is now a museum. Walking through its many workshops, it was as if I could still hear the roar of the ma-chines, smell the lingering stench, and see the toiling workers. The factory was in operation from 1784 to 1959 and at its peak employed 434 people.

DIRECTOR (*voice only*): Stop –

Projected images stop.

DIRECTOR: (*speaking to two actors set to go onstage*) Thank you. (*turning to the New Industrialist*) Could you say something about how long they worked?

NEW INDUSTRIALIST: Sure (*getting back into character after the interruption*) Prior to 1847, workers at the Quarry Bank Cotton Mill worked 13 hour shifts, from 5 AM to 8 PM, plus overtime when necessary.

(*stops, addressing the director*) What's strange is that the museum guide says "Working conditions at the time were very different from today," but I used to work 14 hour days. Who says things have changed? In factories and work sites all over, people work ten or more hours a day, and that doesn't include overtime.

(*back in character*) At Quarry Bank cotton mill workers were also punished: weights hung from the ears, fines, overtime, beatings and verbal abuse were all common—(*remembering*) my boss used to yell in my ear everyday: country girl! ...

DIRECTOR: (*stopping her*) OK, OK – I know... When Quarry Bank Mill was founded, there still weren't any laws regulating working conditions. Later in the 19th century, workers began protesting en masse, destroying machinery, pushing for legal reform, eventually forcing the government to regulate labor conditions. Of course, laws have to be enforced...

BUSINESSWOMAN: We know all about this from handling industrial waste. Director, do you think big capital cares about this stuff? They only care about making profits. I've met any number of investors, and they go on about globalization, and how they need to think globally when they consider production inputs. For them the social problems that come with cheap labor and environmental degradation are merely matters of investment risk. They're not things investors should worry about. The governments should take care of that.

DIRECTOR: Capital treats people like money-making machines – Play that other video from Manchester, the one that shows the beginning of a different historical trajectory–

A group of workers comes onstage and sets up a white cloth as a screen. The workers on the assembly line stop what they're doing and turn to watch. The projection shows Manchester's Chetham's Library. The librarian opens a cabinet and takes out a stack of books. He talks about them as he walks toward the reading room, then opens them.

DIRECTOR: This is England's first public library, Chetham's Library, next to one of Manchester's big churches. When I met the librarian, he said to me "All the way from China are you? Here, I'll show you the books Marx read when he was here." Engels was sent by his father to work in a cotton mill here in 1842, supposedly to get rid of his radical ideas. Several years later he wrote *The Condition of the Working Class in England* based on his experiences. In the summer of 1845, Marx came here from Germany to study. That's where they read that summer. Marx mostly read classical economics, including *The State of the Poor* published in 1797, a study of the lives of the poor since the 11th century. He also read *A Survey of the Responsibilities of the English Upper Classes* and *State of the Nation: Thirty or 40 Factories in and Around Manchester*. The librarian said that this was also the beginning of Marx's turn away from Hegel and philosophy toward economics.

Image: Prints of the Peterloo Massacre.
The sound of applause as the assembly line workers come forward and stand in front of the screen.

ASSEMBLY LINE WORKER A: Word has it that once there were 80,000 people who gathered at St. Peter's Square in Manchester. On August 16, 1819, the infamous Peterloo Massacre occurred. People were demanding electoral reform, repeal of the corn laws, and freedom of association for workers. When the political leader H. Hunt was arrested, in the violent repression that followed, eleven people died and 400 were injured.

The images stop. The screen is lit from behind. They start marching to the beat of a drum.

ASSEMBLY LINE WORKER B: (*marching*) The industrial revolution started in England and spread through Europe. It brought large scale urbanization and gave birth to the working class.

WORKERS (*Gather together from everywhere, singing "Warsaw Workers' Song."*)

Workers have longed lived on the verge of starvation.
Brothers we cannot remain silent!
We are comrades in arms, young and brave;
How could we fear the scaffold?
Our soldiers were cut down in the glorious fight for our cause.
Through our victory song their names will live on in the people's hearts.
Our struggle is sacred and just.
Ever forward brothers!
Our struggle is sacred and just.
Forward ever forward brothers…

Song ends, white cloth descends, people disperse.

ASSEMBLY LINE WORKER A: (*Going back to the line, singing*)
I have always dreamed of another world,
A world without bosses and factories.
Let the workers create a new world!
A meaningful life is within our grasp…

Assembly line workers return to their tables and continue their work.
Several workers remain onstage after the others have left, still marching and hold-ing signs. As they talk and throw down their signs, we see the backs of the signs on which are written "strike," "8-hour workday," "deportation," "NGO," "negotiations," "protecting the status quo," "police," "law," "protecting rights," "unions," "brain-washing" etc.

WORKER A: Before the 17th century, there were no capitalists.

WORKER B: But once capitalists appeared, they began accumulating capital.

WORKER A: First they enclosed the commons and made them into their private property.

WORKER B: And left us only one road: the one leading to the factory.

WORKER A: At the factory, we got to know each other; we organized.

WORKERS: First, we smashed the machines.

WORKER B: They brought in bosses, laws and police to discipline our bodies and regulate our sense of time, and clocks to regularize our movements.

WORKERS: But we kept fighting back.

WORKER A: We stayed united; we kept our hope for a better society. They gave us religion, patriotism, male chauvinism, racism...

WORKERS: We kept fighting back.

WORKER B: They made an empty formalism out of our democracy.

WORKER A: They made bureaucratic authoritarianism out of our revolution.

WORKERS: We kept fighting back.

WORKER B: They gave us social welfare.

The workers stop throwing down their signs. Only one remains, with the word "I" written on it.

WORKER A: They made a consumer society for us. They gave us TV, movies, soft drinks, computers, cheap clothes, mobile phones you have to upgrade all the time...

WORKER B: They created self-centeredness.

WORKER A: They made me this I.

WORKER B: And ceaselessly, they make my desires for me.

WORKER A AND B: (*calling*) I—there's only I.

They continue to throw signs, but they all have "I" written on them. They disperse. The New Industrialist arrives.

NEW INDUSTRIALIST: I learned that Manchester was the first "World Factory." Later, financial capital flowed into the rest of the world, and industries moved where labor was cheaper, eventually landing in China.

(*pauses*) It's said that China is undergoing its own industrial revolution, one that is not only changing our own lives, but the lives of people around the world. Perhaps one day our industrial historians will speak knowingly about it, about the cities and industries and business parks, about the technology and brands and factories...

The New Industrialist picks up the signs and looks at the words written on them.

NEW INDUSTRIALIST: From the very beginning, the "World Factory" has been a labor-intensive form of manufacturing notorious for its atrocious working conditions! With all the changes that have occurred over the past two centuries, how can China assume that it's on the right side of history? How can we know what it means any more to be part of the history of the World Factory? As long as people are making money, does that mean everything's OK?

A song is heard then fades, leaving only tiny spots of light.

STREET MUSICIAN: (*singing Industrial District*)
  Thrown off a train, I ended up in Canton;
  In those southern skies, it never ever snows.
  I moved through the nights, moved through my dreams,
  And in the end where I got was a crowded industrial zone.

  A street of factories, one led to another.
  All I heard there was the din of the machines.
  Signs all around, help wanted ads,
  I wonder which of them will deign to take me in.

(*Industrial Zone, Lyrics/Music: Xu Duo*)

4. Hands of the Assembly Line

The new industrialist moves forward, reaches out her hand, looks, and pretends to have an injured hand.

NEW INDUSTRIALIST: I've seen many hands, many shocking hands, disfigured hands, missing hands... not in Manchester, but in Guangdong, China.

(*Looking carefully at her own hands*) This is a young person's hand, a skinny hand, just skin covering bones—the new skin is still very tender—each finger is deformed, they don't seem to fully extend—the ring finger and pinkie are particularly crooked, as if they're stuck together—and the pinkie is missing a piece—and then there's the deep scar running across the palm –

(*pauses*) I asked him how old he was at the time, and he said it happened two years ago when he was twenty. I intentionally looked away to keep him from feeling self-conscious. He said that when he was in the hospital one day, he couldn't stand the waiting any more so he went to an internet café to chat with his cousin on QQ. His cousin's first question was "Are you typing with your feet?" He said he'll always remember the touching concern shown by his friends and relatives. Everyone was worried that his hand couldn't be fixed. They made him show his hand at job interviews, and he'd stretch it out. Eventually he started working again. The hand that got mangled in the lathe has a big scar, but he served me tea with it. "Will it return to normal?" He said with the right skills it would. I knew he was talking about advanced medical technology, those kinds of skills. He said it so casually.

The New Industrialist thinks of that hand and strains to open her own, extending her fingers over and over—then turns slowly and calmly.
Workers come onstage and together create an assembly line.

BUSINESSWOMAN: (walking into and through the assembly line) In 1913 this kind of assembly line was developed by Ford Motor Company. It's as if you can hear the machinery yelling "Higher! Higher efficiency! Higher profits!" From Detroit the assembly line spread from one city to another and, in the end, it stretched all over the globe.

The New Industrialist leaves the stage.
One by one the workers describe their tasks. As one finishes, the next begins

FEMALE WORKER: Punch three sockets, put it on the lathe and push the button. Take the red head and push the three coated wires through it and push the button. Put the copper wires into a plastic tube and add a plastic connector.

Then add three more different colored plastic connectors. Turn on the electricity, look at the numbers, test for noise, and attach the inspection sticker.

WORKER D: Push the button, put the copper wire into a plastic tube, add the first plastic connector, then the second and third. Turn on the electricity, look at the data, test for noise, and attach the inspection sticker.

WORKER B: Extract a binding wire. Tightly wind the stator connected to the inlaid wire starting at the unwired end and tie securely. Cut off the excess wire. Manually mold the embedded wire stator moving outward toward the packets at both ends until it is uniform in shape in order to facilitate further assembly.

WORKER C: With the left hand select a component for inspection from the assembly line and locate the position of the name decal. Tilt 45 degrees. With the thumb of the right hand affix the name decal, barcode and inspection sticker to the top and bottom covers. With the thumbs of the left and right hands press and smooth the name decal.

ASSEMBLY LINE WORKER B: Extract a binding wire. Tightly wind the stator connected to the inlaid wire starting at the unwired end and tie securely. Cut off the excess wire. Manually mold the embedded wire stator moving outward toward the packets at both ends until it is uniform in shape in order to facilitate further assembly.

Eventually the voices blend and turn to noise as the workers repeat themselves over and over. The voices suddenly stop but the work continues.

FEMALE WORKER: We –

WORKER D: We –

WORKER B: We –

WORKER C: We –

WORKERS: Our hands repeat the same motion for ten hours, pressing the red button.
Ka-chink—Ka-chink—Ka-chink—Ka-chink—Ka-chink—
Our hands do the same thing for ten hours, fitting wires with transparent connectors.
Affix one and step on it, boom—Affix one and step on it, boom—Affix one and step on it, boom–

For ten hours, every movement of our hands is precisely regulated by the clock. There are no smiles, no sighs, no gaps, no breaks. Da, Da, Da, Da, Da, Da, Da, Da, Da ...

FEMALE WORKER: The foreman berates me: Clumsy country girl! You're not on the farm anymore! You need to learn how to behave!

The 50s era film Huang Baomei is projected. It shows a textile worker's hand. In the following scene, workers enthusiastically discuss technology and are given awards. A fashionably dressed passerby, wearing headphones and absorbed in their own world, dances and plays in front of the black and white images of the workers on the screen.

FEMALE WORKER: I am a component of the assembly line. My hands are components for making components. My hand is a component that makes component after component. To make a pair of athletic shoes takes two hundred pairs of hands. How many hands does it take to make a mobile phone? How many hands does it take to make a pair of jeans? How many hands does it take to make a car? We are changing the world, but –

WORKERS: Our hands are empty, our legs are sore, our eyes are wide with wonder—What kind of factory should we have ? What kind of world should we have?

(stops and different workers begin to speak, one after the other)

The hands of the world's workshop come in all colors
In the past American hands replaced English hands
Japanese hands replaced American hands
Taiwanese hands replaced Japanese hands
Today mainland Chinese hands replace Taiwanese hands
Rural hands replace urban hands
Anhui, Sichuan and Hunan hands replace Dongguan, Zhejiang, and Jiangsu hands
Young hands continually replace calloused hands
Black hands, white hands, yellow hands, brown hands, green hands, red hands:
These are the hands of the World Factory.

The workers on the assembly line pass a box to the person on the street. He opens it, and opens another, and takes out the buns inside and devours them greedily. He throws the box on the ground without a second thought. The assembly line produces another box, which he opens with great force. He throws away the box. Inside is an electrical bird that sings. He is fascinated and begins playing with it. But soon he throws it aside and leaves.

5. A Scream, a Body in Pain

The HR manager appears among the audience.

HR MANAGER: Can anyone jump rope? Can you jump rope? Can you jump rope?

The HR manager finally finds someone who can jump rope

HR MANAGER: What kind of work do you do?

AUDIENCE MEMBER: ......

HR MANAGER: How much do you earn each month?

AUDIENCE MEMBER: ......

HR MANAGER: I know of a job that will earn you more, something I'm sure you can do. You interested? You only have to jump rope. Let us go up on stage.

The HR manager convinces the audience member to take the stage and jump rope.

HR MANAGER: You get one *fen* for every jump. At a normal pace you can jump 60 times per minute, 3600 times per hour. That's 36 RMB per hour, at least three or four hundred RMB per day, so eight or ten thousand per month no problem. And we don't require a physical exam...

AUDIENCE MEMBER: ......

A female worker comes onstage and starts jumping with the audience member The HR manager helps the audience member count jumps and tells him/her to collect payment from the director after the performance. The HR manager praises the audience member and sends them offstage for pre-employment training.

FEMALE WORKER: (*alone onstage, jumping and mumbling to herself*) 1 *fen*, 2 *fen*, 3 *fen*, 4 *fen*, 5 *fen*, 6 *fen*, 7 *fen*, 8 *fen*, 9 *fen*, 1 *jiao* 1 *fen*, 1 *jiao* 2 *fen* ... I don't know why I have that dream, the same one every night. The dock, the river, all very familiar, as if I've been there countless times

(*Keeps jumping*) When did I start having this dream? A month ago I worked overtime until 11:30 three days in a row. Then on Sunday morning we had to move into a new dormitory. I was exhausted and sore from head to toe. I couldn't control or stop the pain, as if my body weren't my own. Everyone else was out, the room was empty. All that was pent up inside me came out in a horrific scream. I couldn't believe how loud it was.

(*still jumping*) That sound terrified me. From then on I've been having that dream and screaming, over and over

Keeps jumping rope and counting to herself.
Other female workers can be heard in the background.

FEMALE WORKER A: (*Recorded voice*) There's something wrong with my back, it's extremely painful. I'd only been here a few months when it started hurting. You know, my work isn't as hard as the girls who work on the line, they have to sit there all day. But I don't know why my back hurts so much. Sometimes it's my back, sometimes it's my neck.

FEMALE WORKER B: (*Recorded voice*) You know, no one wants to work in the clean room. So they send the new people in there, and I can't get them to trans-fer me out. It smells so bad in the clean room you can hardly breathe. The acid makes me dizzy and I can't concentrate. If I keep having these headaches, I'm going back home.

FEMALE WORKER C: (*Recorded voice*) If the wafers are damaged, they can't be fixed, so we have to be really careful. There's a lot of pressure—when I'm on the night shift I don't have any energy so I move slowly—when my stomach hurts they give me drugs, I'm not sure what kind—some people say it's birth control or pain killers—sometimes I'm afraid that the supervisor won't give me any, so I've hidden a few.

FEMALE WORKER: (*still jumping*) I've woken up screaming every night for a month. It bothers me hearing other people talk about it. It's the same dream every night: I dream I'm walking toward the dock, to take a boat across a river. The river separates me from my children. I'm worried because I see that the boat is leaving, I'm very nervous. But my body won't move, it's sore and tired, it won't move—I see the boat about to leave, and I'm about to be left behind. It's getting darker, and I'm stuck...

It gradually darkens, leaving only points of light.
The rope falls and the woman squats down dejectedly.
Images are projected: A worker from Hangzhou describes her ideal job: right now, she's just a laborer, but she hopes to open her own cosmetics shop one day... the video cuts to a noisy, smoky, dusty work environment and other images of industrial pollution.

6. The World's Garbage Dump

The Masked Clown comes onstage and sees the images of pollution. Her movements are exaggerated and a bit erratic.

MASKED CLOWN: What's this? Those chimneys, pipes, machines, it's all so grand! Production – production – this is the great age of mechanical industry! That noise you hear is the sound of human progress! That smoke is the dust kicked up by the wheel of history! (*Hears something and stops her exaggerated movements to look at the audience*) What? Smog? What's smog?

Walks around, and suddenly sees an environmental expert in the audience.

MASKED CLOWN: Hey, aren't you Professor Lü, the environmental scientist? The last time I saw you, you were still at the Chinese Academy of Sciences Institute of Psychology, and now you're in environmental studies? Professor Lü, please come up. Just now someone mentioned smog; can you tell us what smog is?

ENVIRONMENTAL EXPERT: (*Comes on stage excitedly, as before*) That's an excellent question. Smog is... smoke and fog, HaHa! Water vapor condenses on tiny particles and turns into tiny droplets suspended in the air (*imitates a suspended water droplet*) This is fog. Smoke is particles of dust and ash suspended in the air (*the masked clown throws powder into the air*), tiny little particles.

MASKED CLOWN: (*Playfully throwing powder at the environmental expert*) Oh, Oh... smog smog, smoke plus fog.

ENVIRONMENTAL EXPERT: HaHa, yes! That's what smog is.

MASKED CLOWN: And where does this smog come from?

ENVIRONMENTAL EXPERT: Smog comes primarily from factories, but different industries create different types of smog, and they affect people in different ways.

MASKED CLOWN: (*Teasingly*) It affects our bodies?

ENVIRONMENTAL EXPERT: Oh yes, HaHa! For example, smelting factories produce smog high in heavy metals, and breathing it can lead to chest pains and swelling in the lungs and sometimes even respiratory failure... and then you die, then you die...

The Masked Clown puts powder on the face of the Environmental Expert, who imitates pulmonary failure.

MASKED CLOWN: (*laughing*) HaHaHa! You poor thing!

ENVIRONMENTAL EXPERT: HaHa! Then in other places with power plants and chemical factories, where garbage is being burned, there are lots of organic gasses in the air. These organic gases contain sulfides and dioxin that damage the human nervous system and cause headaches, vomiting, diarrhea and loss of consciousness. You won't necessarily die from it, but if your nervous system is damaged then you turn into an idiot, an idiot...

The Environmental Expert imitates an idiot.

MASKED CLOWN: (*lauging*) HaHaHa! You've turned into an idiot; there's no helping you now.

ENVIRONMENTAL EXPERT: Then there's the dust produced by mining companies. If you breathe it in, it hurts your lungs, gives you black lung and lung cancer.

MASKED CLOWN: (*laughing, reaches out toward the Environmental Expert's tie*) HaHa!, Black lung, I don't believe that. Let's open you up and take a look –

ENVIRONMENTAL EXPERT: (*nervously*) Go away! You can't touch the Environmental Expert! Listen, this "World Factory" is just a "world outsourcing factory." In a lot of places, like shoe factories, there is a heavy odor from organic gases, and there's a strong possibility that women who work in these places will become infertile.

MASKED CLOWN: Wow, you make all that money, and after you die there's no property to fight over –

ENVIRONMENTAL EXPERT: Our world factory is actually nothing but a world garbage dump!

MASKED CLOWN: Shh! This is a big secret; you can't just tell everyone.

ENVIRONMENTAL EXPERT: Everyone in the factory already knows! You think I'm the only expert–

MASKED CLOWN: What? So Professor Lü is an expert on garbage dumps now? HaHaHa—Turns out we live in a filthy dump! (*pointing to the audience*) Look at them, all dressed up suits, thinking they're so clean when really they're maggots in a latrine, living on shit, HaHaHa –

ENVIRONMENTAL EXPERT: (*Dragging the Masked Clown with him*) Shhhh—
that's the real secret. We're all trying our best to get by in this hopeless world.
You can't just tell people that. Let's go.

7. Far from the City, Farther from Home

The People's Liberation Army March starts playing
"Forward forward forward!
We march across our homeland into the sun
Carrying the hopes of our people; Ever victorious
Sons and brothers of the people
We are the weapon of the people ..."
A young man marches out holding a notebook. He suddenly breaks into wild, child-
like movements, then suddenly stops.

LEFT-BEHIND CHILD: (*Rolling the notebook into a microphone and speaking
loudly*) Dad, mom, I love you! Dad, mom, come back soon!

A crowd appears and watches from the wings.

CROWD: What do you want to be when you grow up?

LEFT-BEHIND CHILD: (*As before*) A worker.

CROWD: Do you miss your parents?

LEFT-BEHIND CHILD: No.

CROWD: Do you like studying?

LEFT-BEHIND CHILD: No.

CROWD: What do you like?

LEFT-BEHIND CHILD: Playing.

CROWD: Do you want to go to university?

LEFT-BEHIND CHILD: Yes.

CROWD: If you don't study now, how will you get to university?

LEFT-BEHIND CHILD: I'll be able to when I grow up.

CROWD: Are you happy when your parents come home?

LEFT-BEHIND CHILD: Yes.

CROWD: Do you miss your parents?

LEFT-BEHIND CHILD: Yes.

CROWD: What do you want to be when you grow up?

LEFT-BEHIND CHILD: A worker.

CROWD: What do you want to be when you grow up?

LEFT-BEHIND CHILD: A worker.

The crowd disperses.

LEFT-BEHIND CHILD: I was born in a small town in Sichuan in 1990. I was raised by my grandmother for a while, my mother's mother; but the relatives laughed and said "How silly for an old woman to be raising her daughter's child!" When I was two my parents took me on a train back to Wenzhou. The scenery there was pretty. But my parents crossed a river, and left in a pedicab. My dad started taking cotton to Sichuan to sell, and mom went south to work.

Workers on the assembly line, humming "Industrial District."

LEFT-BEHIND CHILD: (*Pauses*) In Wenzhou I had cousins, a grandfather and grandmother, and lots of uncles. I went to school during the day and at night grandpa took me to church to pray (*Imitates a pastor and in a heavy accent says "Bless you, bless you!"*) Summer evenings we went up to the roof, spread out mats and looked at the stars, counting the stars. My relatives say that when I missed my parents I would hold their picture and cry. Three or four years later my parents took me to Sichuan.

Squats down, like people used to look at him.

LEFT-BEHIND CHILD: When I got back, people would say "Oh! Look at this little baby! HaHa! Wenzhou pig!" "Sichuan pig!" "Wenzhou pig!" "Sichuan pig!" "Wenzhou pig!" "Sichuan pig!" "Wenzhou pig!" "Sichuan pig!" "Wenzhou pig!" (*Yelling and working himself into a rage*)

(*Calms down from this agitated state*) My mom says that she was determined that I would go to school! In the county seat! The villagers said "It's a waste of money, going that far." When I went to the county seat to study I couldn't see my parents. Different relatives took care of me, or I lived by myself.

(*Pauses*) I remember in 2000 when I was ten, I was watching the Sydney Olympics in the apartment I rented, and when I saw the Chinese flag go up I was so happy, my hands were sweating. Later on, my parents settled down in a different city and brought me to live with them. I went to elementary school there, and middle school, and high school. Then I came to the big city for university.

(*Looking around*) Now I'm back in the Sichuan countryside with no land and no house. The place I rent used to have a tree out front but they cut it down and sold it. Some fields don't have anyone to farm them. The rivers I used to swim in are used to raise ducks and fish. Lots of people go to the city to work or do business, try to make a living.

The crowd gathers again, talking back and forth among themselves.

CROWD: Where is your *hukou*?[2]

CROWD: People in the city don't want their daughters marrying into villages.

CROWD: China has 200 million workers and 61 million kids left behind in the countryside. Over 40 million of them are under 14. Over 30 percent of these parents will be gone for over five years.

CROWD: Three billion trips are made at spring festival, which shows how many parents are separated from their children and from their native land.

CROWD: The workers who come to the city from the countryside are leaving a labor shortage behind them.

CROWD: Don't encourage rural children to go to university, because they'll never return home and that would be a shame.

CROWD: Traditional China lives on in the countryside. If the villages are abandoned, Chinese tradition will fade away.

CROWD: When will we be like the people in the city, really be accepted as urban workers?

---

2   Hukou refers to the household registration record that identifies a person as a permanent resident of a certain area.

The People's Liberation Army March is heard again. The young man with raised hands marches and sings forcefully. The crowd gradually surrounds them, and the circle gets smaller and smaller.

YOUNG MAN: (*singing, but the song gradually falls apart*) "Forward forward forward!/We march across our homeland/Towards the sun/Carrying the hopes of our people/Ever victorious/Sons and brothers of the people/We are the weapon of the people ..."

The singing turns into shouting and ranting, and he finally throws his diary up into the air. The young man quietly walks out of the crowd. He collects the diary and moves to a corner of the stage.

YOUNG MAN: (*opening the diary and reading*) Wu Jiamin, Sichuan Province, Jingyan County, Sanjiao Village, No. 2 Sanjiao St.

The young man holds open the diary showing a picture of himself with his parents in front of their house.
Images: A rapidly changing village along the high-speed rail line and workers inside a factory... In the background can be heard a recording from rehearsals of discussions about production, working conditions, and the working class.

RECORDING: "Even though I've only been in this environment for a short time, I think "operator" or "laborer" is more appropriate than "worker." In the past to be a "worker" was an honorable thing. Now there is no sense of honor, only shame. These operators or laborers belong to the lowest class, the lowest profession."

"They aren't workers. I worked on construction sites for 25 years and had countless supervisors. The supervisors are in it for the money, they're there to tell you what to do. If you don't work for a day or two then they don't want you. That's how it is, we're beggars."

"This is our European business. This is in Chile. This is in the US. And that's how the structure worked. Our head office was over here, and accounting was in Hong Kong. I worked my way up, in billing, and then I started doing foreign procurement billing."

"There are lots of strikes at private companies. But that's mainly a symbolic thing. Do you know why Honda was under so much scrutiny? Because those workers weren't getting minimum wage, they were making more than the average wage for that region; but their strike represented a shift in their awareness of the workers' rights. You can see for yourself, in the Pearl River Delta there are strikes happening all the time."

(English) "Ford was a good employer. He paid his employees well. It's because they reduced their own costs with research on time and movement, and through mass production and assembly lines. He was dictatorial, but people have jobs and they pay well. So lots of people are willing to stay with them."

"It's just a turn-around point. You go out and earn money and come back home all happy. If you don't earn any money, you can still come home, it's a warm place to come back to. Out there, like I said it's just a turn-around point. It's a struggle, and it's all up to you."

"I know a woman who makes packaging for cosmetics. She's been doing it for seventeen years; every day she makes thousands of little boxes. But when people buy those cosmetics, they throw the box out. So her life's work is thrown out after just a few seconds."

"To put it bluntly, labor contractors are just human traffickers. It's a systematic violation of human rights, isn't it? These people don't have any production resources, no tools or anything. So how do they earn money? They just make introductions and then they charge a management fee. But people cannot be bought and sold."

(English) "In the 1970s capital started to shift. Fisher Bendix, who made washing machines, moved from Liverpool to the Far East, like a lot of other capitalists. At the time a lot of people were trying to save their jobs. They were used to standing up for themselves and they were willing to fight. Because their jobs had never been stable, and they had formed themselves into a true working class."

"Work is work, right? They've got to give you what they owe you, nothing less. If they don't then you're not a worker. If you don't give me what I deserve then you're exploiting me, and we've got a problem."

"If you invest in a company that's manufacturing something, you want it to outsource, you don't want it investing in all these fixed assets. So you wind up with this. You want them to use the world factory and not go do it themselves. When this kind of globalization leads to political problems, for investors these problems become a matter of risk."

"It's connected to the national system, anyway, the whole system of household residence. Now this problem, although it's going to be a top-down solution, but still I'm certain that the country will think of a way to solve it, including the problem of workers' children who have to register for entrance exams in their official residences."

(English) "I know a lot of people who are proud to call themselves working class."

"There are lots of silly conspiracy theories out there. Like if you're a migrant worker you will be treated differently in the city."

"In today's China, how are we supposed to understand the notion of "work," after the chaos of the socialist period, and after the conversion to capitalism, and now after globalization? Marx said that labor makes people, this was one of his fundamental principles. So how are we supposed to understand labor today? What does it mean for us?"

The voices become noisy and indistinct.

8. Is That Your Spot?

Workers enter the city, moving among the audience and onto the stage. From the cotton work gloves they're wearing, they pull out long threads, forming a web of linked threads on the stage and above the audience.

FEMALE WORKER: The assembly line brings components and takes them away, brings the world and takes it away. Where are the hands that will replace ours? They say –

WORKERS: (*Saying the names of countries*) Ethiopia, Kenya, Tanzania, Uganda, Bengal, Sri Lanka, India, and Myanmar; Cambodia, the Philippines, Laos, and Vietnam; the Dominican Republic, Mexico, Peru, and Nicaragua.

FEMALE WORKER: The assembly line moves faster and faster, and the blood in my veins pains me more and more, but...

WORKERS: Our hands are empty, our legs are sore, our eyes are wide with wonder. What kind of factory should we have? What kind of world should we have?

The line in their hands breaks and they begin explaining frantically.

WORKERS: We must work overtime; we must make money. We must work overtime; we must make money. We must work overtime; we must make money. We must make money to buy the mobile phones we assemble. We must make money to buy the jeans we sew. We must make money to buy the computers we assemble. We must make money to buy the toys we make. We must make money to buy the shoes we make. We must make money to buy the cosmetics we make. We must make money, just like everyone else in this world. We must make money, just like everyone else in this world.

Suddenly conflict breaks out among them, they push and shove and are about to fight.

WORKERS: (shouting) Is this your spot? This is my spot! Is this your spot? This is my spot! Is this your spot? This is my spot!

But gradually they calm down, sitting back-to-back and resuming their work on the assembly line.

9. The World Factory or the End of Labor-Intensive Production

DIRECTOR (*voice coming from the back*)*:* An American think tank reports that China's role as the world factory will be taken over by 16 as yet undeveloped countries called the PC16. Will these countries turn into the new "world factory"?

The New Industrialist enters.

NEW INDUSTRIALIST: What's this about the PC16? That's just capital lying to you! They just want to scare companies and workers: you want more? Higher wages? Better working conditions and environmental protection? Well, there are plenty of people waiting to take your jobs!

DIRECTOR: Tell them about your trip to Pingchuan and how it affected you.

NEW INDUSTRIALIST: It startled me. They proudly call themselves "new workers." The village is changing. They work in both industry and agriculture. They grow their own grains and vegetables. Now that the persimmons are red and the other fruits are ripe, ecotourism is attracting people from the city. The villagers can't afford to live in the cities, they can't afford the houses they built or the products they've made; but here they can build their own homes. There are no tearful left behind children. Kids live with their parents, and study in their own schools. There is even a worker's university and a worker's museum. Listen, one of the Worker's Art Troupe members Xu Duo is singing his song.

Singing is heard. Xu Duo comes to the front.

XU DUO: In this world factory, you're nothing but a component
And they're slowly grinding you down, grinding away your youth
And they want to kick you out
And then you realize, your rage has no place to go.

The New Industrialist breaks character and returns to normal.

YU KAI: (*laughing*) Thank you Xu Duo! Hello everybody, I'm Yu Kai. My role was originally played by Wang Yi at Grass Stage

Wang Yi enters, Yu Kai exits.

WANG YI: I'm Wang Yi, I design environmental protection equipment for a living. Based on my work experience I've written this (*takes out a paper*) "The World Factory or the End of Labor-Intensive Production." (*reads*) 95 percent of industrial products wind up as garbage, and only five percent find practical application. In order to improve working conditions and ease workers' burdens, we must change the current consumption-driven mode of production. We must promote forms of social cooperation not based on employment and consumption. We must promote production units of under 100 people. We must promote the production of complete products rather than the production of components. We must promote the use of robots and high technology. We must promote shared ownership and use of production resources and democratic forms of management. We must promote public governance, public transportation, public factories, schools and research. We must promote conservation of resources, shared responsibility and communal living.

(*stops and looks at the audience*) This was my plan for the finale of this play.

The Expert controls a group of little blue figures. He makes them dance and looks scornfully at Wang Yi.
The Masked Clown eventually appears and runs toward the audience.

MASKED CLOWN: HaHa! If you do things his way, will you still have iPhones? Will you still have name brands to wear? Will you still be able to play mahjong, watch your stocks and wait to die? If you listen to him your lives will have to change. Scary isn't it? Is that what you want? Are you scared? Is that what you want?

Masked clown laughs madly and leaves.

Xu Duo's song is heard. The entire cast rushes on stage with little blue figures and start singing.
The assembly line workers climb up the scaffolding at the back of the stage holding large numbers of little blue figures that they have made and let them fall.

XU DUO AND THE CROWD (*sing We Quit*):
In this world factory, you're nothing but a component
And they're slowly grinding you down, grinding away your youth
And they want to kick you out
And then you realize, your rage has no place to go
How do you like being a piece of dust?
How do you like floating in the wind?
How do you like having them above you?
How do you like them babbling?
How do you like the incurable ignorance?
How do you like not caring whether or not you even exist?
How do you like feeding on illusions?
How do you like living in a dream?

We quit—we quit—we quit!
Wherever there is oppression there is resistance
The light of a star can start a wildfire
The true path is always world changing
Marching boldly forward for the sake of those who follow...

(*We Quit, Lyrics/Music: Xu Duo*)

During the song Wang Yi picks up discarded gloves and signs from the ground printed with "Strike" or "Unity" and looks at them blankly. Then he walks toward the audience and steps over the seats of audience members, climbing in the dark toward the back and toward higher ground.

The End

How to Work With Things That Really Happened

Hans-Werner Kroesinger

What we are doing in our theatre is setting up works based on documents—and by "documents," I mean that we work with things that really happened. So we take actual things, actual events and we try to create stories. We try to create multiple stories, stories that contradict each other, stories that work on different levels. And in order to give you an impression of what I do, I will tell you about things I have done. But before I do this, I would like everybody to say their names [*Students introduce themselves and give their ages*]. It is important that you say your name and your age—because in the theatre we work with ourselves. Your age tells you something about the timeframe that your life is a part of. It is very different to read about something or to have experienced it. I am much, much older than you. I am 55, so it is a long timeframe that I cover. I have been doing theatre now for thirty years, so I have been in the theatre for longer than you have been in the world.

Over this period, a lot of things have changed in the theatre. I received my training in the drama department of the University of Giessen. Giessen is a very small town close to Frankfurt. The advantage of a small town is that you don't have many disturbances, the only thing you can do in small towns is work. The kind of theatre we were trained for in Giessen, our professors always told us, did not yet exist. "So you will receive a lot of classical training," they said, "but for the theatre we imagine, you will have to make it happen, you have to do it." It is very interesting if you think of theatre as something that is not fixed. You need a lot of professional skills to do it, but in the end, what is happening on stage between you and the audience is always something new. It depends on the timeframe, on what is happening in society. Every period creates new problems. When there are new problems, you maybe have to respond with new forms, because it has to be something that makes sense to you in relation to the age you are living in. It all sounds very abstract, but it is very simple: It has to be interesting for you, and it has to be interesting for the people who come—and it has to tell them something about you and your opinion about the world. But it is not about preaching. It is not like going to church. You think about something that is happening, and you try to give it a form. The audience will take something out of this form that is useful for them. In Giessen, we received a lot of classical training: We learned about breathing techniques, movement techniques, about what actors think when they are playing a part, about what actors don't think when they are playing a part; also about what a director and a dramaturg think while constructing a play. We learned also the ability to describe what is happening on stage. That is a complicated thing, because you have to look very carefully at what is going on. On the stage, there is text being spoken by the actors, but there is always much more than the text. The stage is constructed out of a lot of layers. You have to try to get a vision of all these layers.

The big advantage of our department in Giessen was that we had visiting professors. They were experts in their field. Robert Wilson visited—a prominent director, Heiner Müller came—a major playwright, and then we had a director and playwright who was very important to us: George Tabori. Tabori was Jewish, and he lost almost all of his family during the Shoah. When he came to our department, he was already a very old man, but he had developed his own technique of working with actors and developing plays. He experienced many terrible things in his life, but he made the best comedies I have ever seen. He said that sometimes the only way to deal with reality is comedy, because the comedy opens up the audience's heart. And sometimes you laugh about something funny, and in the next moment, you start to cry, because there is something under this joke which isn't funny. He was looking for these moments, looking to create these moments.

One of the most famous productions that he did was Beckett's *Waiting for Godot.* We all know how it has to look: There has to be a tree on the stage. When George Tabori directed it, there was no tree on the stage. So the people who knew the play from the book were very disappointed; the only thing that was on stage was a very small table. Tabori said this is because this play is about waiting, and usually in theatre, when you develop a production, you spend a lot of time with waiting and repetition. So he said to the actors, let us see what will happen if we just sit at the table and try to do the play in this form. So when do we have to leave the table? When something happens. He had two of the most brilliant German actors of this time doing this production: Peter Luer and Thomas Holzmann. Great actors with great personalities. There is a film about this production. If you know the play, you can see how these two actors reach results with minimal things that are far beyond what you think you can do on stage.

Then we had Richard Schechner from the Performance Group in New York. We had a lot of different visiting professors, different teachers. What is interesting about these various teachers is that each had his own approach towards theatre. So we had a variety of training, and every student had to take out of these different approaches what they considered important for themselves—and with everything you take, you construct your own thing. And during the training, you realize what is useful to you. In the end, you have to make the decision about what is useful to you when you are doing theatre.

I am telling you about various plays I did without showing you pictures, so you have to make up the pictures in your mind. When I finished my training, I was part of the production *Hamlet/Hamletmachine*, which was put on by Heiner Müller. Heiner Müller was staging *Hamlet*, and he was using his old play *Hamletmachine* as a comment on Shakespeare's play. The production was rehearsed over a period of eight months. The play was produced in East Germany (GDR). When we started with rehearsals, the GDR still existed, but when we finished, the GDR was gone—the state had disappeared. There was a wall through Berlin that separated Berlin into East and West. Now all the tourists in Berlin look for the Wall and take pictures there. But in the 1980s, you could enter East Berlin for one day from West Berlin only if you paid twenty-five Deutsche Mark. If you lived in East Germany, you were not allowed to leave the country. You would have been shot at the Wall if you had tried to pass. It was really a divided city with a lot of tension. I grew up in West Germany and I had a special visa that allowed me to stay in East Germany. I could pass the border every day as I liked without paying. I could also stay overnight. If you didn't have this visa, you had to leave East Berlin before midnight. When we started the rehearsals, Heiner Müller had the idea that Hamlet was the son of high party members and that there had been a change in the party and his father had been a victim of this change, with Hamlet disagreeing with the new leadership. His dissent creates the central problem of the play. You can read this play in this way, and it makes a lot of sense. But what do you do if the state disappears and this model of the ruling party is gone? If the people are no longer interested in the party? If the people are interested in going shopping, going on vacation, leaving the country? Your frame of reference disappears. And it is very difficult to perform a play when the reference is no longer there. The performance lasted for eight hours, and sitting for eight hours in a theatre is really a long time. You have to dedicate so much of your time to the theatre. If you work with such a long timeframe, it changes something in the perception of an audience. There will be sequences where the audience gets tired. But because every member of the audience has different interests, they will get tired at different times. So it creates a particular atmosphere or energy in the audience. And this energy you can use. Then the audience starts to think about its own situation in relation to what happens on stage. Our stage designer, Erich Wonder, created a set where the people on stage looked very small. When you looked at the stage, you got the idea that the surroundings were too big for the people, then you watch very carefully what they were doing, they had to invest energy to exist in this environment. This play became very successful, to our surprise, because—situated amid all these events that were going on at that time—the theatre became a place where you could rest and reflect. When a society is changing so quickly, people have to rest somewhere and think about what is going on around them. But of course, you have to do this in an entertaining way. Because theatre, as we know, is also about being entertaining. Entertaining in a way so that people get energy.

There are different methods of creating energy. The most popular thing is to do some song and dance. So people would send 25 people on stage and let them sing karaoke, and then you have this energy. But Heiner Müller did not do that. He had just a bunch of actors, and they were doing funny little tricks. But only small tricks, and they were all happening during one sequence at the same time. As an audience member, you had just got a little bit tired and then suddenly there was so much happening on stage, and because it all happens at the same time, you would miss something. And then for a moment you would feel very uncomfortable because you had paid and you wanted to see everything. And this keeps your energy level up, and you concentrate more, you focus more because you don't want to miss the next scene when something like this is happening. This is a very good way to deal with the audience. You educate the audience to pay attention. In the end, the audience is also responsible for the circulation of energy that happens during a performance. Theatre is always about the action happening between the audience and stage. A good performance is always working with a good audience. But if you want to try something new on stage, you have to train the audience, because the audience has to learn how to see and perceive what you do on stage. There is a text by Brecht on developing the art of watching. If you train your audience, you can achieve more with the things that you do on stage. The audience and the actors construct the scene together.

The kind of theatre that Regine Dura and I are doing has a lot to do with developing the art of watching. When we started our first performances, people said: "It is very interesting, but it is not theatre: There are no characters, there is no plotline, there is no drama. The actors give a lot of information. It is very complicated to follow, and I have to concentrate too much. I have to work during your performance as an audience member. Maybe it is visual art. Maybe it is visual art with actors." So, in the first three or four years, the critics argued a lot about whether it was theatre or not.

The good thing about this quarrel was that it existed and it made people curious: Every year something new was happening, and people would come to see it, and sometimes people would come to see the show twice because it was so complicated. And sometimes, people seeing a show for the first time would leave after 15 minutes because it was too complicated for them. Some people prefer having something relaxing. They might ask: "Where is the song and dance?" They realize no song and dance is coming and so they say: "Let's go and have some dinner!" That was not easy for the actors. It's a strange experience for the actors when the audience leaves during a performance. But sometimes it is necessary, since the people on the stage do not have the same interest as the people in the audience. In shaping your audience, you also develop the people you can work with. The interesting thing when one audience disengages with the theatre is that they are replaced by another kind of audience. When we started our theatre in the 1990s, many people had no more interest in theatre. They said, why should I see "Waiting for Godot?" He is not coming, and I know that. This is not a surprise. They lost interest, but they were very interested in what was going on in society.

In Germany, we had the fall of the Wall in 1989 and reunification in 1990. For one part of society, the state had disappeared. For the other part, the state had grown bigger. Suddenly, there were 20 million new people in the country, speaking the same language, but having very different experiences, because they grew up in a completely different system. It also changed the western part of Germany. The society had to face new problems. Some of these problems were related to history, to German history—and you had to find a way to communicate this. In the kind of theatre that Regine and I are doing, we try to deal with these problems. We deal with German history and its impact on our country, on our society and its relation to the world.

The first documentary-style play I did was a play about Adolf Eichmann, called *Q&A—Questions & Answers*. The Germans killed six million Jews in concentration camps. Most of the german concentration camps were in Poland. So one had to transport the Jews from Germany and other countries to the concentration camps and gas chambers in Poland. One had to organize this, and the man in charge of the organization was Adolf Eichmann. He was responsible for bringing the Jews to the camps. He was very good at this. After the war, if they had caught him, they would have killed him immediately. So he went underground and ran away to Argentina, where he lived for about 15 years. The Israeli Secret Service, associated with the IDF, tried to catch him. They were looking for him all over the world. But they could not find him. One day, one person received the information that there was a guy in Argentina working for a German Company. Of course, his name was not Adolf Eichmann. He had a different name: His name was Ricardo Klement. He was living in Buenos Aires in very poor circumstances. And because Eichmann stole a lot of money, they expected him to live in rich circumstances. So they were not sure if this was really him. But they found out that he was living together with the former wife of Adolf Eichmann. They thought this could be a hint that it was him. But they were not sure if it was him, because he looked different. So they placed him under observation for two months, following everything he was doing. One day this man came home with a beautiful bunch of flowers, a really expensive bunch of flowers. It was not his wife's birthday, not his child's birthday, also not his birthday. So they wanted to know why he came with these flowers. And then they found in the papers that this was the day when Adolf Eichmann married his wife. And they said, why would he spend all this money if he was not Adolf Eichmann. Then they kidnapped him in a secret operation from Argentina. They took him from the street and flew him from Argentina to Israel. In Israel, they took him to court. But before you take someone to court, there is an interrogation, and the investigator tries to find out what has happened. Eichmann was sitting in prison and was not allowed to see other people. There was an Israeli officer from the national police who was Jewish German, who had grown up in Berlin, and was one of the best interrogation officers the Israeli police had. So they assigned him to do this interrogation. His name was Avner Less. He said, "I don't want to do it because they killed all of my family." But his superiors said, "You have to do it because you know Berlin and Germany."

And now imagine you have a period of half a year when these two people meet almost every day. Eichmann knows that in the end, he will be killed. So for him, it is important to talk as long as possible, and he does not know what the other knows. So they start talking, and at the beginning, he is lying all the time, and Less tries to catch him out. There is a team of people checking Eichmann`s information. Towards the end, he gets more and more real information out of Eichmann. If you imagine Eichmann's situation: He is sitting in this prison and has no contact to anybody. The only person he sees is this interrogation officer. This creates a kind of intimacy between these two people. As a human being, you need contact. You have to talk to people; you cannot be alone all of the time. They do this interrogation, and Eichmann describes how difficult it was to get the trains to get the Jews to the camps because the army also needed trains for its soldiers to send them to the front lines. So Eichmann is very proud that he managed to get these trains to bring the people to the death camps. He says, "I am not responsible for the killing. I just did the transport." A very strange logic. They met all these days. Sometimes Less feels really sick, because what the other person says is so terrible. But of course, he cannot show how much he dislikes him; as then the other person would stop talking. There was one day when Less had to go to see Eichmann, which was the birthday of his father, who was killed in Auschwitz. He is sitting there, and he is interrogating the officer who is responsible for the transport. He is full of anger and full of despair. Eichmann realizes that this day something is different. So he asks him, "Is something wrong with you?" Less says, "It is my father's birthday, and he was killed in the camps"—and Eichmann looks at him and says, "That's terrible!" It is a very interesting moment if we take this moment for real, that Eichmann—at this moment—really has sympathy for this guy whose father was killed. But he is not making the connection that he is the one responsible for the killing. That is a very theatrical moment: It is a moment full of tension, full of energy. When you experience something like this on stage, it does something with you. You start thinking: Something is happening on an emotional level and an intellectual level.

In theatre, this is what you are looking for: You are searching for something that works emotionally and intellectually. And you have to give it a form. When the interrogation was over, they put Eichmann before the court. And there he could no longer see Less. The trial against Eichmann lasted, I think, about four months. During this trial, it was the first time in Israel that there was a public discussion about the Shoah. A lot of the Jews that came to Israel did not talk about the Shoah. It is the year 1961. During the trial, there is one more meeting between Less and Eichmann in the courtroom. Before the trial, these two people always met in a small, closed room—you could say in privacy. Suddenly they are in a big courtroom: There are 600 people in the audience, international media from all around the world, film cameras—it is a major public event. One of the journalists who was there during the trial described that you could feel a link between these two people, something that you could not touch, like a strong connection. Two people who knew a lot about each other. That is also a very theatrical moment. How can you transfer it to the stage?

They sentenced Eichmann to death. They hang him, burn him, and put his ashes in the ocean so that there is no grave, no place where you can remember him. I found this a very interesting subject for theatre. There was a transcript of this interrogation. It has 3,600 pages. It is a huge volume of paper: six books. On one part of the page, it is in German; on the other, it is in Hebrew, and Eichmann had to sign every page to authenticate the content. On 3,600 pages, you find his signature. The same signature that you find under the document that authorized the deportation of the Jews. When you read through the papers, there is a special kind of logic in his language: The logic Eichmann has is not connected to the killing. He is talking about solving problems and that he is very good at solving problems. In one part of the papers, Eichmann mentions that 1,800 Jews were deported to Auschwitz, where they were killed. But Eichmann's focus is on the problem of getting 30 wagons for transportation. He is not talking about the people. He is talking about solving the problem. You realize that Eichmann starts talking once Less enters into this kind of logic. You read more than 40 pages, whose content is about the killing of people—but you just read about solving problems. This is very interesting language, because it avoids the reality it is dealing with. So when I set up this play, I decided: This language will be at the center of the play. We will create a special place where the audience can be a part of this interrogation.

And now imagine you have a space double the size of this one [*gestures to the room*] and you have a very big table, 15 meters long, and on one side of the table sits Eichmann and on the other side of the table sits Less. And on each side of the table are 30 chairs for the audience members. So you sit together with the actors at the table. This is one space. In this space on the table, you have a microphone into which the actors speak and a camera that picks up the images of the actors.

You have a second space, where you have very small tables, and there is a lightbulb hanging from the ceiling over each of the 30 tables. Two members of the audience sit opposite each other very closely. There are no actors. There is just the sound of the interrogation that is being performed live by the actors in the first space; you just listen to its text, and you see a technician who is working with a recording machine. From the visual point of view, it is very interesting, because the movement of the wheels of this recording machine resembles train wheels. And you can make a lot of interesting sound effects just by moving these wheels. This was the second space. There is a third space, where you have three television sets. You have documentary footage from the trial on one set; on the second monitor, you have the actor playing Eichmann; and on the third monitor set, you have the actor playing Less. The audience is placed in a normal theatre situation, sitting in rows. They all watch the monitors. The only sound they have is from the documentary footage. They don't hear the actors talk, but they see original material.

We also did something very impolite: We dressed the actor who was playing Less like Eichmann. So when you just watch the surface, you see a man in a black suit, and you think it is Eichmann in the black suit. The other guy is just wearing a pullover. If you don't pay attention to the body language, you think the guy in the black suit is Eichmann.

And now imagine that there is an audience in each of the three spaces when this play starts. You have an audience together with the actors; you have an audience together with the voice of the actors; and you have an audience together with the images of the actors. The play is structured in three sequences, in three acts. The audience will move around the building, but they will not meet. The audience is on different routes, and they go on different journeys through the play. There is one group that starts with the image. They get a lot of background information. Then they go to the next space, and suddenly they are sitting at small tables and listening to the voices of the actors while sitting opposite each other at such a small distance, and so they think of the actors as also sitting that closely opposite each other at a small table. Then they enter the third space, and suddenly they see the large table. They sit together with the actors at the table.

There is something about the human being which is very interesting: Nobody wants to sit next to the bad guy; because you want to be on the good side. But, if you don't pay attention, you think that the guy in the pullover is the good guy. When the space opens, the audience rushes to the guy with the pullover. They want to be as far away as possible from the bad guy. And when the performance starts, they realize: "Oh shit, I am sitting on the wrong side." You can see it in their body language. They start to become uncomfortable, since the actors are really so close to them that if they reached out their arms, they could touch the audience. This creates a very special kind of energy in the audience. That is one trip. The second possible journey is when you start together with the actors in the same space. Of course, this is very nice, because you are usually not so close to the actors in the theatre. Then you go to the next space and you just listen to the actors' voices, and you have to pay more attention because you only have this voice. In the last space, the voice is gone, and you see only the images of the actors. And you have all this documentary footage. The people on this route were always very disappointed because they feel like you have taken the actors away from them. Back in those days, people liked to go to the theatre because they wanted to spend time with the actors. And they were already so close to them, and suddenly, their bodies are gone. So they were unhappy. But sometimes, in theatre, you have to be unhappy. And the last group started with the voices and then got the presence of the actors, and then, in the end, they saw the documentary footage. This is the most intellectual way to experience this performance.

What was interesting was that we separated the audience into three groups. The audience is clever, so they realized that if you go on a different trip, you experience a different play. So the people who liked it wanted to see the other trips, too. They came back and saw it another time, and so they had a real encounter with the material, with the performance. You know it from yourself, if you see a show a second time, you learn different things about the performance. This is a way to train the audience. And it is very good for the box office, because people buy another ticket. When you work with these limited crowds of 100, 120 people, you have to ensure that you sell tickets. This is not our main intention, but it is important to consider. That was the first play we did in this documentary style. It was quite successful. There were a lot of people who came, and we toured it through other cities as well. And since then we have continued to do this kind of theatre.

STOLPERSTEINE STAATSTHEATER

Documentary Theatre

Hans-Werner Kroesinger

TEXT Regine Dura

https://tinyurl.com/Kroesinger-Stolpersteine

ENGLISH TRANSLATION FROM THE GERMAN David Tushingham

WITH Veronika Bachfischer, Antonia Mohr, Jonathan Bruckmeier, Gunnar
   Schmidt
DIRECTOR Hans-Werner Kroesinger
ARTISTIC ASSOCIATE Regine Dura
DRAMATURG Annalena Schott
STAGE, COSTUME & VIDEO DESIGN Rob Moonen
MUSIC Daniel Dorsch

PREMIERE June 21, 2015, at the STUDIO (Badisches Staatstheater Karlsruhe) to
   mark the 300th anniversary of the city of Karlsruhe, Germany
COMISSIONED BY Badisches Staatstheater Karlsruhe
PERFORMANCE RIGHTS Hans-Werner Kroesinger/Regine Dura, Berlin
ORIGINAL DOCUMENTS Generallandesarchiv, Karlsruhe

The audience enters the theatre. The scene consists of a large table with seats arranged around it. The four actors keep the audience from sitting there. They start to sing the song, "Abschied."

ANTONIA: Culture is not the private passion of the supposedly "cultivated." Culture is not something to be kept shut up in bookcases or painted in oils and framed on walls.

GUNNAR: Instead it is the wealth of relationships which every single comrade of the Volk has with his earth and soil, with his new home, which connects to all the things and experiences that are dear to him, which bring him joy and refresh his soul.

JONATHAN: Culture therefore belongs to the entire Volk. It should not sit enthroned like a cuckoo on a cloud high above life as it is lived to provide literary aesthetes with a few hours of cleverness.

VERONIKA: The art of the stage must take its place at the centre of the Volk, to bring every comrade the sharpest interpretation of the work the poet has created which his soul demands in a time of celebration beyond his material everyday life. This is the work of bringing the entire Volk together in celebration, and is unique in its scale.

GUNNAR: You who are economically better off and have had access to works of German art for some time should declare that you regard art and culture as a great treasure belonging to the whole of the Volk and that those with higher incomes should therefore pay higher prices to enable those who are worse off financially to attend.

ANTONIA: Everyone should learn to appreciate the cultural values and works of our Volk as an art warm with life and close to the people and gain new strength from these hours of seriousness and jollity to apply to everyday work.
    "Art is not international!"

GUNNAR: If it were, there would be Gothic cathedrals in India or Indian pagodas in Germany.

JONATHAN: If it were, Chinese theatre which is completely foreign to us would be entitled to a home in Germany and vice versa.

VERONIKA: If it were, we would be unable to talk about Viennese waltzes, Spanish dances or Russian ballet.

ANTONIA: Art is national!

JONATHAN: Only because the Nordic people can only feel in a Nordic way, does a Nordic face look out at us from all Nordic works of art

GUNNAR: and not a French one!

ANTONIA: And only because the German must draw in a German way do all his works of art reveal the soul of the German Volk.

VERONIKA: Art is national and the more national it is, the greater international recognition it receives!

ANTONIA: Now we stand at the beginning of a difficult struggle, a struggle for the soul of the German Volk and its culture.

All: Fight with us!

The scene is opened to the audience. Everyone goes to the long table, including the actors and sits down.

Lilli Jank

GUNNAR: Personal file LILLI JANK. Actress. A letter from Lilly Jankelowitz to the Director of the Baden Regional Theatre, Ludwigshafen, 2 April 1928:

VERONIKA: Esteemed General Director of the Karlsruhe Regional Theatre.
Permit me to take the liberty of asking whether your opera company will be casting the voluntary role of a soprano in the coming season. In which case, please allow me to apply.
I am the daughter of Adolf Jankelowitz from Gera, who fell in the Great War, and have studied since 1924 at the Regional Music Academy in Weimar, in the singing masterclass. During my studies I was awarded a scholarship by the state of Thüringen for outstanding musical ability.
I request confirmation whether the esteemed General Director is willing to consider my application and when it might be possible to present myself in person.
With deepest respect.
Yours faithfully,
Lilli Jankelowitz.

GUNNAR: On 4 April 1928, two days later, the reply from the Baden Regional Theatre arrives:

JONATHAN: To Miss Lilli Jankelowitz, Ludwigshafen.

Dear Fräulein!

All roles in the opera during the coming season have been cast. There is no voluntary position available which is in any way paid. For the purpose of further training it might be possible to consider you for entry to our theatre academy. However, we cannot offer any prospect of remuneration. If you should decide to enter the theatre academy as a pupil under these terms, we request further notification.

Respectfully yours,

Baden Regional Theatre

Signed Waag, General Director.

GUNNAR: One week later on 11 April, Lilli Jankelowitz writes back:

VERONIKA: Esteemed Director of the Baden Regional Theatre Karlsruhe.

Many thanks for your kind letter of 4th of this month. I am most willing to enter your theatre academy as a volunteer or pupil in accordance with the regulations. With deepest respect.

Yours faithfully,

Lilli Jankelowitz.

GUNNAR: On 28 August, 1928, she writes again;

VERONIKA: Esteemed General Director of the Baden Regional Theatre Karlsruhe.

I hereby respectfully request whether it might be possible to waive part of my tuition fee. As my father died in the war and my mother can only support the costs of my stay here with difficulty, I would be most grateful if you could heed my request.

With deepest respect.

Yours faithfully,

Lilli Jankelowitz

GUNNAR: She receives this answer on 1 September:

JONATHAN: Dear Fräulein!

In reply to your letter of 28 of the previous month we must reply that sadly it is not possible to waive a portion of your tuition fee for the theatre academy. However, we are willing to compromise by dividing tuition into monthly instalments and crediting fees you have earned against this so that you need only pay the balance at the end of the month.

Respectfully.

Waag, General Director.

ANTONIA: 1928. Adolf Hitler makes a two hour speech in Karlsruhe in the Festival Hall, on the site of the present day Schwarzwaldhalle in front of around 3,000 people, many of them party members from the wider region of Baden and the Palatinate, on "Ideology and the Daily Struggle."

ANTONIA starts to hum "Das Wandern ist des Müllers Lust"

GUNNAR: Karlsruhe 1 September 1928

Humming ends

VERONIKA: Honoured General Director of the Karlsruhe Regional Theatre.
I hereby inform you that my name—Jankelowitz—has been shortened to Jank, and I intend to keep this from now on.
With deepest respect.
Yours faithfully,
Lilli Jank

GUNNAR: There is a hand-written note in the file:

JONATHAN: Thank you, Lilli Jank. So someone finds a place to sit by her wits.

ANTONIA: In the 1929/30 season Lilli plays 14 different small parts in theatre and opera productions including a fairy in 'Faust 2' and Eleonore in 'Käthchen von Heilbronn'.

GUNNAR: Baden Regional Theatre Karlsruhe. Contract of service. Miss Lilli Jank is employed as a beginner by the theatre and opera of the Baden Regional Theatre in Karlsruhe. This contract starts on 16 August 1930 and ends on 15 August 1931. The member is entitled to:
  1. A fee for each performance in which the member appears in one or several roles of: 4 Reichsmark guaranteed at least 25 times per year for the 1930/1931 season.
  2. For a second or third performance taking place on the same day the member is entitled to remuneration of one half of the fee laid down in the guarantee for the relevant season.

ANTONIA: In the 30/31 season Lilli Jank sings roles including Pirate Jenny in Brecht's 'Threepenny Opera' as a fully recognized company member.

GUNNAR: Small but prominent!
Baden Regional Theatre Karlsruhe. Contract of Service.
Miss Lilli Jank is employed as an actress and singer (soubrette for theatre and opera) by the Baden Regional Theatre in Karlsruhe. This contract begins on

16 August 1931 and ends on 15 August 1932. The member is entitled to:
1. An annual salary of 1,400 Reichsmark
2. A fee for each performance of 5 Reichsmark, guaranteed at least 200 times per year, or 2,400 Reichsmark annually.

ANTONIA: "As a lisping Klärchen in the Weißer Rössl, Lilli Jank is a suitable partner for audience favourite Hermann Brand," says one Karlsruhe newspaper on 21 September 1931.

VERONIKA: (*lisping*) Why is it Sigismund is so divinely handsome?

GUNNAR: Are we doing Brand's file too?

ANTONIA: Later.

JONATHAN: Shortly before the end of her second season, the Artistic Director, that's this man Waag, to the Minister of Culture and Education:

GUNNAR: Miss Jank has developed into a reliable and useful company member with some excellent performances particularly in the operetta. Miss Jank is single and as a result of her engagement in the operetta has unusually high dressing-room expenses. (Make-up and costumes.) We therefore wish to offer a modest increase to her last agreed salary of some Reichsmark 300 net per year. We request approval.
Signed Waag. General Director.

ANTONIA: During this period there is a production of the operetta 'Zur goldenen Liebe' by the composer of the 'Weiße Rössl' Ralf Benatzky. "Among the soloists," writes one euphoric reviewer, "the production is carried chiefly by the singer Lilly Jank, for whom the libretto also offers a splendid acting role." And of her role in Schubert's 'Drei Mäderlhaus' they write: "Far beyond the requirements of the part, Lilly Jank as Grisi was supremely confident of the effects of her mocking satire even when clearly exaggerating."

JONATHAN: Two weeks later, the Minister of Culture and Education replies to the General Director of the Baden Regional Theatre's letter regarding his request concerning the singer and actress Lilli Jank, formerly Jankelowitz:

ANTONIA: Your request is refused.

"Das Wandern ist des Müllers Lust"—humming.

VERONIKA: On 14 September 1930 the NSDAP becomes the strongest party in Karlsruhe with 26 percent of the vote, almost eight percent above their national result of 18.3 percent.

GUNNAR: In 'Der Führer', Baden's militant paper promoting National Socialist politics and German culture, the following advertisement is published at the time:
The Führer as the helmsman. Even in a force 12 gale, our militant paper is the best helmsman for Adolf Hitler's movement. It won't give in to the moneybags of the Jewish department stores, it won't accept any fiddling by the so-called Federation of Jewish War Veterans like the "neutral" press, which is in thrall to the Jews.

The humming stops.

ANTONIA: Hermann Brand

Jonathan stands and walks around the table.

JONATHAN: 1932. Politics is becoming very diverse. There are fights in the streets, those with different opinions are abused, meetings become battles. Riots and trouble prepare the city for the Third Reich to come.
     The gentlemen of the theatre orchestra whisper to each other: "It's almost time—the Doctor made an internal speech two days ago where he called on all party officials to make the necessary preparations to takeover power."
     The Doctor is that grandee of lower life forms with a limping soul from Berlin. The party was the N.S.D.A.P.—The Nazis.
     Most members of the theatre orchestra have secretly been party comrades for years. Now it is 1933. Suddenly they have the courage of their convictions.
     I have to sing a couplet in the 'Weiße Rössl'. It is the revival. Dissonance comes from the pit. The gentlemen of the orchestra are deliberately playing the wrong notes. Their cold sabotage works. They have a little celebration instead of accompanying me, the Jew Hermann Brand, and think it's wonderfully amusing.

GUNNAR: The Jew Brand will soon have sung his last!

JONATHAN: Many of my fellow actors begin to align themselves on the side of the future rulers. They cautiously keep away from Jewish acquaintances and from me, their Jewish colleague. You never know!

ANTONIA: It is an injustice to the German Volk that those with no inner calling wish to perform theatre for our own Volk for money. It is also an injustice to

German actors deprived of means and opportunities to practice their profession and serve the good of the Volk.

JONATHAN: The city's policemen march in step in ordered rows down the main street—following a swastika flag—thus breaking the oath to the serving Republican government they were once so happy to swear as honourable soldiers. At the other end of the long main street they turn around and march back along the same route through a line of indifferent bystanders.

Gunnar, Veronika, Antonia stand up.

GUNNAR: THE GLORIOUS BREAKTHROUGH.

VERONIKA: HITLER.

ANTONIA: GERMANY'S CHANCELLOR.

ANTONIA: Torchlight parade in honour of our Führer in Karlsruhe.

JONATHAN: A nation awakes –

VERONIKA: Boundless enthusiasm of the populace –

GUNNAR: 2,500 Brownshirts march.

VERONIKA: All at once, like a storm, from somewhere, possibly from the poorest attic, the song grows of our comrade Horst Wessel (*Antonia hums the melody of the propaganda song "Die Fahnen hoch"*). On every pavement people stand with their arm raised and sing, and for a brief time the traffic is silent.

GUNNAR: Boundless enthusiasm overcomes the masses. Windows are thrown open, the masses cheer in a way Karlsruhe has not heard since August 1914. To celebrate that the Volk has been freed! Slowly the troops pass through Amalienstraße, past the Kaiser memorial, towards Kaiserstraße, accompanied by a vast crowd.

JONATHAN: And cheered on.

ANTONIA: The trams can't move, cars are stuck, traffic has come to a standstill. The shouts of 'Heil!' roar and thunder rolls through the endless rows of marchers far into the neighbouring streets. Karlsruhe shows that it is national socialist. Free of vermin, Karlsruhe shows its true face.

GUNNAR: At the junction of Kronenstraße and Kaiserstraße the red rabble from Dörfle, young lads, are back. Communists have no business being on the streets.

ANTONIA: We won't be talking much longer!

JONATHAN: To untold cheers from the populace, the troops march through Waldhornstraße to the Schlossplatz. Gauleiter Köhler speaks.

ANTONIA: Comrades, Germany lives through you and lives in you. Germany, Germany above all in the world.

All: GERMANY! (*Jonathan last*)

VERONIKA: Thousands sing the song with their arm raised. It is like an oath.

ANTONIA: Doubters be warned, death and destruction to our enemies.

All: HEIL! HOORAY! HEIL! HOORAY!

JONATHAN: Erm?

All: HAIL! HOORAY!

Gunnar, Veronika and Antonia sit down again one after another.

JONATHAN: The swastika flag is raised over the roof of the theatre. And has been hanging there—it seems—for two days in succession. Two days of the fourteen I think this nightmare will last. I make an appointment with the Artistic Director. He has always been kind to me and receives me straight away now.
  "Sir, this is the second day that the swastika flag has been flying over the theatre, you will understand that as long as that flag is hanging there I have to refuse to appear in this building."

GUNNAR: "It's good of you to come and tell me that. It makes things easier for me. Today I have been instructed by the Ministry of Culture to place you on temporary leave. I have to recast all the parts you are currently playing."

JONATHAN: "That's fine by me, this spell won't last long."

GUNNAR: "One can't know that. I have tried to make it clear to the gentlemen from the Ministry that I can't imagine this theatre without you. But the gentlemen won't budge."

JONATHAN: The Artistic Director shrugs his shoulders and takes a concerned look out of the window at the dome above the stage where the swastika flag behaves like all flags: it is flapping busily in the wind. He shakes my hand. I stand up and leave thinking: two weeks' holiday will be very nice.

Antonia starts to hum "Das Wandern ist des Müllers Lust."

ANTONIA: One afternoon in April 33 a gang gathers, going from street to street to the shops which are owned by Jews.

JONATHAN: Kaiserstraße, Karlstraße, Herrenstraße.

ANTONIA: The rowdy mob, joined by adolescent posh boys, smashes windows, knocks over displays and forces the shops to close.

JONATHAN: Werderplatz, Steinstraße, Schützenstraße.

GUNNAR: Jewish businesses are boycotted and marked with a yellow sign on a black background. Party members are encouraged to photograph anyone breaking the boycott.

JONATHAN: Kriegsstraße, Erbprinzenstraße, Nebeniusstraße.

Veronika and Gunnar start to distribute leaflets.

ANTONIA: Among the German Jews there are a few audacious believers in the rule of law who protest to the authorities and demand compensation. They are usually treated like the lawyer in Munich whose shoes and trousers are removed and is then dragged through the streets barefoot in his underwear with a placard around his neck on which it says:

JONATHAN: "I am a Jew and will never complain about the Nazis again."

Jonathan repeats this line softly during the following text

ANTONIA: Outside Germany this photograph of the lawyer who is accompanied by a platoon of Nazis—the picture of this disgraceful procession appears in all the illustrated newspapers.

JONATHAN: Nobody intervenes. Every country can ultimately do whatever it likes with its Jews.
   On another day, a hunt is declared on Social Democrats. Every country can also do whatever it likes with its Socialists.

Leaflet

For the first time the actors sing Das Wandern ist des Müllers Lust—with lyrics.

VERONIKA: The transportation of Dr. Adam Remmele, previously a miller by trade, former Regional President, Minister of Culture, Justice and the Interior; State Secretary Ludwig Marum; Government Secretary Stenz; Sally Grüne-baum and Detective Sergeant Furrer from the State Prison in Riefstahlstraße to Kieslau, will be made via the following streets: Riefstahlstraße, Mühlburger Tor, Kaiserstraße as far as Police Headquarters on Tuesday, 16 May 1933, between 11 and 12 o'clock in the morning.

ANTONIA: It almost seems as if the entire capital of Baden has made a rendezvous to bid their red comrades a final farewell. The crowd in the square outside the prison assumes giant proportions. Police cars drive up and collect the convicts, flanked by SS men. When the gate opens and the cars drive into a wall of people, it flares up. A shrill, raging concert of whistles begins, booing thunders across the square. Thank God the hour has come when even the comrades of the Volk will finally open their eyes. Today they will see how rotten and foul everything is. The cars, which are surrounded by a thick SS cordon, can only get underway slowly. They pass at walking pace between a wall of people. Choirs have posted themselves on street corners, playing the miller's song non-stop and the masses join in.

GUNNAR: There is a minor incident outside the Marum's house where the Jew Marr has to the cheek to shout:

JONATHAN: "Goodbye Freedom!"

GUNNAR: It only takes a moment to shut his insolent Jewish mouth.

JONATHAN: Watch out, or you'll be sent to Kieslau.

GUNNAR: So the procession continues past the regional parliament, the Regional Ministry and the red building that used to belong to the metalworkers. Just before noon, they reach Police Headquarters, from which they drive at speed to their destination of Kieslau.

Singing breaks off.

JONATHAN: My brothers and I stand there dumbstruck. None of us says what he is thinking. I think: it's not nice being a coward. It's nice to be brave. But being battered to death by a mob for being brave, that's not nice at all. That evening I am sitting in a café with my colleague Nelly Rademacher. The place is very busy. A giant comes in through the revolving doors with a much smaller companion. Both walk past my table. It's obvious which party they belong to from their haircuts. The big one says loudly:

ANTONIA: "There he sits, the dirty Jew!"

JONATHAN: Then he comes to my table and growls:

ANTONIA: "You dirty Jew, you've provoked me, you're coming outside!"

JONATHAN: I get up and leave. The two are coming after me. The short one lunges at me before the revolving door and slaps me in the face. My fist hits his nose. He slowly slides down the wall and onto the floor. I quickly spin through the revolving door. I'm in the street and now I really am in trouble. There are four SA men waiting outside who jump on me immediately. One of them knocks me to the ground. I stand up to avoid more blows from these thugs in a cowardly retreat when suddenly I am held firm by powerful arms from behind me. I turn round—two policemen have tight hold of me—like iron. I'm one against four. They arrest me and take me to the station. Here they start finishing me off "legally."

Jonathan turns away from the table.

GUNNAR: Get this Jew out of a German theatre!
So far we have waited in vain for a reply as to what the Baden Regional Theatre has undertaken in order to prevent incidents such as the one conjured up by the Jew Brand in Kaiserstraße last week from happening again. This is not the first time this Polish Jew has bothered passers-by in the street in the coarsest way. Proving provocation on the Jew Brand's part is hardly necessary. We thank God on bended knee that the time has finally come for an awakening to pass through the German Volk, and we hope the moment is not far off where those aliens and parasites harmful to the image of Germany can be deported to where they belong. We must sweep away the filth with a broom of iron!

Brutus writes in a reader's letter to the Führer:

ANTONIA: The Jew doesn't have the right fingers for work and what his mind offers is always rotten.

Jonathan turns back to the table.

JONATHAN: Torn from sleep I'm on the phone at four in the morning: "Is that the police station? Waldstraße 68 here, ground floor. Brand. Please can you send someone to check everything is in order. The door bell is being rung continually and there is fighting at the front door. It's being going on for 10 minutes."

Antonia starts throwing paper and erasers at Jonathan.

ANTONIA: "Yes, that's perfectly in order, open the door—it's the police who are trying to reach you."

Gunnar stands up, walks towards Jonathan.

GUNNAR: "You are State Actor Brand,"

JONATHAN: "Yes?"

GUNNAR: "We have to search your house for weapons and forbidden literature."

JONATHAN: "Help yourselves." We go into my room. The armed escort remains in the hallway. He soon gives up looking for weapons.

GUNNAR: "What are you doing now, Sir?"

JONATHAN: "I'm waiting to see what happens."

GUNNAR: "If I were you, I wouldn't wait—do you understand me??—There are plans for you—get out of here!"

VERONIKA: "Aren't you taking any luggage?"

JONATHAN: "No, I don't want to be noticed at the station. Keep well. Nobody's going to bother you. You're Poles. I've got a German passport. We'll see each other again soon—Goodbye!"

Jonathan goes to the auditorium.

GUNNAR: From the Führer, 15 March 33. Karlsruhe.
Exterminating the demon Jew.
The cleansing operation, begun in the Culture Ministry by removing the Jewess Fischel as Director of the Baden Art Gallery, is to be continued. A general ban on recruitment has been decreed covering all operations of the Ministry of Culture and Education with immediate effect. This ban includes the Baden Regional Theatre. In one area on which we have had to shine a critical light for some time, at the Baden Regional Theatre in Karlsruhe, Dr Wacker has already put things to rights. The acting Culture Minister has given the General Director of the Baden Regional Theatre the following decree:

ANTONIA: "In amendment to the agreements and mandates granted under decree No. A. 3407 of 28 February 1933 No. A. 3407, it is determined that

1. Any extension of the contracts expiring at the end of the current season with conductor Schwarz, solo repetiteur Stern, actress and operetta soubrette Jank, and head of stage design Thorsten Hecht is to be refused.

Gunnar stands up and takes Jonathan's seat at the end of the table.

2. With regard to negotiations over new contracts with the following members of the solo staff, distance will be provisionally taken from:
Chamber singer Schöpflin
Chamber singer Schuster
Chamber singer Strack
Chamber singer Fanz
Singer Haberkorn
3. The indefinite leave granted to State Actor Brand is hereby confirmed.
4. Notice is also given that on 15 March 33 the Commissioner for the Ministry of Culture and Education has ordered the placing the Artistic Director of the Baden Regional Theatre Dr. Hans Waag on immediate leave. All management duties are transferred to Ministerial Advisor Senior Government Secretary Dr. Asal until further notice.

VERONIKA: For months the brown shirt has dominated the image of Karlsruhe's streets and it is now loved and trusted among the populace as much as the uniform of the old 109ers, whose tradition will be carried on and faithfully upheld by our SS regiment 109.

GUNNAR: It's early, but thousands already line the Schlossplatz where the formations of the National Front to Celebrate the Awakening of the German Volk have assembled. A forest of flags gleams over the so-called Stresemann-platz. Platoon stands behind platoon, the army sport sections of the steel helmets fall in. The 20 war veterans from Karlsruhe enter, joined by countless numbers of workers from the NSBO (National Socialist Workplace Organization) with their special sections: tramways and postal service.

VERONIKA: Then, greeted by cheers from the ecstatic comrades of the Volk, the Karlsruhe police march into the square. Three police officials lead with swastika banners and flags of black-white-red, the colours of the new Germany. In deep ranks the twelve thousand men: SA,

GUNNAR: Police,

ANTONIA: Steel helmets,

VERONIKA: and SS.

ANTONIA: Orders echo. The standard bearer of regiment 109 holds his eagle higher.

GUNNAR: The wind grabs hold of the cloth. The formations line up behind each other to march into the city to the Schlossplatz. Comrades of the Volk stand in the streets and cheer.

VERONIKA: People wave out of windows to the men marching, the traffic has to be stopped, so that no lives are endangered amid the throng...

ANTONIA: Everywhere the brown fighters appear, they are greeted with boundless enthusiasm,

VERONIKA: and everywhere the dark uniforms of the police are seen, in advance of the banners of an awakening Germany, the enthusiasm erupts through the streets and surges across the rooftops.

ANTONIA: The route of the march to the Schlossplatz leads through Karl- and Friedrichstraße, Erbprinzen-Kaiser- and Waldhornstraße. Masses of people clog the streets, streaming through side streets to the faraway square.

VERONIKA: The steps of the columns reverberate powerfully and the sound of the choirs echo rousingly over the masses of people. The procession of these 12,000 people is like a metaphor of battle.

GUNNAR: Endless jubilation as the police choir joins in the sonorous game. Torches blaze in the background in the fists of the SA men.

ANTONIA: shining over blood-red swastika banners.

VERONIKA: shining over victorious standards,

GUNNAR: shining over the glorious flags of Bismarck's Reich. The flags of the Baden soldiers' associations are represented in large numbers.

VERONIKA: And in all the faces burns a joy, an enthusiasm appears to grow within itself as if it's never going to end. Then the Reich's appointee Gauleiter Robert Wagner speaks

Gunnar, Antonia and Veronika turn towards Jonathan.

JONATHAN: "We want to restore inner peace and inner order to the Volk of Baden. These are the foundations on which we shall build the state. What we have encountered in Baden is no easy legacy. Empty coffers and nothing but debts. Plus corruption, theft of files, wiping away the traces of years of mismanagement. We are willing to see our cleansing operation through to the bitter end. We want a spirit of joyful responsibility to move into every single office. Nothing rotten may remain to hinder reconstruction. Our Volk must be filled with one spirit, one belief, one will. With this new awareness we can then attack the task of reconstruction. Heil Hitler."

GUNNAR: On 20 April33 it's the Führer's birthday! In honour of Adolf Hitler the "Hitler Lime" will be planted in the Schlossplatz.

Jonathan walks slowly to the table, passed Gunnar, whose original seat he takes.

VERONIKA: On 10 May the new city council names Adolf Hitler and Robert Wagner honorary citizens of Karlsruhe. The Marktplatz is renamed Adolf Hitler Platz, and Gottesauer Platz becomes Hermann Göring Platz.

ANTONIA: Strasbourg.

GUNNAR: "The Jews stick together."

Gunnar gives Jonathan a letter.

JONATHAN: That's a nice line, thought of by non-Jews. It's not true. The Jews in Strasbourg, whose support I am expecting behave like good Frenchmen when I ask them in German for help. They do not love anything German. To them I am a German. A German the Germans don't like. *Jonathan spreads business cards on the table.* What have I to do with them? I happen to be of the same religion as them. It obliges them to do no more than help me with some business cards. I've been living for a month now in a tiny room in a former nunnery in Strasbourg. At four o'clock one night there is a knock at the window. In the street next to a heavy suitcase, stands Nelly.

VERONIKA: "We can get to Basel in Switzerland in two hours. A character actor at the theatre there has died suddenly: it's a great opportunity for you."

During the next line Jonathan climbs over the table to Veronika.

JONATHAN: We travel together to Basel. Those were the days. Jews could travel across borders without any fuss.

Antonia goes to what was originally Gunnar's seat, collects the business cards and then returns to her seat.

JONATHAN: The director meets me. "I was a character actor at the State Theatre—your character actor has just died. About the vacancy –"

GUNNAR: "I'm sorry but you're too late. This vacancy was filled a year ago. How is your Artistic Director?"

JONATHAN: "He's been fired. He was too late deciding to fall into line."

GUNNAR: "So, so—these Nazis have no sense of humanity. Their dynamic is purely destructive. As a human being, homo sapiens has a mission to remain human. In one word, humanity! Tolerance! Ethics!—Sir, it has been a pleasure."

JONATHAN: He offers me his hand. I stand up and leave. A pity, I would have liked to stay with this humane man.

Gunnar returns to his original seat.

JONATHAN: Nelly tells me the news from Karlsruhe:

VERONIKA: "Our theatre's 'leading man', who used to be an almost daily guest in the house of our highly artistic Rabbi has declared:"

GUNNAR: "I thought the matter through properly last night, for a whole hour, and I must admit the National Socialists are right about everything. I'm absolutely for them."

VERONIKA: "And what about your friendship with the Rabbi?"

GUNNAR: "That's over, obviously! I can't afford it. I would lose my job. I'd advise you to stop visiting Brand's parents so often. You are an Aryan after all. If you go visiting Jews, it won't go down at all well. The National Socialists are in power now and, after due consideration, I can only say they want the best for us. I've also signed up as a party member. We have to think of the Volk."

VERONIKA: "Is that what you really think?"

GUNNAR: "It's absolutely what I think. Although, what happens—if things change—I don't know."

JONATHAN: The party has its eye on Nelly. Her post is being read. Not only her friendship with me is suspicious. Her whole behaviour is provocative. She uses all kinds of tricks to avoid the new German salute. She will not raise her arm to those two idiotic words which everyone growls at each other everywhere. "Heil Hitler!" *Gunnar turns to Antonia and uses gestures to re-enact the following text.* She won't ever cross the street without carrying an umbrella in one hand and a little suitcase or muff in the other. How can she raise her arm in the herd's symbolic greeting weighed down like that? But Germany's new rulers have their eyes open. Even an actress like Nelly is important enough for them to spy on. Snotty young boys who can't be trusted to say any more than "We've saddled the horses!" now become important members of the company because they belong to the party. It is these lads who pounce on Nelly: "You're going to learn how we salute in Germany!" (*ANTONIA: Yes, sir*) She remains incorrigible. However, she is soon able to feel the omnipotence of the snitches. She is gradually phased out of the repertoire. She no longer gets any parts. This is paving the way for her sacking. But a suitable reason for dismissal needs to be found. The Artistic Director demands proof of her ancestry. She supplies it.

During the following text, Antonia goes to Veronika's seat and collects her files then returns to her own seat.

She cannot be fired for artistic reasons. From the Ministry of Culture—not the Artistic Director—she receives a notice that her contract will be dissolved at the end of the season for reasons of "cultural realignment." So now she has it in black and white that she is a hindrance to culture. In her place the theatre she is forced to leave will hire someone "culturally aligned." Culture has been saved.

For this text Veronika walks around the table next to where Johannes was originally sitting and kneels on the table.

VERONIKA: Death is great.
  We are his,
  Our mouths laughing.
  When we think
  We're in the midst of life,
  He dares to cry
  In the midst of us.

All climb onto the table, come together and sing the Song "Was kann der Sigismund dafür..."

GUNNAR (*turns around*): German men and German women!

Antonia, Veronika, and Jonathan turn around.

In the name of Baden State Theatre I would like to welcome you all most heartily. It is a particular pleasure for us to see that you have followed our summons today in such numbers. Allow us to give you a taste of what our theatre has to offer.

Our theatre follows two guiding principles:

The idea of a national theatre

And the idea of theatre for the Volk.

Our desire for culture and the programme to deliver it are there, forces are ready, everyone in their places. Preparations for work and the work itself are performed willingly and happily by every single one of our working community, loyal to the wishes of our Führer and Reich Chancellor. We offer our hand in trust, to lead you into purer territory, the land of what is true, good, and beautiful, the land of German poets and thinkers, the delights of German music—follow us and visit your theatre en masse.

ANTONIA: Your theatre, without which the spiritual life of the state capital and residency could not be imagined, and which is ideally suited to carry Karlsruhe's reputation far beyond the city boundaries. We are conscious of serving this city and serving this country, rooted in the same earth as its poets and composers. We shall therefore hold a Baden week to coincide with South-West German Homeland Day, whose highlight will be a visiting opera performance with singers born in Karlsruhe.

GUNNAR: Restructuring our literary department under Propaganda Leader Becker will ensure that we are more in touch with intellectual trends in literature and music in future than we were before.

VERONIKA: From the start of the new season the N.S. [National Socialist] Cultural Congregation, the Union of the German Stage, the League to Fight for German Culture and the N.S. Organization "Strength Through Joy," will also contribute.

GUNNAR: Make sure you get good seats in plenty of time. You definitely won't regret it.

ANTONIA: And remember:

JONATHAN: It also creates jobs. The health and well-being of around 400 families depends on a flourishing State Theatre, and you in turn depend on your beloved Karlsruhe artists,

ANTONIA: who for their part consider it an honour to be able to perform for their beloved Karlsruhers.

So let's go to the State Theatre!

GUNNAR: Let the play begin.

VERONIKA: Signed Himmighoffen, new General Director, Baden State Theatre Karlsruhe.

Everyone climbs down off the table, Veronika at the end of the table (originally Jonathan's seat), Jonathan in Veronika's seat, Gunnar in his original seat. Music becomes louder!

VERONIKA: EMMA GRANDEIT

GUNNAR: Personal file Emma Grandeit 57a 896.

The Minister of Culture and Education to the General Director.

25 April 33.

Re: Law for the Restoration of the Professional Civil Service

Jonathan selects a folder of laws.

JONATHAN: Civil servants who are not of Aryan descent are to be retired.

Everyone looks at Gunnar, who takes a couple of steps back.

JONATHAN: Paragraph 1 does not apply to civil servants (*Gunnar stands still*), who served at the Front during the First World War for the German Reich or its allies or whose fathers or sons fell in the World War. (*Gunnar returns to the table*)

GUNNAR: In accordance with sections 3, 7, and 15 of the law of 7 April 1933 "the contracts of employment with General Music Director Krips, State Actor Brand, and prompter Grandeit are dissolved, and they are dismissed from their duties at the Baden Regional Theatre.

Signed. Dr. Wacker."

Have we got the Wacker file?

VERONIKA: No.

JONATHAN:It was lost in a fire.

On 4 May 1933, the prompter Emma Grandeit writes:

Gunnar and Jonathan decide Antonia is Emma Grandeit.

ANTONIA: Esteemed Mr. Senior Government Secretary!
   From various sources it has been drawn to my attention that a rule exists whereby 1 1/2 percent of the staff may consist of Jews. As I want to leave no stone unturned in attempting to retain my position, may I politely request that you bear me in mind while in applying this rule if at all possible, especially in view of the fact that my contract runs until 1 September 1934. Thanking you in advance.
   With deepest respect,
   Emma Grandeit.

GUNNAR: Dear Mrs. Grandeit!
   This questionable rule applies only to Jews attending schools and universities. As you have already been informed, your dismissal in accordance with sections 3, 7, and 15 of the Law for the Restoration of the Professional Civil Service was made on 7 April 1933. Amendments to this order which has already been made are not possible.
   Respectfully,
   Asal, Senior Government Secretary, Professor.

VERONIKA: On 27 April 1933 the Baden Regional Theatre becomes the Baden State Theatre Karlsruhe and on the noticeboard to the left of the entrance to the canteen, the following notice can be found:
   On Thursday, 11 May 33 from 2120–2130 hours an air raid drill will take place during which a blackout will be carried out across the city of Karlsruhe. For this purpose, it is also necessary for the theatre building to be blacked out. External lighting is forbidden for the duration of the exercise. Before the performance begins, Director Pruscha will step in front of the curtain and explain to the audience the measures which will have to be taken in the theatre building as a result of the exercise. The curtain will be brought down at around 2115 hours. The house lights will immediately be switched on. When the exercise begins, the State Power Station will switch the house lights off, so that only the emergency lights remain on. The audience will be requested to remain in the auditorium. The conductor and orchestra should also remain in their seats and the performers on stage. The end of the exercise will be indicated by the house lights coming on. The performance may then continue. If emergency lights are switched on in dressing rooms and other spaces it must be checked immediately whether the windows are covered. If this is not the case, the lights must be extinguished immediately. The purpose of the exercise can only be achieved if every member willingly supports it.

While Jonathan is reading, Antonia writes. When he has finished, Jonathan walks over to Antonia to give her her reference, then returns to his seat.

JONATHAN: Reference for Emma Grandeit: June 1933. Karlsruhe, State Theatre.
Mrs. Emma Grandeit has worked at the Baden State Theatre in Karlsruhe for many years and proved herself to be a quite excellent prompter. This view is shared by all the company members, especially those who are busiest and under most stress, but also by the directors, because she genuinely understands the art of prompting: of being reliable, sympathetic, and at the same time unobtrusive, tireless, and supportive in rehearsals, alert and calm during performances. She has been an equally reliable worker in both theatre and operetta. We regret that she leaves against her will and wish her the very best.
Felix Baumbach.
Resident director, Baden State Theatre.

ANTONIA: Karlsruhe, 25 June 1933.
Dear Mr. Artistic Director,
Permit me to trouble you with regard to the following matter: I have worked at the State Theatre as a prompter for seven years and now because of my non-Aryan descent I was dismissed on 30 June. The enclosed copy of my reference supplied by resident director Baumbach says everything about my good qualities as a prompter and a person, and the other company members tell me every day that they would be delighted if I could stay.
I have recently heard from many sources that there will soon be changes regarding the Jewish question. I would very much regret losing my job unless it is really necessary.
As I understand it, no steps have yet been taken in decisive positions because your support has been anticipated with regard to this question.
I have been married since the beginning of 1914, my husband is an actor, Aryan, here, has not had a regular job for six years, he served in the war for 3 ½ years, 1 ½ years at the front. My brother was severely wounded in the war, my brother-in-law was killed, another brother-in-law was shot by the Poles in Upper Silesia on suspicion of being a German spy.
I come from a family which has sacrificed a great deal for the Fatherland and has been resident in Germany for many generations. I myself have never felt anything other than entirely German.
And I therefore cannot understand that I would not be worthy of practicing my profession at a German theatre.
I therefore ask you, dear Mr. Artistic Director, if you should see any chance of my being able to stay, assuming of course that you would be so kind as to support my case, and to urge the General Directorate here to wait before filling my position. This position is now free once again because the lady viewed as my potential successor turned out to be inadequate during her trial period.
The theatre would also save around 2,000 Marks if I were to remain because my contract runs until September 1934 and I should receive 75 percent of my pay during this time.

I would be most grateful if you were able to do anything for me and would also request that you inform me of the same.

With deepest respect,

Emma Grandeit.

JONATHAN: To which the Minister of Culture, Education and Justice—Culture and Education Department—replies:

Karlsruhe, 13 July 1933 to Mrs. Emma Grandeit.

Jonathan throws the file at Antonia.

GUNNAR: The Law for the Restoration of the Professional Civil Service only permits very specific exceptions for the retention of persons of non-Aryan descent in state employment. These exceptions cannot be extended. In particular it is not legally feasible to interpret the rule about service at the front any wider than that the official or employee concerned must have personally served at the front. I am therefore unable to act on your request despite your professional performance, which I am happy to confirm here was fully recognized at all times at the Baden State Theatre. Asal.

VERONIKA: From the Baden Press: State Theatre Day

Veronika walks around the table to Antonia.

Among the many events which took place in the course of Saturday, one of those which took pride of place was the Baden State Theatre's promotional day entitled: "The Theatre for the German Volk."

JONATHAN AND GUNNAR: Hooray!

VERONIKA: From half past three to half past four there was a concert on the balcony of the City Hall by the band of regiment 109 conducted by Kapellmeister Dankwart, while at the same time the police band under Music Director Heisig let their cheerful tunes be heard outside the State Theatre.

Jonathan and Gunnar walk up and down on their side of the table.

JONATHAN: The centrepiece of the promotional event is the early afternoon rally at Adolf-Hitler-Platz, where the topic is the theatre's duties in the new state.

VERONIKA: In his address, resident director Felix Baumbach begins by explaining that no theatre can survive without the living echo of a congregation, without a deep connection between the community of performers and the community of the audience. Especially now, in this new state, these communities have to come together more easily.

GUNNAR: Evenings on which the great works of a Kleist, a Schiller, a Goethe, or a Hebbel are performed on stage must be holidays. But the repertoire of the Baden State Theatre will also do justice to world literature, as far as it possesses essential cultural values. Clearly the poets of this new time must also find their way to the stage open. Cramps, kitsch and unclean experiments are banned, but the State Theatre will find room in its programme for plays which bring daylight, which provide the audience with relaxation. Karlsruhe loves its theatre and it will find its community of visitors who provide the foundation which make it possible for the theatre to fulfill its great and joyful task.

JONATHAN: Propaganda director Fritz Becker emphasises that it is not the Baden State Theatre's intention on this promotional day to address individual comrades among the Volk and to go begging. The day is guided by an artistic conscience. This propaganda is in the service of the Volk. The State Theatre must leave its reservations behind in order to give its achievements the recognition they need. In addition to this, the promotion also has the intention of fostering the community of the Volk because the life-affirming works of our great writers give them the tools to do so.

GUNNAR: The target which the Directorate of the State Theatre aims to achieve is a serious one and especially in this period it requires the assistance of the audience.

JONATHAN: The theatre turns particularly to youth, to awaken the flame of enthusiasm in their hearts. In this way our State Theatre can achieve its lofty task of reaching the Volk through youth.

GUNNAR: The young must come and be enthused by the greatness of German art. No-one should be ashamed of this enthusiasm, because these are our best who are capable of being enthused.

JONATHAN+GUNNAR: Hooray!

Gunnar, Veronika, and Jonathan are now at the end of the table opposite Antonia.

JONATHAN: From the personal file of Emma Grandeit.

During the following Antonia moves away from the table.

ANTONIA: Karlsruhe, 19 July 1933. To the General Directorate of the Baden State Theatre.

Dear Sirs,

I intend to move to Breslau, my husband's native city. As I no longer have any prospect of employment, my husband hopes to secure a livelihood through old acquaintances in his home town, which is impossible here. As things stand, once my contract has run out, we would become a burden on public welfare.

My wages, however, are hardly enough to support three adults, especially after 30th September when the cut of 25 percent comes into force. We therefore do not know how we can pay for the move and our additional expenses in another city until we have found accommodation, etc.

I am therefore taking the liberty of turning to you with the request to approve a payment to cover the removal expenses which I estimate to be between four and five hundred marks.

I hope that you will understand that we wish to try to establish a modest livelihood elsewhere and that you will be able to help me by granting my request. I would be most grateful if you were able to come to a decision as soon as possible so that I can give notice to leave my apartment.

With sincere thanks for your kind response in advance, I sign this with the greatest respect,

Emma Grandeit

JONATHAN: 20 July 33:

GUNNAR: Dear Mrs. Grandeit,

I regret that I am not in a position to comply with your request, much as I would like to help. The rules for implementation of the Law for the Restoration of the Professional Civil Service make no provision for assistance with removal costs. Consequently I am unable to fulfil our request.

Respectfully,

Asal, Senior Government Secretary.

ANTONIA: Dear Mr. Director,

If you don't want me to commit suicide, then I am asking you to inform me <u>as soon as possible</u> what sum I shall receive from the pension fund and <u>when</u> I shall receive this money. I want to move away from here at the beginning of September.

I am at the end of my strength. If this last chance to move away from here after all the failures is also taken away from me, then I shall commit a desperate act.

Respectfully.

Emma Grandeit

GUNNAR: Dear Mrs. Grandeit!
There is no reason at all for you to upset yourself because of this questionable matter. You will receive the money due to you in any event. You must however bear in mind that I can only process one thing at a time. I shall resolve the matter in the course of the week. You will then be notified immediately.
Respectfully,
Asal, Senior Government Secretary.

The actors sing the song "Salzkammergut."

ANTONIA: Gentlemen, now that is degenerate.

GUNNAR: Today the Baden State Theatre has become the theatre of the Volk and nothing else ever guides it other than the thought of serving the Volk.

JONATHAN: The new era brings new powers to the fore, valued German individuals give the Volk a new artistic sense following years of stagnation and decline, youthful enthusiasm which has been strengthened in the struggle has thrown tired decadence and antiquated formal discipline overboard, and the German artist can now create freely for his kind and according to his artistic conscience.

VERONIKA: With the national awakening of 1933, today's theatre has become a cultural power of unprecedented importance, as at no time has the stage's value in creating a Volk been more clearly recognized and commended to the hearts of the Volk more urgently than in these days by our Führer. Now what is sick and problematic is no longer of interest, only what is healthy is of interest now, irrespective of victory or defeat.

GUNNAR: Dear Mrs. Grandeit,
We remind you of our letter of 27 September 1933 and request that in determining whether a payment is due to you from the Baden State Theatre for the month of October you provide us directly with an official certificate of your income in the said month.
General Directorate of the Baden State Theatre

ANTONIA: Breslau, 11 November 1933
Re: Law for the Restoration of the Professional Civil Service
In reply to your letter of 9 November I regret to inform you that I have not received any letter of 27 September from you. I therefore do not know what it concerns. However, I assume that you have placed me under the obligation of constantly presenting you with official certificates that I have not earned anything. I am now asking you to tell me precisely who is supposed to issue me with these certificates, because I have no idea how I should obtain such a

certificate. In the meantime I am therefore sending you a sworn affidavit that I have not earned a single penny to this day. I assume that this will suffice temporarily as I hope you do not believe me capable of perjuring myself for the sake of a few marks.

At the beginning of October I directed an enquiry to the cashier as to what sums I might withdraw here. As I received no reply I have withdrawn what I have calculated to be my salary regularly at the bank here, convinced that these sums have been transferred to the official bank. I therefore request that you transfer these sums to the bank as soon as possible, including the first instalment for November. I should add that you know very well that it is impossible for me to find any kind of employment in Germany because of the Civil Service Law. It is therefore quite impossible for me to ever be in a position to earn even a penny. And if this were nevertheless the case by some accident then I would declare it and not leave myself liable to prosecution.

I stress once more that I have not received a letter from you dated 27 September I can, however, explain the way in which this letter may have been mislaid. It will have been addressed to Karlsruhe and then left with the porter until it was mislaid.

I assume this as your letter dated 9 November was initially also addressed to Karlsruhe, even though I specially informed you of my new address on 25 September and had also sent my address to the cashier's office. I enclose the envelope as proof.

Perhaps it will be sufficient if I constantly send you affidavits that I have had no earnings. That will give you greater security as you can immediately have me charged with perjury if I should turn out to have lied.

Emma Grandeit.

Breslau I. Junkernstr. 28 II

Antonia slams the file on the table.

Appendix: Affidavit.

I hereby affirm on oath that following my dismissal from the Baden State Theatre until this day I have not earned a single penny and I hereby declare that I shall give notice to the Baden State Theatre of any sum which, contrary to expectations, I may earn in future.

Breslau, 11 November.

Emma Grandeit.

Veronika and Jonathan direct the following lines to Antonia.

JONATHAN: "The improvement which was clearly visible at the Baden State Theatre in its first season will be continued in the coming winter: that is the unconditional wish of the General Directorate. The first year in Adolf Hitler's

Germany, the start-up year as it has significantly been called, has been a year of discovery—of seeking and finding. A wealth of experiences and a renunciation of everything un-German has been the rich reward of this period."

VERONIKA: Himmighoffen, the new General Director, Karlsruhe. Season opening at the Baden State Theatre 1934

ANTONIA: STATE ACTOR PAUL GEMMECKE

VERONIKA: Name?

GUNNAR: Gemmecke

VERONIKA: First names?

GUNNAR: Georg August Friedrich, but they call me Paul

VERONIKA: Job description?

GUNNAR: Actor

VERONIKA: Place of residence?

GUNNAR: Karlsruhe, Yorkstr. 41, Flat 5

VERONIKA: Place and date of birth?

GUNNAR: Kassel, 13 December 1880

VERONIKA: Have you been a member of the Communist Party or Communist Aid or support organizations (including the so-called National Communist movement—the "Black Front")—and if so, when?

GUNNAR: No.

VERONIKA: Have you been a member of the Social Democratic Party, the Iron Front, or other social democratic or republican support and satellite organizations, particularly the Federation of Republican Teachers, the Union of Socialist Teachers, the Liberal Teachers' Union, the International Socialist League, the Free School Union of Germany, the Young Socialist Workers, the Red Falcon, the Federation of Socialist Students, the Federation of Republican Students, the German Association for Peace, the League for Human Rights, the Peace League and other international or pacifist societies, associations or consortia, and if so, when?

GUNNAR: None.

VERONIKA: Were you part of a trade union?

GUNNAR: The Co-operative of German stage employees, No. 31378.

VERONIKA: Of which political parties have you ever been a member?

GUNNAR: None.

VERONIKA: Are you or were you a member of the NSDAP, the NS, the SS, the steel helmets, the Technical Emergency Service or other bodies in support of the elevation of the nation, and, if so, when? (to be confirmed by presenting the relevant certificates

GUNNAR: No.

VERONIKA: To which political societies or lodges, orders etc. have you belonged or do you belong and, if so, when?

GUNNAR: None.

VERONIKA: Are you descended from non-Aryan or specifically from Jewish parents or grand-parents?

GUNNAR: No.

VERONIKA: Closer details of your ancestry. Your father's name?

GUNNAR: Gemmecke.

VERONIKA: First names?

GUNNAR: Heinrich Ludwig Friedrich

VERONIKA: Status and profession?

GUNNAR: Train driver

VERONIKA: Place and date of birth?

GUNNAR: Gronau near Göttingen, 30 April 1850

VERONIKA: Place and date of death?

GUNNAR: Kassel, 27 November 1934

VERONIKA: Religion?

GUNNAR: Protestant

VERONIKA: Married at?

GUNNAR: Mörshausen, Melsungen district

VERONIKA: Married on?

GUNNAR: 6 October 1877

VERONIKA: Mother's maiden name?

GUNNAR: Kurzrock

VERONIKA: First names?

GUNNAR: Rosine

VERONIKA: Place and date of birth?

GUNNAR: Mörshausen, 5 February 1856

VERONIKA: Place and date of death?

GUNNAR: Kassel, 11 September 1905

VERONIKA: Religion (and any previous religion)?

GUNNAR: Protestant

VERONIKA: Grandfather's name?

GUNNAR: Gemmecke

VERONIKA: First names?

GUNNAR: Georg Heinrich

VERONIKA: Status and profession?

GUNNAR: Master blacksmith and estate manager

VERONIKA: Place and date of birth?

GUNNAR: Gronau near Göttingen, 2 December 1811

VERONIKA: Place and date of death?

GUNNAR: Gronau near Göttingen, 16 December 1884

VERONIKA: Religion?

GUNNAR: Protestant

VERONIKA: Grandmother's name?

GUNNAR: Gemmecke, born Friedes

VERONIKA: First names?

GUNNAR: Friederike Louise Charlotte

VERONIKA: Place and date of birth?

GUNNAR: Gronau near Göttingen, 24 January 1814

VERONIKA: Place and date of death?

GUNNAR: Gronau near Göttingen, 30 May 1842

VERONIKA: Religion?

GUNNAR: Protestant

VERONIKA: Grandfather's name?

GUNNAR: Kurzrock

VERONIKA: First names?

GUNNAR: Johann Heinrich

VERONIKA: Status and profession?

GUNNAR: Master blacksmith and estate manager

VERONIKA: Place and date of birth?

GUNNAR: Hefelür, 13 December 1822

VERONIKA: Place and date of death?

GUNNAR: Mörshausen, 4 February 1860

VERONIKA: Religion?

GUNNAR: Protestant

VERONIKA: Grandmother's name?

GUNNAR: Kurzrock, born Horn

VERONIKA: First names?

GUNNAR: Anna Gertrud Micabeth

VERONIKA: Place and date of birth?

GUNNAR: Mörshausen, 31 October 1823

VERONIKA: Place and date of death?

GUNNAR: Mörshausen, 1 November 1887

VERONIKA: Religion?

GUNNAR: Protestant

VERONIKA: Are you married?

GUNNAR: Yes.
I affirm that the information above is to the best of my knowledge correct. I aware that by knowingly providing false information I might expect summary dismissal, the withdrawal of employment or a disciplinary hearing for the purposes of my dismissal. Georg August Friedrich, known as Paul Gemmeke.

Gunnar goes to the others to hand out questionnaires.

VERONIKA: The information provided and the <u>three</u> certificates attached give no reason to doubt the Aryan descent of the State Actor Paul Gemmeke. Heil!

JONATHAN: Heil!

ANTONIA: Heil!

GUNNAR: Heil!

Jonathan comes around the corner of the table.

JONATHAN: Because my home at Yorkstraße 41 is on the garden level and has no window onto the street, today I asked Mr. Paul Gemmeke, State Actor at the State Theatre here, who lives in my building, if I might be allowed to fly my new swastika flag on his balcony.

    Herr Gemmeke refused with the remark that his wife is a Jew and that raising the swastika flag on her balcony would represent a slap in the face to her fellow believers.

    G. did emphasise that he supports the government and that he would be willing to fly a black, white and red or yellow, red and yellow flag.

    Heil Hitler!

    Signed H. Griesshaber

VERONIKA: Hugo Griesshaber, Karlsruhe, Yorkstraße 41, to the district leader of the NSDAP in Karlsruhe. Karlsruhe, 30 April 1933.

ANTONIA: "Fly the flag to proclaim Hitler's victory! All the necessary equipment at the cheapest prices, including flagpoles are available from Party Comrade S. Auppinger, Specialist supplies. Buchenweg 3b, Kühler Krug.

Sold in the east of the city by Party Comrade Grafinger, Bellchenstraße."

ANTONIA: Germans buy from Germans! Advertise in the FÜHRER!

VERONIKA: SA-equipment—SS-equipment—Badges for office holders etc. Top quality—from Party Comrade K. Schopfer, LAHR, Kaiserstr. 137 upstairs

JONATHAN: Permit me to ask politely whether the Culture Ministry is aware that the State Actor Mr. Paul Gemmeke, of Yorkstraße 41, is married to a Jew.

    On 30 April this year Mr. P. Gemmeke refused to allow me as owner of the house to place a swastika flag on one of the two balconies to his flat to mark 1 May 1933. I gave written notice of these facts to the NSDAP district leadership in 1 May 1933, a copy of which is enclosed.

    Heil Hitler!

    Signed H. Griesshaber,

    Block warden Mühlburg district and Sergeant in Reserve Motor Brigade 1/109.

VERONIKA: In response to your submission of 10 October 1933, on behalf of the Ministry I must inform you that the fact that a state employee is married to a

Jew is not in itself legal grounds for premature termination of his employment. For the engagement of new officials or employees this fact would be a definite hindrance. A copy of your submission has been sent to the General Director of the Baden State Theatre in Karlsruhe to check whether State Actor Gemmeke's political attitude might be appropriate grounds for the termination of his contract of service at the next available opportunity. Gemmeke's behaviour in this regard will be watched.

Signed on behalf of.

Antonia passes a laurel wreath to Veronika, who slowly gives it to Gunnar.

ANTONIA: Dear Mr. Gemmeke!

Today 25 years have flowed by since you became a member of our artistic institution. With an unfailing delight in your work and an unstinting sense of duty, you have consistently placed your valued abilities in the service of our theatre and made a not insignificant contribution to the reputation which the Baden State Theatre enjoys. We urgently desire to express our thanks. We combine these with the wish that you will be able to pursue your profession in mental and physical health for many years to come.

Heil Hitler! Himmighoffen

Veronika passes Gunnar the laurels.

GUNNAR: But come, you brave sons of Teutons,
in this grove of silent oaks
and let us thank Wodan for the gift of victory!

Dear Mr. Artistic Director!

Your affectionate lines on my 25 years of work at our institution gave me great pleasure. I thank you most warmly.

Heil Hitler,
Yours faithfully,
Paul Gemmeke.

Gunnar climbs onto the table, keeping one foot on the chair.

It remains for us to hasten to the Rhine
So that none of the Romans may slip away
From Germania's holy ground:
And then—let us courageously depart for Rome itself!

Raises wreath.

JONATHAN: In Kleist's 'Hermannsschlacht' we have in Paul Gemmeke a genuine actor who never loses a word at any volume.

VERONIKA: The basic notion of Kleist's great drama, the gathering strength of the German Volk to defend itself against the damage of foreign influence is as current today as it was in Hermann's time and in the time of the writer Heinrich von Kleist. With brief intervals, greedy hands have always tried to grasp Germanic, German property and duped comrades of our own Volk were internal enemies and welcome tools of those from outside. The image of a Volk divided was always the same—the Volk's greatest need, however, gave rise to a Cheruscan prince, who emerged as its saviour. Are we not witnessing the same events today? The great agitator has come. In its hour of greatest need the German Volk has once again been sent a saviour, whom it cheers in thanks!

JONATHAN: Why Kleist?

VERONIKA: In Heinrich von Kleist a poet has been revived who became the creator of new and eternally meaningful dramas of popular and state con-sciousness for Germany. And it is precisely that which now brings us so close to the poet and warrior Kleist, and above all so close to the warrior.
    In 'Prince Friedrich of Homburg' he addresses a problem which often affected Kleist himself, the relationship between the individual and the state. That is the essence of this work, the deepest meaning of the drama which unfolds between the Prince and the Elector. The state, which manifests itself through the laws derived from its nature and its existence, is in this case the Elector. And it is to his authority that the Prince must bow if he as an individual wishes to live in this state. And this state is not a welfare institution, not a "nanny state" whose task is fulfilled by providing its citizens with all their daily requirements. Instead it is a state of demanding, binding laws, a state of urgent necessities.
    While the Prince may have been victorious in battle, this was by chance rather than a victory derived from the clear necessity of sober consideration. And as a consequence he is of no use to the state.

GUNNAR: "This victory I like not, a child of chance,
    which falls into my hands, I wish to uphold
    the law, mother of my crown,
    which will bear me a race of victories."

VERONIKA: says the Elector.

Only when the lost dreamer, who overhears the battle plan, who wins the battle and Natalie's affections intoxicated by his own self-possession, only when this person becomes a man who bows to the law with earnestness and awareness, only then is the Prince a worthy member of the collective of the Volk. Because now this collective will no longer be exposed to the chance derived from his wilfulness, but it shall thrive on the laws derived from it. Hermann the Cheruscan embodies the state to come, as the Great Elector embodies the existing state and the law.

A worthy person will, however, always see the necessity of the state and its laws as a result of his own responsibility and thought and will then bow to that law also. Only those of no use at all to the state will fail to gain this path. The Prince, however, finds his way through the dreams of his youth to a responsible leader in support of the laws of state.

ANTONIA: And this is why the State Theatre is right to launch its season with Kleist's 'Prince Friedrich of Homburg'.

GUNNAR: Into the dust with all the enemies of Brandenburg.

JONATHAN: Theatre Section of the Reich Theatre Council Berlin to the General Director of the Baden State Theatre in Karlsruhe. 4 April 1936.

I request a confidential report on the artistic abilities and other personal characteristics of State Actor Paul Gemmeke.

Heil Hitler!

On behalf of the Leader of the Theatre Section.

ANTONIA: Baden State Theatre to the Theatre Section of the Reich Theatre Council Berlin 8th April 1936.

State Actor Paul Gemmeke, who has been in the company of the Baden State Theatre since 1 September 1909, is employed in the category of principal supporting actor (and for character parts at the discretion of the General Director). His artistic achievements cannot be described as above average. He does, however, discharge his duties with skill and artistic sensitivity. On a personal level we know of nothing negative. His wife is apparently, according to rumours, non-Aryan. The contract of the above may be terminated each year on 1 January with effect from the end of the season.

Heil Hitler! Himmighoffen

JONATHAN: Notice of marriage.

Gunnar on the table. During the following Jonathan pushes him out.
GUNNAR: On 15 July 1912 I married Martha Kern, religion Jewish.

Karlsruhe, 25 December 1936,

Paul Georg Gemmeke

ANTONIA: To the President of the Reich Theatre Chamber Berlin.

State Actor Paul Gemmeke visited me in my office and explained that he had received a letter from the Reich Theatre Chamber to the effect that he had to cease his employment immediately due to non-reliability and non-suitability according to the Theatre Law. Permit me to ask whether Mr. State Actor Gemmeke, who has dutifully reported the matter to me, is entitled under the law of appeal to continue to perform his duties until a final decision has been made on the appeal which he has since entered.

Heil Hitler! Himmighoffen

GUNNAR: Now, Oh immortality, you are all mine!

You shine through the bandage on my eyes.

JONATHAN: Employment of N.S.D.A.P. members.

We draw particular attention to the President of the Reich Theatre Chamber's instruction that all German theatre directors should voluntarily and without delay integrate at least one veteran comrade of the National Socialist movement in an appropriate function within the organization of their theatre. The theatre directors should regard it as a matter of honour that no deserving and qualified party comrade should be left on the streets unemployed.

Signed. Leers, Chair of German Theatre Union.

GUNNAR: Now, Oh immortality, you are all mine!

You shine through the bandage on my eyes

With the brightness of a thousand suns!

VERONIKA: To the President of the Reich Chamber of Culture, Reich Minister Joseph Goebbels.

As State Actor Paul Gemmeke of the Baden State Theatre in Karlsruhe informs me, he has been forbidden from practicing his profession on German stages by an order of the Reich Theatre Chamber as he is married to a Jew. If, as is beyond my powers of judgement, good artistic performances, 27 years of loyal service at the former Court and now Baden State Theatre and the fact that neither he nor his wife maintain relations with Jewish circles, might be considered when making the relevant decision, I would support State Actor Gemmeke being able to remain in the company of the Baden State Theatre until further notice.

On behalf of the Minister of Culture and Education

GUNNAR: Now, O immortality, you are all mine!

You shine through the bandage on my eyes

With the brightness of a thousand suns!

Wings grow on both my shoulders –

JONATHAN: In reply to your letter of 31 December, I hereby inform you that, having checked your information and all the relevant steps, I regret that for fundamental reasons I do not see myself in a position to amend or lift the order made against you by the Theatre Section and therefore the Reich Theatre Chamber.

On behalf of the President, Reich Propaganda Minister Goebbels.

Signed Hinkel.

GUNNAR: Now, O immortality, you are all mine!
You shine through the bandage on my eyes
With the brightness of a thousand suns!
Wings grow on both my shoulders
Through the silent ether my mind soars –

ANTONIA: To the President of the Reich Chamber of Culture.

I most respectfully inform you that Mr. Gemmeke has already stopped performing as he is ill with flu and that of course no further appearances will be made by the person named.

Heil Hitler! Himmighoffen

GUNNAR: Now, O immortality, you are all mine!
You shine through the bandage on my eyes
With the brightness of a thousand suns!
Wings grow on both my shoulders
Through the silent ether my mind soars,
and like a ship seized by a breath of wind –

ANTONIA: Following the decision by the President of the Reich Chamber of Culture on 14 January 1937 there is no question of any further artistic employment of the State Actor Paul Gemmeke. As the person named has not applied for retirement we request a decision as to how we should proceed in this regard.

Himmighoffen. General Director.

JONATHAN: As his practising the profession of actor on a German stage is now legally forbidden, payments to State Actor Gemmeke should be ceased with immediate effect.

On behalf of the Minister of Culture and Education.

GUNNAR: Now, O immortality, you are all mine!
You shine through the bandage on my eyes
With the brightness of a thousand suns!
Wings grow on both my shoulders
Through the silent ether my mind soars,

and like a ship seized by a breath of wind
which sees the brave harbour town sink
all life seems to expire in the twilight:
Now I can still make out colours and shapes –

ANTONIA: Dear Mr. Gemmecke!
We enclose a copy of the order made by the Minister of Culture and Education on 26 February 1937 for your attention. Accordingly we have strong grounds to terminate your terms of service under section 626 with effect from 8 March 1937.
From 8 March 1937 you will be paid an advance of the pension to which you are legally entitled.
Heil Hitler! Himmighoffen.

GUNNAR: And like a ship seized by a breath of wind
which sees the brave harbour town sink
all life seems to expire in the twilight:
Now I can still make out colours and shapes
And now all that lies below me is fog.

VERONIKA: Residence:

GUNNAR: Karlsruhe

VERONIKA: Family status (married, widower, single, separated, widow):

GUNNAR: Married

VERONIKA: First and surname of spouse (maiden name):

GUNNAR: Martha Kern

VERONIKA: Pension for 27 years of service Reichsmark 4,020
Per month Reichsmark 335
Emergency tax deducted Reichsmark 64.50
Net 270.50

ANTONIA: <u>Announcement</u>
State Actor Gemmeke died suddenly last night as a result of angina pectoris. The General Directorate thanks him for his many years of distinguished service at the Baden State Theatre.
Honour his memory.

Karlsruhe, 25 May 1937.
General Director of the Baden State Theatre.
Himmighoffen

VERONIKA: Later research conducted in the 70s by the Office for Restitution among surviving former members of the Baden State Theatre revealed that it can be assumed that the person named took his own life as a result of the measures which had previously been taken against him.

GUNNAR: Paul Gemmeke, born 1881, dismissed 1937.
"Mixed marriage"
Humiliated/Deprived of his rights
Died 25 May 1937.

Veronika and Antonia enter the gap between the two tables during the following.

JONATHAN: To his honour, the Mayor of the Regional Capital of Karlsruhe.
From NSDAP local command, West II. Kriegsstr. 151.
Karlsruhe, 7 October 1940

Antonia joins Veronika between the tables.

ANTONIA: As we have seen, in the coming days the city administration intends to hang posters in the trams which forbid Jews to use seats inside the cars. In future they must use the forward platform. This change is welcomed. However, the rule ignores one thing: Where are German mothers supposed to go with their prams?

VERONIKA: According to the existing regulations, prams and luggage may only be placed on the forward platforms of the carriages. German women with their children are now obliged to associate with Jews. For years German women have been warned to beware of contact with Jews and now it is demanded that they occupy the same platform as the Jews.

ANTONIA: A general ruling is required here. In future Jews should not be allowed to use the tram.

VERONIKA: If the city has been instructed to allow Jews to use the trams for financial reasons, in an emergency another rule can be found here.

ANTONIA: The people of Karlsruhe are called upon to make a one-off donation of ten pfennigs per person per year if the city cannot bear the financial consequences of the Jews not being allowed to use the tram.

VERONIKA: The city really cannot make a better deal, and German women and their children would be prevented from coming into contact with this dirty race.

VERONIKA and ANTONIA: Heil Hitler!
Local Commander.

The actors bring out suitcases:

GUNNAR: Karlsruhe, 20 September 1942.
Registered mail.
Re: Emigration.
By order of the Karlsruhe State Police Control Centre we inform you that you have been selected to take part in an evacuation transport on one of the last days of September. You are required to wait in your home on 28 and 29 September for collection by the Gestapo.
We request that you read and follow the instructions below carefully and prepare for your departure calmly.
Appeals to be exempted from the transport are futile, as each case has already been checked thoroughly by the authorities.
All transportees will be visited in good time by trusted persons who will provide information about any queries and help to fill out the declaration of assets (see II).
I. Confiscation of assets.
Irrespective of the rules in the next paragraph you may not dispose of any assets, i.e., you may not sell, donate, pass to others for safekeeping, or destroy anything of any kind.
II. Declaration of assets.
All securities, savings books, insurance policies, and other documents relating to assets left behind in possession of the transportee are to be attached to the declaration of assets.
III. Taking means of payment, documentation, and luggage with you.
Every passenger must hold the sum for the ticket from his place of residence to his destination readily available to buy a ticket on the day of travel. You are most urgently warned not to take forbidden objects or more than the permitted sum of money with you. Passengers should expect thorough searches to be made of their persons and luggage. Each passenger may take either one suitcase or one rucksack with them. Trunks are not permitted. All items of luggage must be permanently marked with the name and previous address of the owner. Experience has shown that many emigres do not choose the correct items to pack for travel. Essential objects are often forgotten and instead things are taken which are of no use at their destination and represent an unnecessary burden. It is not necessary to take as much as possible but rather those

objects which are genuinely needed in the appropriate quantities. Bear in mind that you must carry your own luggage and that no designated luggage car is available.

VERONIKA: Theresienstadt, 7 June 43. Martha Sara Gemmecke to Goldine Zweifel, Bahnhofstr. 26, Karlsruhe

GUNNAR: My darlings,

I'm glad to be able to send you a sign of life. Cards and parcels from outside do reach here and are handed to the recipient promptly.I hope all my darlings are healthy and cheerful. Mother has left me all alone; I regret that she closed her eyes for the last time on 30 August. I am working very hard in a law office. Now you know my address I hope to hear good news from you regularly so I need not worry. Do not forget me, even if you don't hear from me for a long time. I am thinking of you and our friends in common.

Dearest wishes,
Martha.

VERONIKA: Theresienstadt. 3 March 44. Martha Sara Gemmecke to Goldine Zweifel, Karlsruhe.

GUNNAR: My darlings,

The cute little munchkins really raised my spirits. Rosy, my namesakes, need not worry about following in your footsteps. I would be pleased to hear news of you more often. Thanks for visiting the grave—couldn't find your cousin without a first name. I was especially pleased with the fat and jam. Please note latest address for swiftest delivery.—Now I will drink a glass of Hag-Kola to your health and thank you for everything—including the warm cap which fits me well. Warmly.

Stay healthy.
Yours, Martha

VERONIKA: Theresienstadt 21 April 1944. Martha Sara Gemmecke to Goldine Zweifel in Karlsruhe.

GUNNAR: My darlings,

Many thanks for the latest food. The apples from the garden were extremely refreshing. At preserving time do you think of my help as often as I do of yours? I did not get the reply promised from Herrenstraße to the card I sent two months ago, why? Show my cards around to friends, I can't write to everyone but they can write to me. I often think of Mrs. Schrot. I was happy to volunteer on the farm on ten free afternoons last autumn. Her memorial day is 26 August. Except for Mrs. Müller, there's nobody you know from Karlsruhe here.

Stay healthy all of you and a thousand warmest greetings.
Yours, Martha

JONATHAN: Letter from Goldine Zweifel, Karlsruhe, to Martha Sara Gemmecke, Theresienstadt, from 16 May 1944. Returned: addressee deported to Auschwitz on 16 May 1944.

VERONIKA: In the book of remembrance for Jewish citizens of Karlsruhe the following can be found about Lilly Jank: (*narrative voice*) Even after her dismissal was brought about by the Nazis, Lilly Jank remained in Karlsruhe. From the beginning of 1934 she lives in a girls' home in Strasbourg. According to the compensation files Lilly Jank is unemployed in 1935/36.

In January 1936 Lilly is staying in Zurich. She claims to be preparing to emigrate to Palestine. At around the same time her friend Emmy Seiberlich, who has already emigrated to Canada, is trying to secure an entry permit for her there. Possibly because of her plans to marry Dr. Viktor Wahl, Lilly drops her plans to emigrate. On 19 March 1936, the couple marry in Basel. They move into a home together in Strasbourg. There their son Silvio is born on 31 December 1936. The outbreak of the Second World War causes her to flee to the south of France, to Vichy.

Two weeks after the Allied landings in Normandy on 6 June 1944, the Wahl family is deported to Germany on 22 June 1944. Viktor Wahl dies in Ohrdruf.

Lilly, Silvio and his grandmother, Lilly's mother-in-law, are taken to Bergen-Belsen concentration camp, and shortly afterwards, in July 1944, to Ravensbrück, where both women die in October 1944. Lilly Jank is 37 years old. Her son Silvio survives.

What remains are two Stolpersteine at Stephanienstraße 59 (outside the theatre—*where she never worked, at least not on this site*):

HERE LIVED (or. HERE WORKED)
LILLY JANKELOWITZ
KNOWN AS JANK
BORN 1907
ESCSAPED TO FRANCE 1936
DEPORTED 1944
BERGEN-BELSEN
RAVENSBRÜCK
DIED OCT. 1944

Gunnar and Antonia move to the rear of the table for their interview.

VERONIKA: Emma Grandeit to the new Artistic Director of the Baden State Theatre

ANTONIA: Hamburg, 10 September 1946.

Dear Doctor!

I congratulate you on your appointment as Theatre Director in Karlsruhe. I believe that the job will make you very happy and that you will manage to return the theatre back to the high artistic level to which Karlsruhe has been accustomed for generations.

I myself am back in the theatre after an involuntary break of twelve years, at the Hamburger Kammerspiele, which our current director Ida Ehre continues to run now in the spirit of Erich Ziegel.

I feel very happy here and because there are two prompters I have a very pleasant life. We do not perform many productions as they run for a very long time.

My husband still does one-man shows like he used to but is also acting at the theatre so he is very busy at the moment. As he is acting almost every day, he has had to miss or postpone a lot of shows. My son is a stage designer for Dr. Sattler, who employed him during the last 12 years, even in senior positions, although he was not allowed to at the time. All three of us are working in the arts, we have also been bombed out, and I was in a concentration camp too, but I got over that a long time ago.

And now I come to the request I have of you: I have registered my compensation claim for these 12 years and need supporting information from the theatre itself or someone who knew me from that time. After repeated requests the theatre has finally replied to the compensation commission that all the papers were burnt and nobody knows anything about me. However, I am sure that you will still remember me. In any event I enclose copies of two references by Baumbach and Trenck to jog your memory. I would ask you to confirm the following for me:

1. That my salary during the war would have been no less and indeed possibly higher than it was when I left Karlsruhe.

2. That I was employed there from 1926 until 1933 and would probably never have been dismissed as there was no criticism of me personally or professionally.

I would be most grateful if you could provide me with this information that the authorities have requested along with the documents I have and that you send them to me using the theatre's letterhead. I would also be very pleased to hear about you personally, what happened to you in the past years and what your current plans are.

Perhaps you would be able to contact Mrs. Ervig about the information. I have written to her to this effect, and she is bound to remember me from before.

Thank you in advance for your efforts and please let me know as soon as possible.

With best regards, also from my husband,
Yours,
Emma Grandeit

GUNNAR: Today is the 3 of December 1986. I am together with Mrs. Lola Kloeble-Ervig in her home. I would like to know from you, Mrs. Ervig, how you experienced the start of the persecution of the Jews, using the Regional Theatre as an example. There were a number of Jewish company members at the time.

ANTONIA: There was Lilly Jank. She was a soubrette, who danced very nicely. And I was very sorry about her as I was sitting on the bench in the theatre when Lilly got the letter.

GUNNAR: You were there?

ANTONIA: I was there. And then she had a tragic fate.

GUNNAR: May I ask what was written in the letter? For what reason was she sacked?

ANTONIA: Yes, I can't say it word for word but it would have been that she was not tenable. That would have been said.

GUNNAR: Was her contract simply not renewed?

ANTONIA: Yes: they could stay until the end of the season. And then Lilli Jank ran away to Belgium.

GUNNAR: At the end of the 33 season? How old would she have been?

ANTONIA: On, I should think—not yet 30. Mid-20s. And she married a doctor there, I heard, but then when the Germans marched in she was caught and died apparently, which made me very sad as she was a very nice young and talented colleague ... she had a tragic end ... only her son Silvio survived.

Antonia clears up.

GUNNAR: (...) Mrs. Ervig, there were some other Jewish members of the company then.

ANTONIA: Yes, there was the prompter, Mrs. Emma Grandeit, who was a pure Jew but very conscientious and above all a very intelligent prompter. I was very sorry about that because I liked her a lot as a person.

Veronika pushes the table away.

GUNNAR: Can you tell me, do you remember how that happened? Did it happen very quickly after the coup or only in the course of the spring or summer of 1933 that the Jewish members simply weren't there any more?

ANTONIA: Hermann Brand, who was the best-known of the actors, went straight away. And I even think he went voluntarily and didn't feel the growing threat, he was a pious, orthodox Jewish man. His mother lived in the east of the city and he only ate kosher meat. He had the disadvantage that he was a little hostile to people who were Aryan or blond, though for no reason. Because we always thought it was terrible the way these notorious blue letters were handed out to our colleagues. What could we say to console them?

GUNNAR: Now you yourself, if I remember correctly, were very blonde?

ANTONIA: Yes.

GUNNAR: Didn't he like blondes?

ANTONIA: No, he didn't. He thought all blondes were anti-Semites. Well I certainly wasn't, I will tell you later that I had very, very dear, close friends, bank director Stern, who were Jews and I was so sorry when I met Mr. Stern in the Kaiserstraße and spoke to him and he said: "Miss Ervig, you'd better walk on the other side, it will harm you if you walk along with me."

Jonathan and Gunnar clear away the files while Antonia listens.

VERONIKA: My apartment in the south of the city is dark, cold and damp, I always say, but simply beautiful. High ceilings, wooden floors, a shower in the kitchen. All the charm of bygone days in which I would rather have lived than now. Earlier it was a house for craftsmen, I was told, with workshops on the ground floor around the courtyard and then private apartments on the upper floors. I never wondered about all the different people who had lived here, because it is my apartment, and the idea that it was once someone else's home is rather spooky. My sister has six Stolpersteine outside her front door. She's never looked at them properly. The idea of everything that might have happened in her peaceful family home is too much for her to bear. Of course I've always been able to understand that attitude to a certain extent but I've criticized it far more. And then I'm sitting in my living room one evening after three years, hear the birds singing, look out into the gorgeous inner courtyard and ask myself for the first time, whether it also happened here. And I imagine that here -

GUNNAR: Let's come back to Hermann Brand.

ANTONIA: Older people from Karlsruhe will definitely remember Hermann Brand because he was a brilliant comedian and a man who really supported Karlsruhe.

GUNNAR: He emigrated to Switzerland?

ANTONIA: Yes. And he worked his way up to become Artistic Director of the Lucerne Theatre. But then he seemed homesick for Germany.

VERONIKA (JONATHAN and GUNNAR): Hello Karlsruhe!!! Hello Baden-Württemberg!!! Hello Germany!!! I can see a lot of flags! Where are the patriots? (Here) Where are the defenders of the German fatherland? (Here) Where are the friends of freedom? (Here) Of democracy? (Here) Where are the opponents of Islamification? (Here) Of jihad? (Here) Of the Salafists? (Here) Of beheadings? (Here) Of honour killings (Here) Of oppressing women? (Here) And of abusing the asylum system? (Here)

ANTONIA: Anyone who doesn't love Germany.

ANTONIA, JONATHAN and GUNNAR: Should leave Germany! Anyone who doesn't love Germany, should leave Germany! Anyone who doesn't love Germany, should leave Germany!

JONATHAN: Send them to Siberia!

ANTONIA, JONATHAN and GUNNAR: Out! Out! Out!

JONATHAN: We know that we're right! Right is a good word. Be right. Enforce our rights. Yes.
1, 2, 3—

ALL: Thank you, Police. 1, 2, 3—Thank you, Police. 1, 2, 3—Thank you, Police. 1, 2, 3—Thank you, Police.

VERONIKA: There's a street party against Kargida I tell the sweet old man who I've been talking to about the best ground temperature to grow cucumbers or how deep to sow nasturtiums. He smiles gently. It would be nice if you could come, we've been demonstrating for weeks but there are so few of us. I can see why (*Antonia, Jonathan, and Gunnar freeze*), he says and keeps on smiling. What can you see? Well, he says, all anyone ever speaks round here is Turkish. And in the supermarket over there, he points in the direction of the Russian supermarket, they only speak Russian. But we're speaking German, I say, get on my bike and ride away. (*Freeze dissolves*).

All the files must have disappeared off the table.

GUNNAR: Mrs. Ervig, do you have any personal memories of the Reichskristall-nacht or the boycott of 1933 when SA members would stand outside Jewish businesses?

ANTONIA: No, all I saw was their "success" that the good carpet shops, Veit or Goldfahrt, who actually had the best fashions, had their windows smashed.

GUNNAR: After Reichskristallnacht?

ANTONIA: Yes. At the time I lived in Waldstraße, directly behind the synagogue. We could see the synagogue from the roof terrace.

GUNNAR: Did you see it burning?

ANTONIA: Yes.

GUNNAR: No one put out the fire.

ANTONIA: No, no. They said it was the anger of the Volk. But I have to say colleagues weren't aggressive to anybody or only acted passively. We were all very sorry, because they were all good artists and there was nothing they could do about it.

JONATHAN: I stumble on something in Karlsruhe. In the south of the city, where I live, it's usually dogshit. There are little junk shops. There's the Werderplatz with its dubious characters and sun-seekers. And there's the Indian fountain as a legacy of the ethnological exhibitions. That's how Buffalo Bill came to Karlsruhe. Human beings were put on show. In the zoo.

    The Indian fountain was designed in 1924 and was an instant hit. "We're not Red Indians" I can hear from a long way off. There are no more signs of the Wild West in Karlsruhe. But from time to time I come across people in the south of the city who I need to take a closer look at. Could it really be that Native Americans once lived here? That they fell in love here? Becoming Baden Indians? Genuine south city Indians?

GUNNAR: Every morning when I stumble out of the house, to take the kids to school, I also stumble over Leopold, Alice, and Gertrud.

    When I saw a group of people on the pavement outside out house 18 months ago and joined them, I saw that they had just finished laying a Stolperstein for the Kullmanns, who had lived in the house next door before they were deported.

I had always thought: in such an old building, in the middle of the city, there were bound to be Jewish families living there before '33. Leo the Jew (as he was called) and his family—I looked them up—were not religious.

Like us. He was a lawyer and later a judge at the Regional Higher Court in Karlsruhe and was active in the SPD. Like my father. That's why some of the people laying the Stolperstein had red carnations. The local branch of the SPD had donated the Stolpersteine.

"Why are you so secretive?" I ask the group as they break up, "I would have liked to join in."

"No, we've had some unpleasant experiences with that—letting the residents know—there have been some unpleasant incidents. Not everyone wants one of these Stolpersteine outside their front door."

Perhaps some people have the feeling that they had dispossessed the earlier Jewish tenants?

The judges and lawyers were the first to lose their jobs in 1933 and who then had to see how they were going to live. The Kullmanns sold their furniture and I can see them carrying their—in my imagination beautiful—furniture through our door and onto the street.

Leo steps onto the street, and stretches out, not noticing that on the spot where he's standing there are three little Stolpersteine in the pavement with their names on them.

ANTONIA: First stop Herrenstr. 22. Here are the Stolpersteine for Sophie and Helene Ettlinger and Rosalie Lonnestädter. I kneel down and clean and polish the Stolpersteine.

I carry on. At Ständehausstr. 2 there are Stolpersteine for a total of eleven members of the Baden regional parliament including Dr. Ludwig Marum. They are all quite clean already. But I give them another go anyway. An elderly woman, I think mid-70s, stops and thanks me.

Kaiserstraße 103, Esther and Leopold Schwarz. A woman looks at me uncertainly, laughs, asks why I am cleaning the street and asks if I have to do that—when I put a flower down at the end, she thinks it's sweet. Lina Hirsch, Kaiserstr. 166. When was the last time "memories were polished" here? Even scrubbing repeatedly, I can't get the chewing gum off.

I look for, find and clean: Kaiserstr. 145, Kaiserstr. 201, Kaiserstr. 34a, Kaiserstr. 49, Lammstr. 15. At Yorckstr. 41 I look in vain for a Stolperstein for Martha Gemmeke.

Veronika, Gunnar, and Jonathan freeze.

I wonder who is going to "polish up" the Stolpersteine at Nokkstr. 2, which are almost black already and only make pedestrians stumble if they know they are there. They commemorate the married couple Otto Josef and Lilly Charlotte Löwenthal and their son Heinz Hans, who were deported first to Gurs on 22 October 1940 and then on 4 September 1942 to Auschwitz, where they died.

Freeze dissolves.

I notice that the edges of the Stolpersteine gradually begin to take on the colour of the street. Brass oxidizes and loses its shine over time. Eventually they will disappear into the road surface. Will anyone then remember that people remembered?

GUNNAR: Now I am standing over the dark, oxidized Stolpersteine: "Come on guys! Get a move on, we're running late!"

Through Kriegsstraße into Hirschstraße, then up Waldstraße. And just past Aldi on the left-hand side, I really do stumble. Every morning. Inside.

In a clothing shop there are cool clothes with the word 'LONSDALE' written on them. A way for Neo-Nazis to recognize each other. If you wear an unzipped jacket over the writing, all that can be seen of 'LONSDALE' is NSDA. You can imagine the rest.

The Stolpersteine are a good size.

Ought to fit in your hand nicely.

A shop window like that won't be any problem for them.

A good image: the Kullmanns' Stolperstein surrounded by LONSDALE shirts and broken glass.

—I didn't think of that.

GUNNAR: Mrs. Ervig, the rumours went around that contracts were not being renewed—and it was clear that the reason was that they were Jews. Did other people just ignore this?

ANTONIA: The people at the theatre I spoke to were all shocked and horrified. But there was nothing one could say to console them or anything. But they carried on acting with us just as they had before.

GUNNAR: Until the end of the season.

GUNNAR: Mrs. Ervig, you mentioned in our preliminary interview that the Jewish General Music Director Josef Krips was not allowed to conduct on 1 May, I believe?

ANTONIA: Yes, he wasn't allowed to conduct at all. And I have to tell you the funny situation arose that all three of the conductors were Jews and it was the Führer's birthday on 20 April and we were supposed to perform 'Meistersinger'.

And as there was no other way, they got Josef Keilberth to do it, who was a repetiteur then, and very young, a beginner. He jumped straight onto the conductor's podium.

GUNNAR: For that reason. And then became a conductor and soon afterwards General Music Director?

ANTONIA: Yes, of course. Until he then...

GUNNAR: So he was practically—without intending to be so—a beneficiary of the persecution of the Jews.

ANTONIA: Yes, that's right. Though you can't blame him. I mean, sometimes in life you're just lucky.

The End

RED

A Documentary Performance

Wen Hui and Living Dance Studio

https://tinyurl.com/Wen-RED

ENGLISH TRANSLATION FROM THE CHINESE Zhuang Jiayun

WITH Jiang Fan, Li Xinmin, Liu Zhuying, Wen Hui
CHOREOGRAPHER Wen Hui
DRAMATURGS Kai Tuchmann, Zhuang Jiayun
AUTHOR Zhuang Jiayun

WORLD PREMIERE December 25, 2015, at the Power Station of Art, Shanghai, China
ALL RIGHTS Wen Hui and Living Dance Studio

[Our performance is constituted by two elements: An ONSTAGE part, in which the performers act and an ONSCREEN part, in which we project the interviews that we conducted during our research process for this play.]

ACT ONE. MARCHING FORWARD[1]

ONSCREEN. Seven interviewees are being asked to discuss their memories of The Red Detachment of Women. *The interviewer, Wen Hui, is not present onscreen. Only her voice can be heard.*

Interviewee 1: Liu Zhuying, former performer in The Red Detachment of Women, *a retiree from the Kunming City Song and Dance Troupe.*

WEN: Did you perform in *The Red Detachment of Women*?

LIU: Yes, I did.

WEN: When was that?

LIU: In 1970. We were recruited from the dance school to perform *The Red Detachment of Women*. I'd say this piece of ballet was a part of us while growing up.

Interviewee 2: Cui Weiping, Scholar from Beijing.

WEN: Did you perform in *The Red Detachment of Women*?

CUI: No. But I have always been a devoted attendee of performances of *The Red Detachment of Women*. I also believe I understand this piece of revolutionary model ballet completely.

Interviewee 3: Zhang Xian, Art Activist.

ZHANG: I didn't perform in the model ballet. When I was in the factory, I worked for the Propaganda Office. Part of our job was to promote this kind of performance.

---

1   Marching Forward, *Xiang Qianjin*, is the theme song of the 1961 film *The Red Detachment of Women*, directed by Xie Jin. The revolutionary model ballet under the same title was based on Xie Jin's film. The lyrics begin with: "Forward, forward. The responsibilities of the soldiers are heavy; the women's hatreds are deep."

Interviewee 4: Wang Huifen, former performer in The Red Detachment of Women; *played the female protagonist—Wu Qinghua; a retiree from the Kunming City Song and Dance Troupe.*

WANG: This character fits me well. She's wild. I took the role very seriously. I played "for real" and fought "for real" onstage at the time. On that kind of stage, under that kind of circumstances, that was how I portrayed the character.

Interviewee 5: Liang Xiaoyan, founder and advocate of an educational NGO.

LIANG: I studied the piece, but I can't remember if I got eliminated during the rehearsal process. But I indeed danced the part with "The River of 10,000 Springs" on stage. I remembered that! I was very familiar with all the music, to say the least.

Interviewee 6: Yue Gang, Associate Professor of the Department of Asian Studies, UNC Chapel Hill.

YUE: I never watched a complete production [of *The Red Detachment of Women*]. I saw parts of the production by the Qinghai Province Song and Dance Troupe. When I was serving in the General Logistics Department in the army, I also saw a few excerpts of the revolutionary model ballet performed by the army cultural work troupe.

Interviewee 7: Zhang Laishan, former performer in The Red Detachment of Women; *played the male protagonist—Hong Changqing; a retiree from the Yunnan Province Song and Dance Troupe.*

ZHANG: All the dancers were put in groups of three: A, B, and C. I was in Group A. Compared to other dancers, I participated in the most rehearsals and the most performances. I worked the hardest. Someone from the National Ballet of China ... Was it Li Chengxiang [one of the choreographers of *The Red Detachment of Women*]? I can't remember ... He came to Yunnan and watched my performance. Then he said, "This dancer looks exactly like Liu Qingtang [a household name during the Cultural Revolution because of his performance as the male lead in the model ballet]! His performance is so compelling!" That was the first time I ever got that kind of comment. The way he struck a post was exactly the same! Thanks to his comments, I was able to perform on the most important occasions. Perhaps I performed a couple of hundred times. I got to perform more than anyone else in my song and dance troupe.

ONSCREEN. A special edition hard copy of The Red Detachment of Women *is shown. The audience can see the pages turning slowly, and the positive and negative characters from model opera are shown.*

ONSTAGE. Wen Hui explains the principle of "The Three Prominences."

WEN: On May 23, 1968, in honor of the first anniversary of the establishment of the Revolutionary model opera , Yu Huiyong, a standing committee member of the Shanghai Municipal Revolutionary Committee, published an article in *The Wenhui Daily*, entitled "Let the Stage of Literature and the Arts Forever be a Battlefront for the Propagation of Mao Zedong Thought."

For the first time, he proposed the principle of "The Three Prominences." He argued, according to the instructions of Jiang Qing [Madame Mao], "The Three Prominences" should be regarded as one of the most important principles when creating characters. That is, among all characters, prominence is to be given to positive characters; among positive characters, prominence is to be given to heroic characters; and among heroic characters, prominence is to be given to a main heroic character. To sum up, the goal of the Revolutionary model opera is to create magnificent, fully developed, bright, and impeccable worker-peasant-soldier characters. This is the primary task of socialist arts.

Wen makes a gesture, indicating the start of the demonstration.

WEN: For example, in terms of staging techniques, positive characters should be placed at the center of the stage, given all the light possible, to bring out the stage effect of "Close, Big, Bright!" By contrast, negative characters should be placed near the corners of the stage and kept in the shadows for the most part, aiming at the stage effect of "Far, Small, and Dark." The principle of the "Three Prominences" was influenced by the principles of classical aesthetics, building up a hierarchy of characters. Hong Changqing—this is the leading heroic figure in *The Red Detachment of Women*. These heroic figures reflect the will and desire of the proletarians. They are meant to occupy the stage!

I started learning to dance in the 1970s, during which the Three Prominences dictated the artistic standards of the Culture Revolution. Twenty years later, in 1994, *Living Dance Studio* was born. We also have fundamental guiding principles when creating dance: we don't create characters, we don't play roles, and we don't need prominences. Each of us brings our own identity, memory, and personality onto the stage, and we share our experiences with the audience. In this particular space, each of us is an individual. We are all equal.

ONSCREEN. Wang Huifen's stage photos from the 1970s are shown. Wang shares her story about playing the role of Wu Qinghua.

WANG: I remember my energy and strength, and with that kind of pace! I wasn't trained to walk that way. Maybe I just got it from my character. They all said, "How come you walk so powerfully and so handsomely?" Yes, I still remember that clearly.

ONSCREEN. Zhang Laishan's photos from the 1970s are shown. Zhang recalls how his performance was appreciated.

WEN: Have you ever imagined yourself as Hong Changqing [the male protagonist]?

ZHANG: No. I have never thought of myself as him. But I followed the director's instructions to create such a heroic figure.

ONSCREEN. Liu Zhuying's photos from the 1970s are shown.
ONSTAGE. Jiang Fan and LI Xinmin approach Liu's photos. Liu Zhuying begins her story about being Young Soldier No. 18.

LIU: This photo was taken in January 1971, when we were at the Guizhou Province Song and Dance Troupe learning the model ballet—*The Red Detachment of Women*. I was selected among other members to play Wu Qinghua [the female protagonist]. I was very good at the character's movements and techniques, but I never got the chance to play the part on the stage. I was short and didn't grow much more. The principal characters of the Revolutionary model opera, for example, Wu Qinghua, Hong Changqing [the male protagonist], and the company commander [the second female protagonist], were supposed to be tall and good looking. Later, I always played minor roles, such as young soldiers, young slave girls, and young inmates.

I still remember, in Scene 2, the detachment of women formed a line on stage. The eighteen of us lined up according to our height. I was No. 18. As other dancers grew taller, they changed positions every few weeks or months. All of them were placed in a different position in the lineup. But I remained No. 18 and never changed.

ONSCREEN. The pages from the special edition hard copy of The Red Detachment of Women *are still turned slowly. A piece of blackboard is shown.*
ONSTAGE. Li Xinmin tells a story about her schoolbag.

LI: The other day, flipping through this book, I stopped when I saw the page with the blackboard on it. It reminded me of a time when I was in fourth grade. The year was 1999, when I was only 11 years old. I will never forget that afternoon, just two days before the final exam. After school, my teacher said to me, "Li Xinmin, go back home and talk to your parents. It's time for your tuition fee: 88 yuan, tomorrow." I still can remember how I felt at that moment, humiliated and ashamed, because the teacher said those words in front of the entire class. But I dared not speak a single word. After everyone else was gone, I sat in the classroom by myself. Moments later, I made a decision. I laid my cotton schoolbag on the desk; it was sewn by my mother. I took out all my books and pens, and left them in the drawer, one by one. Then, slowly, I folded my bag into a tiny piece, as small as my palm. And, slowly, I walked out of the school and never returned.

ONSCREEN. *Liang Xiaoyan discusses the popularity of model opera works.*

LIANG: What impressed me most was that, back then, we could recite all eight revolutionary model plays, including every melodic passage from the beginning till the end. I could do that. You know why? It was because that the scripts of all these plays were published in *The Red Flag Magazine*, and at that time, we were required to study all of them. We learned by listening to the radio. Around that time, there was nothing else. And whenever the radio was turned on, there was at least one station that played the model plays repeatedly. You could learn the plays by heart. Children have excellent learning skills; they can remember everything simply by listening to it. Even when we were in our 40s or 50s, we could still sing all those parts one by one at our parties. You could tell the popularity of those model plays. But then, when we were young, our thirst for knowledge was misdirected toward learning these model plays.

ONSCREEN. *Wang Huifen introduces a photo of her dancing on the threshing ground.*

WEN: Which one are you?

WANG: This one!

WEN: Is it the one over here?

WANG: Yes.

WEN: When did you take this photo?

WANG: In 1971.

WEN: 1971?

WANG: Between 1970 and 1971.

WEN: Between 1970 and 1971?

WANG: During that period, I danced *The Red Detachment of Women* more than 200 times.

WEN: Where did you perform it?

WANG: In the theatres of Kunming, mainly in local theatres.

WEN: I see. In the theatres of Kunming?

WANG: We mainly performed in Kunming, but we also worked as a propaganda troupe and brought the theatre to the rural areas.

WEN: Did you also perform in the rural areas?

WANG: Yes, and when we danced on the threshing ground, we still needed to perform on tiptoes on the soft mud.

WEN: How did you dance on the threshing ground?

ONSTAGE. Liu Zhuying demonstrates how she danced on the threshing ground.

LIU: Let me tell you how we stood on tiptoe. The woman in the video recording, Wang Huifen, and I were in the same troupe. Most of our productions of *The Red Detachment of Women* were staged in factories, military units, and rural areas. Wang just mentioned that we performed "more than 200 times." We performed much more than that. In rural areas, we danced on the threshing ground. At that time, the ground was covered with mud instead of cement. Mud can be hard or soft. When the tips of your toes hit the soft mud, in scenes like Dancing with Broadswords, you can easily sprain your ankle. But we were young and full of energy. We just kept on going and never stopped. That was how we danced.

ONSCREEN. The pages from the special edition hard copy of The Red Detachment of Women *are still being turned. Then, a blocking diagram of its choreography is shown.*
ONSTAGE. Jiang Fan introduces a basic stage diagram.

JIANG: The diagram here shows the basic structure of a stage. The short line is the curtain line, and the long curve is the proscenium line. The part of the stage that extends out from the proscenium line is referred to as the apron. A removable deck can be built on the apron to reveal an area beneath stage level: the orchestra pit, which is usually used in productions that require music. Here, the four short lines refer to the stage's curtains: borders no. 1, no. 2, no. 3, and no. 4. The eight numbers outside the frame remind me of the folk dance lessons I took when I was little. The teacher told us that there were eight points in the room: 1, 2, 3, 4, 5, 6, 7, and 8.

For instance, when performing a traditional Mongolian dance and working on arm-swinging movements, the dancer moves their gaze from Point 2 to Point 8. Feeling surrounded by the vast prairie landscape, they return their gaze from Point 8 back to Point 2, then face toward Point 1, move toward Point 3, jump to Point 8, and then look at Point 2. In ballet, when performing a port de bras, the dancer faces Point 2, intakes a breath, and turns their head toward Point 8. Then they turn toward Point 7, take a breath, and turn their head toward Point 1. The entire movement of port de bras ends at Point 1.

In *The Red Detachment of Women,* Wu Qinghua leans out of the trees, attentively, looking slowly from Point 8 to Point 2. Then she faces Point 3 and makes a forward lunge, with her right hand lifting the edge of her blouse and her left hand making a fist. Then she gazes from Point 3 to Point 8, and Point 3, and Point 8, and 3, 8, 3, 8, 3, 8, 3, 8 … In modern dance, the stage has multiple points, just like the dust particles in the air. Multiple points … Multiple points … 1! Multiple points … 3! Multiple points … 7!

ACT TWO. GETTING INTERTWINED

ONSCREEN. The pages of the special edition hard copy are still slowly turned. The audience can see all kinds of fists are shown.
ONSTAGE. Wen explains "clenching the fist" as the theme movement.

WEN: In *The Red Detachment of Women*, "clenching the fist" is the most common stage action. In choreography, this is called the theme movement or the "seed." When I interviewed Jiang Zuhui, one of the choreographers of *The Red Detachment of Women*, she told me that in the first version of the prologue, the hand movements of the two inmates of Wu Qinghua were quite relaxed. She told me: those women looked extremely elegant and sorrowful. They wanted to rush out of their confinement. They shouldered all the sufferings and were as deeply oppressed as is possible to be, but still yearned to stand up, get out, and become emancipated. But in the later version, the revolutionary model ballet, the women's hand movements were all changed into fists: I want to break the chains, get rid of the oppression, and overthrow the regime! But how could that be possible?

ONSCREEN. The pages are turned slowly. The signature movement in the revolutionary ballet— "head-kick jeté" [or, the "Plisetskaya head-kick"]—is shown.
ONSCREEN. Cui Weiping, Zhang Xian, and Yue Gang discuss this particular "head-kick jeté," in turn.

CUI: The movement left me with an unforgettable image: It is like fire dancing in the air. I think it symbolizes freedom.

ZHANG: That head-kick jeté! This highly skilled movement was captured and made into a staged photo, which was then widely circulated. In the live performance, the dancer was in the air, and it was over in the blink of an eye. In the live situation, it's impossible for you to catch the moment and grasp the techniques. But the stage photos captured it and reminded you that it was all about dance skills and levels of difficulty.

YUE: The most classical movement! Well, there was a dancer on the poster. I still remember her name: Xue Jinghua. She completed a high head-kick in the air. That movement was circulated via posters. With that image in mind, when you had a chance to watch the model ballet, you would pay great attention to how the dancers unimaginably exceed the limits of the body. Their dance brings a form of exquisiteness—the beauty of pure space and pure form. It truly has nothing to do with the Revolution.

ONSCREEN. The pages are turned slowly. Props such as all kinds of swords are shown.
ONSTAGE. Liu Zhuyin and Li Xinmin share their stories about swords. Their stories are juxtaposed.
Liu tells a story about Dancing with Broadswords.

LIU: This broadsword was a prop for every soldier of the Red Army, male or female, in *The Red Detachment of Women*. The performer's body would be this long when extended with its grip (*gesturing*), with a piece of red silk hanging down from here. In Scene 2, Hong Changqing leads the female soldiers in broadsword practice. He does this, and the soldiers respond like this. He strikes a post like this, and the female soldiers clap. After demonstrating a few moves, Hong signals the women to begin the practice. Then we start dancing. During rehearsals, we were told to "be filled with affections of the proletariat," "to be filled with class hatred and national enmity ..."

Li Xinmin tells a story about the swords made by her father.

LI: My father was a blacksmith. When I was little, he made a sword this long, which was used to chop wood. At the ages of 12, 13, and 14, I did a lot of farm work with my mother. During those days when we went up to the mountains to chop wood, I liked those trees that were long and mighty. I was only this tall at that time, a tiny body with great ambition. However, I could only handle the trees that were as wide around as my arms. My father made another knife, about this long, which was used to kill the pigs. My mother kept this butcher knife under her pillow all year round. My father passed away young, leaving only women in the family—my mom, my elder sister, and me. It was not safe for us to stay in the village. I went home for the Lunar New Year last year; my mother and I still sleep together on the bed. My head felt something: my mother still keeps that butcher knife under her pillow.

ONSCREEN. *The footage from the 1961 film* The Red Detachment of Women—*a close-up of the female protagonist [Wu Qionghua, aka Wu Qinghua], played by Zhu Xijuan—is shown.*

ZHU (*as Wu Qinghua*)*:* I run! I just run as long and as far as I can!

ONSCREEN. *Yue Gang, Liang Xiaoyan, and Cui Weiping discuss the image of Zhu and her performance.*

YUE: Of course, the most memorable part is Qionghua, the one who always tried to run away.

LIANG: Qionghua's eyes are unforgettable. Zhu Xijuan [the film actress] is not that beautiful, but her eyes are so piercing and bright. That left me with the strongest memory.

CUI: The totality of the character cannot be necessarily subsumed under the overarching film narrative. This character deeply touched the hearts of her audience. To me, Zhu Xijuan embodies a sense of wildness.

YUE: From the perspective of filmmaking, this part [Qionghua's constant running away] is most personal. It hasn't yet been integrated into the grand history of the Revolution. Each time she got caught and beaten, she tried to run away again. Later she finally made it and met Hong Changqing [the male protagonist]. At that point, the narrative about the Revolution began, and then the personal narrative was integrated into the grand narrative.

ONSCREEN. *The female protagonist in the filmic revolutionary model ballet is bound by chains and shackles.*
ONSCREEN. *Wang Huifen shares a story about her performing Wu Qinghua's escape.*

WANG: She was tied up to that pillar. Look at the hand gestures. She is struggling, stubborn, and persistent! "I will run away; even if you beat me to death, I will keep running away." My wrists and arms were all painted with scars. Yes, I was tied to the pillar and tried my hardest to escape. That's the feeling! I was doing my utmost to run away. The prison door was over there, so I was trying to get to that spot. This is the final posture! Yes, this is the one!

ONSCREEN. *In the filmic revolutionary model ballet, the ballerinas are in army uniforms and holding guns.*
ONSCREEN. *Yue Gang and Zhang Xian discuss the sexualized body images in the revolutionary model ballet.*

YUE: In the army, you can imagine that women were completely absent, except in the hospital. There were very few women until we moved to the city. You can argue that, in that particular historical condition, a unique visual window on females was opened up [through the model ballet]. For those young soldiers, the model ballet provided an entirely different kind of image, the one that had nothing to do with the Revolution. In a way, it is pretty pathetic. Too much effort was devoted to creating the Revolutionary model opera as a form of social mobilization, but the messages the audiences received were exactly the opposite.

ZHANG: The audiences needed to develop some visual interest in all those cultural products that were available during the Cultural Revolution. Ballerina soldiers in their shorts and leggings must have been one of the reasons the audiences became interested. Later, the audience watched *Lenin in October* and the ballet *Swan Lake* repeatedly, because there was nothing else to watch. No other possibilities at all!

WEN: How old were you at that time?

ZHANG: I should have been 17 by then.

WEN: This was during your adolescence then.

ZHANG: Yes. It's hard to say if I would do something at night because of the erotic imagery [from *The Red Detachment of Women*]. My memory is quite blurry now, but I think it could have been possible back then. You could get the vague idea that the staging could be perceived as a bit sexual. The handsome look of the [female] commander might have interested many female audiences ... As a matter of fact, they looked like celebrities. They represented a standard of beauty during the Maoist era: good-looking, muscular body, heavy eyebrows, and big eyes ... The male ballet stars were not quite the same as those male Peking Opera stars. It seems that they were somehow connected with body image. Even though it was about the representation of the Red Army, but the model ballet also provided you with the image of that female commander, a female commanding officer with masculine charm, forceful body, and a uniform that left her half-naked. This could be where audience's guilty pleasure came from.

ONSTAGE. Li Xinmin plays with the fabric of the screen while Zhang Xian's interview is shown.
ONSCREEN. Wang Huifen recalls a story about weaning her baby.

WANG: I have another story to share with you. I had just given birth less than a month before. We got a task to perform Act II of the ballet in the stadium. You know I had just gone through pregnancy and had a baby, but I was asked to perform right after all this. I was breastfeeding at the time. Although I was pretty thin, I had a lot of milk. But the troupe official asked me to take some Chinese medicine and to have an injection that would help stop the milk. And I hadn't rehearsed for more than a year. The official said, "You must come back to rehearsal tomorrow; just get the injection." My teachers were afraid that the injection would hurt me. But the performance was approaching. What could you do? Whatever. I went to the rehearsal the next day. When we had a break during that first day of rehearsal, I saw that my milk had leaked onto the floor. The male dancers wondered why the floor was wet! I knew it was my milk. My clothes were completely wet too. But there was much less milk on the second day. After another full day of rehearsal, my milk was all gone on the third day. I'm not lying to you at all. I didn't even have the injection. Just imagine the extreme physical exhaustion dancers have to go through. This is indeed my personal experience.

ONSTAGE. *In the meantime, Li Xinmin wraps herself in the fabric of the screen when Wang Huifen talks about her experience. Then, Wen and Jiang perform their "pas de deux."*
ONSCREEN. *The pages are turned slowly. A series of ballet movements are shown.*
ONSTAGE. *Jiang Fan explains the movement transformation from traditional Chinese dance to (model) ballet.*

JIANG: When I was reading the special edition [of the hard copy of *The Red Detachment of Women*], I found the technical vocabulary fascinating. When I studied ballet at the conservatory, the instructors all used ballet terminology, such as *battement tendu, battement frappe, pas de bourrée, arabesque.* However, in this book, all the movements—such as *back golden-crown kick, crane-standing posture, crouching step, short quick steps with tiptoes, and the flag*— are described in the terminology of Chinese traditional dance. For example, over here, the No. 16 move—*crane-standing posture*—has four variants. The basics are: put your feet together, hold the supporting leg, draw the working leg tightly to the supporting leg (feel the inner thigh muscles), and point the toes up toward the calf. When facing Point 2, the two arms gesture to indicate a flag, and the fingers form a special gesture called the orchid fingers. The hand gesture of the orchid fingers involves lowering the middle finger in a circle to meet the thumb, with the other three fingers slightly turned up to indicate petals. Chinese traditional dance stresses the presentation of a twisted torso. To do this, one must stabilize the supporting leg, pull the lateral thigh of the working leg upward, and twist the crotch. Tilt the right side of the chest and pull the left shoulder back, then add *the flag* gesture with the arms and the orchid fingers with both hands. If you touch your toes with your fingers to form a half-moon shape, this is known as *crane-standing posture.* It is an *attitude* in ballet. The aesthetics of ballet require dancers "to open, stretch, and straighten" both working and supporting legs, concentrate on the line from the top of the head straight down to the toes, and keep the body upright. *The flag* is transformed from the fifth position of the arms in ballet, with arms extended above the head, maintaining a gently curved line, as if a drop of water is dripping from the upper arm to the fingertips. This is an *attitude.*

In the model ballet, *crane-standing posture/attitude* integrates the arm movements of ballet with *the flag* from Chinese traditional dance. But the hand gestures, which seemed too feminine, were replaced by an extended palm gesture that presents masculinity. This movement is called *the crouching step*, one of the basic movements of Chinese Martial Art. Ms. Liu, what is the next move?

LIU: (*Demonstrating*) A crouching step followed by a crane-standing posture.

JIANG: When I watched the clips of the solo dance of Wu Qinghua, I noticed that her left hand is in the shape of the masculine palm gesture, whereas her left hand is presenting the orchid fingers ... A stage of unconsciousness, maybe?

ONSCREEN. *Wang Huifen tells a story about getting a divorce.*

WANG: I will share with you another story. My husband didn't support my dancing. I was selected to dance the lead part in *The Red Detachment of Women*. His colleagues joked about it, "look, your wife was taken by others." So he didn't support me performing the model ballet. I was very stressed out during the rehearsal because of the pressure he put on me. We fought constantly. One time he threw my bag and pointe shoes out of the window, and they got stuck hanging from a tree. A worker from the propaganda troupe helped me reach those things on the tree, so I could go to the rehearsal in Kunming.

Another time, my husband didn't allow me to go to rehearsal at all. I sneaked out while he was asleep. He woke up and ran after me without even putting his shoes on. And he blocked me on my way to the theatre. He simply didn't allow me to go to rehearsals. Our troupe official told me to divorce him. "He doesn't support your career; why would you want to stay with him? Just divorce him!" Then I drafted a divorce petition and gave it to the troupe official. Well, that surely scared him. He wrote a self-criticism letter. After that, he never stopped me from going to rehearsals and didn't interfere anymore. That's the story. Later I thought: I married you, but I didn't sell myself to you. The way he loved me was completely wrong.

ONSTAGE. *In the meantime, during Wang Huifen's story, Jiang Fan continues to perform the contradictory movements of the two hands.*
ONSTAGE. *Liu Zhuying tells a story about gauze and dancing* en pointe.

LIU: I still remember the days when we were trained in pointe technique. Back then, we didn't have any fancy stuff to wrap our toes. Each of us came up with different creative ways. Most of us just used gauze. Sooner than you might think, our toes became abraded. Gauze would get stuck on our skin with the blood from our toes. When we removed the gauze, we were pained to tears. However, at that time, we had a motto: "Perform the revolutionary plays and be the revolutionary people. Play the heroes and learn from them. Fear neither hardship nor death!"

She repeats slowly.

Fear neither hardship nor death ... fear neither hardship, nor death ... fear neither hardship, nor death ... (getting faster) fear neither hardship, nor death ... fear neither hardship, nor death ... The following day, everyone came back to rehearsal with their pointe shoes. We practiced nonstop until our entire bodies were sweaty. We stomped *en pointe*; stomped, stomped, stomped, stomped, and stomped ... until we began to feel numb. That was how we danced.

ONSTAGE. In the meantime, other dancers exhaustively perform a series of movements in response to the slogan of "fear neither hardship nor death." Later, Liu Zhuying closes the curtain.

ACT THREE. LOOKING BACK

ONSTAGE. Dancers perform Wen Hui's choreography of "The Headless Us"; approaching the audience.
ONSCREEN. Interviewees give accounts of how "nostalgia" works. Again, Wen Hui, the interviewer, is not present onscreen. Only her voice can be heard.

ZHANG: This is his first move. After he turns back, there is a jump ... oh I can't remember it.

WEN: Of course you can!

ZHANG: I don't remember those minor moves... then Hong Changqing pointed out the right direction [to the people]. He gave the silver dollar coins to the poor. "What happened to you guys? What happened to these people?" Liu Qingtang had a special move! ... Oh, I can't remember other moves.

LIANG: I had somewhat complicated feelings about the revival of *The Red Detachment of Women*. When I was offered the ticket to the revival, at first, I wanted to refuse, but then I wanted to give it a try. So I went to the theatre, and I got a good seat, close to the stage. It must be ten years ago—I can't remember which year exactly. But I remember at one point, towards the end of the ballet, I began to feel very uncomfortable. I left before the end.

CUI: If you are open-minded about it and take it as one type of cultural phenomenon, one genre among many genres, I don't see any problems. I'd suggest that we don't simply throw them [the model plays] away altogether. They are more complex than the ideologically charged cultural products. It's much more complex …

YUE: The complicated part of this period of history is that the people who experienced it, including me, are still full of confusion, affliction, and even humiliation. This is particularly so for the Chinese intellectuals. It is hard to imagine that anyone would genuinely celebrate that period. For a nation that went through such a disastrous event, it would be truly tragic if amnesia were to overtake things.

ONSCREEN. Zhang Laishan teaches the kindergarten kids how to dance.

ZHANG: One, two, and look at me! Smile and turn around. One, two, three, four, do a backbend; do the splits. Move, and move. Very Good. Go to your position. Don't move! Raise your head! Good! Smile, get ready! Music, please!

ONSTAGE. When the music of "The River of 10,000 Springs" rises, Liu Zhuying opens the front curtain. Jiang Fan stands still in between the curtains.
ONSCREEN. In the meantime, Zhang Laishan continues to teach the kids.

ZHANG: Pay attention to your facial expression. OK. Then smile, OK. Don't relax; keep your smile! Keep the legs straight! OK, your facial expression! Smile! Bid farewell to the Red Army! You must bend over quickly! Bend! Jump! Go! Move faster. Your facial expression! Come on!

ONSTAGE. Jiang Fan slowly moves away from the curtain, struggling to strip off any trace of discipline.
ONSCREEN. The pages from the special edition are turned slowly. Another blocking diagram is shown.
ONSTAGE. Wen explains a choreographic treatment entitled "The Stars over the Sky."

WEN: Here is the blocking diagram of *The Red Detachment of Women*. Look at those neat, orderly formations. This one is called "The Stars over the Sky." It's a kind of choreographic composition that is used to exhibit a festive and celebratory atmosphere. Such staging choices can be seen on any grand stage in China these days: the Olympic opening ceremony, the Spring Festival Gala, the

National Day TV Extravaganza, the May Labor Day Celebration, the June 1 Children's Day Celebration, the July 1 Communist Party Founding Day Celebration, etc. The choreographic treatment is quite similar in Act II of the model ballet, the part about celebrating the unity of the army and the people. I wonder if this has become a legacy that will pass effortlessly from one generation to the next.

How about we try it onstage.

ONSTAGE. Wen and Jiang demonstrate The Stars over the Sky. *Other dancers gradually join them. The neat and orderly formations dissolve into chaos. Later, Wen starts talking about public square dancing (guangchang wu).*[2]

WEN: When I interviewed the former dancers from *The Red Detachment of Women*, I found many of them have been quite active in public square dancing. This made me curious about what kind of connection there might be.

LIU: When I choreograph the public square dances, if those dancing grannies forget their moves, I ask them to dance them ten times.

ONSTAGE. Every woman raises her hand repeatedly.

LIU: If they still can't remember the moves. No more words, just do 20 more repetitions!

ONSCREEN. Cui Weiping discusses the phenomenon of public square dancing.

CUI: There could be some connection between the cultural activists back then and those in the present time. But I don't think you can argue that the emergence of public square dancing resulted from the contributions of the main players in the Cultural Revolution. I believe the people are the main force behind the public dancing activities. Yes, there might be some connections among those former rural mobile film projection activities, the model plays of the Cultural Revolution, and today's dancing in the public space. In the culture promoted by the communist party, the culture of the masses has always been regarded as a positive tradition. In other words, the culture of the masses has never been reduced to a joke. It is accepted, sanctioned, and even supported by all levels of the government.

---

2 Public square dancing (guangchang wu) is a community dance that is part of everyday life in China nowadays. Middle-aged and elderly Chinese women make up the majority of the dancers. They dance together in open-air public spaces to exercise or to further participate in dance competitions and performances. Some studies suggest that this kind of public dance can be read as a resurrection of Maoist collectivism.

ONSCREEN. Cui Weiping gives comments on discipline.

CUI: There are different types of disciplines, within which you find different cacophonies and sounds. But there is always spontaneity. When you think about it, the practice of discipline is either political, depoliticized, or commodified. Other activities, such as doing homework, can also be considered "discipline." Or maybe you don't move at all, which is also a form of discipline. These dialectic relationships between discipline and anti-discipline, and between the political and the anti-political, didn't exist only during the Cultural Revolution. I think they exist in all times and all cultures. They have created the circumstances under which the body becomes the target for competition; it is a process in which the self is continuously transformed and moved to a new level.

ONSTAGE. In the meantime, the dancers' movements gradually slow down. They slowly approach the screen.
ONSCREEN. Wang's concluding reflection is presented.

WANG: Looking back, it was purely accidental for people like me to step into the art of dance. But then you began to experience all aspects of life. Thank you for offering me a chance to remember the past. Thank you for bringing back my memories. At this stage, what is left for us is memories. Recently, I have been spending days in the hospital with my husband. Looking at the people who reach the final stage of their lives. And today, I have a chance to remember the past. So, thank you for giving me a chance.

ONSTAGE. The dancers continue to approach the screen.
ONSCREEN. Liang Xiaoyan concludes her reflection.

LIANG: We argue that China needs nongovernmental power. This country needs more social subjects to contribute to the development of a good society. We went through the Cultural Revolution. How would you define the Cultural Revolution? The Cultural Revolution didn't allow the existence of a society. We were a country in which society was absent. Except for the vertical, top-down administrative system, we didn't have any horizontal connections. Every part of the society was subordinate to the hierarchical system. So the country was about dominating and being dominated, rather than fostering a society based on cooperation and facilitation. We need a society in which more people are engaged subjects, and we should walk away from a society of dominating and being dominated. We should enable more people to become the subjects of society and develop society, which enables us to grow. Therefore, we must make this society more dynamic, balanced, collaborative, and equal. These are not abstract ideas but need to be actualized through specific social practices and actions. To accomplish these goals, more and more people have to get involved.

ONSTAGE. The dancers approach the audience when the chronology of the Revolutionary model opera is presented on the screen.
ONSCREEN. The chronology of the Revolutionary model opera and The Red Detachment of Women.

1963:	Jiang Qing, Mao Zedong's wife, began to take an interest in developing revolutionary plays that "help the masses to propel history forward."
1964, September 26	*The Red Detachment of Women* was premiered by the National Ballet of China at Beijing Tianqiao Theatre.
1965, March 6	The term Yangbanxi (model theatre) appeared in the Shanghai newspaper *Liberation Daily* to reference *The Legend of the Red Lantern*.
1965, November 10	Shanghai's *Wenhui Daily* published Yao Wenyuan's article, entitled "On the New Historical Drama 'Hai Rui Dismissed from Office.'" The production and publication of the article have been seen as marking the start of the Cultural Revolution.
1965, May	To *commemorate* the 25 anniversary of Mao's "Talks at the Yan'an Forum on Literature and Art," the eight model plays were staged in Beijing. For 37 days, 218 performances were given, with nearly 330,000 people in the audience.
1967, May 31	The entire repertoire was listed for the first time as "eight revolutionary model theatrical works (Geming Yangbanxi)" in an editorial entitled "Excellent Models for Revolutionary Art and Literature" in *The People's Daily*.
By 1967	Eight *revolutionary model* theatrical works were produced, including two ballets (*The Red Detachment of Women*, and *The White-Haired Girl*), five model operas (*The Legend of the Red Lantern, Shajiabang, Taking Tiger Mountain by Strategy, Raid on the White Tiger Regiment, On the Dock*), and one revolutionary symphony *Shajiabang*.

| 1966–1976 | During the Cultural Revolution, professional and amateur troupes and theatrical propaganda teams brought the revolutionary model plays to all levels of factories, villages, government institutions, schools, army units, etc. |

| 1972, February 24 | During his visit to China, Richard Nixon and Mrs. Nixon were accompanied by Jiang Qing and Zhou Enlai to the revolutionary model ballet *The Red Detachment of Women*. |

| 1976–1992 | From the end of the Cultural Revolution to 1992, *The Red Detachment of Women* disappeared from the stage. |

| 1992, May 23 | To *commemorate* the 50th anniversary of Mao's "Talks at the Yan'an Forum on Literature and Art," The National Ballet of China revived *The Red Detachment of Women* based on its 1964 premiere version. |

| 2014, September 23 | To celebrate the 50 anniversary of the premiere of *The Red Detachment of Women*, The National Ballet of China held a commemorative performance at the Great Hall of the People. Since its debut, the ballet has been staged more than 3,800 times by the National Ballet of China. |

The End

From the Red Detachment to the Women: A Postscript

Zhuang Jiayun

Life and Dance

Most Chinese urban independent theatre and performance makers have been connected in some way to the Beijing-based *Caochangdi Workstation* (*Caochangdi Gongzuozhan¹*) and the *Living Dance Studio²* (*Shenghuo Wudao Gongzuoshi*).³ They attended the body workshops conducted by choreographer Wen Hui and borrowed the Workstation stage to rehearse their own projects. Some presented their earliest pieces at the festivals held at either the Workstation or the Young Choreographers' Project. I was probably the last one to enjoy the opportunity to work as an artist at Caochangdi and did so mainly in the summer of 2014, right before its demolition.⁴ That was also my first collaboration with Wen Hui. Without a lived experience of working with the *Living Dance Studio*, I could not understand this kind of creative process, which bears all the marks of inspiration, rapture, and everyday triviality.

    Caochangdi Workstation, a significant incubation site for innovations in unconventional theatre and performance in urban China, lives on in spirit. However, in the middle of our first round of rehearsals for *RED* (*HONG*), its physical body

---

1   Caochangdi is the name of a Beijing neighborhood.

2   A precise English translation of *Shenghuo Wudao*, would be Life Dance. The most accurate translation, however, shifts "life" into a present, continuous form; thus, Living Dance.

3   The definitions and issues surrounding "independence" have been thoroughly discussed in a few scholarly works. They are not the focus of this essay. *Caochangdi Workstation* was an arts organization founded in 2005 by documentary filmmaker Wu Wenguang and choreographer Wen Hui. It later became the home base of *the Living Dance Studio*, cofounded by Wu and Wen.

4   Because of the accelerated urbanization and gentrification in Beijing, even in this alternative neighborhood near the North Fifth Ring Road—where artists, art dealers, students, and migrant workers are the main residents—*Caochangdi Workstation* eventually succumbed to rent increases. Dissolution was its only option.

ceased to exist. When I returned to Beijing in summer 2015 for the second round of rehearsals, the cast had changed, and the rehearsal space was Wen Hui's living room. New to the team were two women of the post-'80s generation: Jiang Fan and Li Xinmin.[5] Both have laughed and cried along with the ups and downs of China's market-oriented, commercialized system. But they know little, if anything, of the Cultural Revolution that dominated the mid-1960s to mid-1970s.

Wen Hui suggested: "Let's start all over again." That remark sparked my epiphany. Our living condition, the moment we found ourselves in, would determine the direction of the dance.

From the Red Detachment of Women

The inspiration to create *RED* came from three sources. The first was a trove of documentary materials related to *The Red Detachment of Women (Hongse Niangzi Jun)*—audiovisual clips, publications, memorabilia from the original revolutionary model ballet, interview footage. These were incorporated to evoke a special territory of memory and reactivate a living and lived archive within specific bodies: those of the performers and those of people who experienced the Cultural Revolution.

The second combined the desire to understand the complex feelings of people who experienced the politicized art and aestheticized politics that held sway during the Cultural Revolution, along with the desire to explore the in/congruity between the state's discourse and the everyday cultural lives of the people.

The third was the idea to use the dancers' bodies as a departure point. Varied connections with the original model ballet, in content and movement and staging, would allow *RED* to anatomize the original choreography and explore here-and-now experiences as dancers and survivors, together, revisit that turbulent decade. Tasks both new and stimulating befell me with the arrival of the two new members. *With its all-women ensemble, RED* could and should add another layer to the complexity of women's reality in China today. It should function as a way to reflect on how the socialist imagination prescribed gender equality and women's liberation, which were embedded in Maoist state feminism and disseminated through the revolutionary model opera . Accordingly, we played the collected documentary materials to the younger performers, pausing whenever they felt inclined to share their thoughts or express themselves through movement.[6] I also created a tabular list of the known past experiences and current realities of

---

5   The other two performers are Liu Zhuying (b. 1955), a former performer in *The Red Detachment of Women* and a retiree from the *Kunming City Song and Dance Troupe,* and Wen Hui (b. 1960).

6   Jiang Fan also helped create a series of diagrams about the ways that Chinese classical dance, for training purposes, created a system of movement vocabulary that drew upon classic Western ballet as well as traditional Chinese opera and martial arts.

the two generations of female performers, including each of their distinct experiences with and understandings of *The Red Detachment of Women.*

Then we heard, quite by accident, that *United Heart Home of Hope* (*Tongxin Xiwang Jiayuan*), an NGO founded in 2003 with the goal of supporting women and children in the migrant communities on the outskirts of Beijing, was singing *Marching Forward* (*Xiang Qianjin*), the theme song from the 1961 film *The Red Detachment of Women,* at all of their meetings.[7] We immediately decided to interview Ma Xiaoduo, the organization's founder. Ma freely admitted that she did not remember much of the model ballet from seeing it in elementary school. But she recounted being exceptionally moved by a single occurrence in the plot: The female protagonist's change of fortune after she joined the Red Army-led women's detachment. To Ma, *The Red Detachment of Women* is about how women should transform themselves to free themselves from oppression and misery. *United Heart Home of Hope* was formed with exactly the same vision of self-salvation.[8]

The development of the script of *RED* in 2015 was strongly directed at and dedicated to women in general and the four female performers specifically. However, in addition to using the original model ballet to engage with the decade-long social and cultural chaos initiated by the Cultural Revolution and examining the cultural products praised by the revolutionary discourse of class struggle, I wonder how *RED* can reflect the ways that women in today's China face ideological orientations that are official, if different, and engage in new forms of political, social, and gender-specific struggle.

Looking Back

Act Three, "Looking Back", aims to both show the past generation's reminiscences onscreen and to demonstrate, through four performers' current stories, their vibrant and tenacious presence onstage. My deepest regret is that this part could not be developed as planned due to inadequate initiatives, opportunity, budget, and rehearsal time. Since "the author is dead" and the performance text refuses further development, can only replace some of these current stories from the original script into a postscript.

Liu Zhuying could not care less if any connection exists between revolutionary model opera and *guangchang wu* (*public square dancing*).[9] To her, the latter is

---

7   The 1961 film, *The Red Detachment of Women*, was directed by Xie Jin. The revolutionary model ballet of the same title was actually based on this film.

8   *United Heart Home of Hope* includes numerous divisions such as a convenience store, a second-hand shop, a kindergarten, and others. Because of its complicated relationships with various neighborhood committees and local governments, the organization has been forced to relocate five times in 10 years.

9   Public square dancing (*guangchang wu*) is a community dance that is part of everyday life in China nowadays. Middle-aged and elderly Chinese women make up the majority of the dancers. They dance together in open-air public spaces to exercise or to further participate

neither a mobilization of mass culture in an era of depoliticization nor a cultural form of reconstruction of Maoist collectivism. She only complains that the middle-aged female dancers are not professional enough, in either spirit or technique. As a local official in charge of cultural activities, her main purpose in organizing large-scale public square-dancing activities is to maintain stability in sensitive times. This goal is best accomplished if public spaces are filled with energetic, if amateur, dancers.

Jiang Fan resigned her position as a choreographer and dancer at the *Shanghai Opera House Dance Troupe* in 2015 and moderately enjoys her freedom from the state-owned performing arts institutions and their suffocating leitmotif projects. She makes a living by choreographing musicals and has collaborated with *Shanghai International Dance Center* as an independent artist. During the creation of *RED*, she recognized the continuity between the revolutionary model opera of 50 years ago and today's leitmotif works that eulogize the Party's revolutionary history. The more artistically independent she becomes, the more she must think about how to balance the market, audience interests, and the degree to which the present can be transmitted through individualized artistic references.

Like Wu Qinghua, the female protagonist in the model ballet, Li Xinmin desperately fled her hometown (Huamulin, in rural Yunnan Province) to Kunming and then to Beijing. Since the demise of *Caochangdi Workstation*, when she lost her dwelling in the city, she continued to make documentary films, worked in an NGO for migrant domestic workers, sold fruit with friends, and, with her long-time artistic partner, created an autobiographical documentary theatre piece, *Timeline* (*Fanhui de Lu*). However, unlike Wu Qinghua, she made peace with her past and decided to go back to Huamulin, where she is about to get married and is expecting her first child. She still thinks *The Red Detachment of Women* has little to do with her life and regrets spending so much energy on *RED*.

We see very little of Wen Hui's personal memories and narratives in *RED*. She keeps creating new pieces and touring old ones around Europe, the site of her "independence," and conducting workshops on the body as an archive in universities all over the world. In December 2018, she commemorated the twentieth anniversary of the independent theatre and performance movement in urban China with *Paper Tiger Studio Beijing* (*Beijing Zhilaohu Xiju Gongzuoshi*) and *Niao Collective* at the Beijing Inside-Out Art Museum. This work functions as a physical manifesto that echoes independent artists' ongoing rewriting of theatre and performance history in modern China. Nonetheless, even as she works with all forms of activity around the phenomenon of memorization, she chooses not to mention

in dance competitions and performances. Some studies suggest that this kind of public dance can be read as a resurrection of Maoist collectivism. *See* Jayne, Mark, and Ho Hon Leung. "Embodying Chinese Urbanism." In Chinese Urbanism: New Critical Perspectives. Edited by Mark Jayne, 189–201. London, New York, NY: Routledge, 2018.

in public two losses of her own: That of *Caochangdi Workstation* and that of Wu Wenguang, her artistic and life partner.

A Nightmare

When *RED* was staged at the Asia Society in New York in November 2018, I moderated a pre-performance dialogue.[10] Some interview footage that was not included in the final documentary performance was shown to the audience. From this footage, I selected Ma Xiaoduo's recollection of her nightmare:

> For years, I have had the same nightmare: I am in the middle of the bridge and cannot cross it. The bridge starts crumbling, and I have to hold tight. That kind of nightmare is a reflection of repression. Sometimes I feel like I am going to screw it. I need to bring it down. I want to be freed. I *feel* I am being repressed. It's like when the red light is on, you are stopped there and cannot move. Just because you are a rural woman, just because you are a woman, everyone can keep walking, but not you. I was blocked all the time. Anyone could do things, but not you. So this is a kind of battle. Whenever I listen to *Marching Forward*, I feel the power.

At the end of that footage, I also added a clip from the demonstrations by workers at Jasic Technology in Shenzhen on July 24, 2018, in which the female workers sing *Marching Forward.* It is in this kind of drastically urbanizing and industrializing Chinese society that we may better understand how the model ballet, albeit in a problematic way, can still serve as a form of feminist intervention—and, as such, how it can continue to inspire women to challenge their gender and socioeconomic oppression.

Bibliography

Jayne, Mark, and Ho Hon Leung. "Embodying Chinese Urbanism." In *Chinese Urbanism: New Critical Perspectives*. Edited by Mark Jayne, 189–201. London, New York, NY: Routledge, 2018.

---

10 Two distinguished scholars who personally experienced the Cultural Revolution, Chaohua Wang, an independent scholar majoring in modern Chinese literature and intellectual history, and Zhen Zhang, a poet, scholar and associate professor in Cinema Studies and History at New York University were the guest speakers at the dialogue.

Don't Be Yourself.
Notes on the Impossibility of Documentary[1]

Boris Nikitin

Translation by Kai Tuchmann

PART ONE: THE DOCUMENTARY AND ITS IMAGES

1

Good morning. My name is Boris Nikitin, I am a theatre director, writer, and curator. I was born in Switzerland—which is also where I live. In my work, I have been dealing with the construction of reality and identity for many years, especially in non-fiction genres like the documentary, but also in news, politics, economics, law, and advertising. My approach towards the documentary, and this is probably also the reason why I am standing here before you today, is critical, and my work has been characterized by this critical attitude for some years now. There are many reasons why I have adopted a critical approach towards the documentary—one could also say of non-fictional representations of reality—but— so I believe—there is also a biographical background, which I would like to briefly detail, because it can be informative for the understanding of what follows: When I was 20 years old, that was in 2000, I came out as a gay man; and with that, I began not only to discover my own sexuality, but at the same time to question the reality in which I lived, which I had been taught, and in which I had believed until then. It felt like a surreal judgment to be in a body that desired the same sex—a circumstance that I tried to bend around with all the willpower at my disposal in order to conform to what I believed to be reality. Social norms, we all know, are very powerful forces that affect our bodies and psyches in such a persistent way that we often forget that they once had a beginning and were not always there. Often these are powerful collective habits that have their roots in legal systems; sometimes they are laws that remain in force to this day.

By coming out, I finally succeeded in interrupting this social delusion—I would also call it a fiction—which is based on historical, and in some places still

1 The revised version of Nikitin's Beijing lecture presented here was made possible by a grant from ITRT Studios Basel/Berlin.

current, law, that being gay makes me something inferior and despicable. This is one of the reasons why since then, I have viewed reality as a potential propagandist product. This is not just a mind game for me, but a tool to not have to think of reality as something closed and inevitable, but to be able to think of it as something possible. As something that I can change.

I am telling you all this—perhaps a little strangely right at the beginning of our seminar—because I would like to think together with you today about reality, about its representations and their effects. The question of the document will play an important role, and at some points, we will also touch on the question of the juridical. The seminar will discuss how these representations and their repetitions—because there can be no representation without repetition—influence our idea and perception of reality. And it will ask how we can shift the grammar of representation through our artistic work and thus open up spaces in reality.

2

Kai Tuchman told me that the focus of this year's seminar is to connect the history of Beijing with questions of site-specific theatre forms and that you want to examine site-specific as a particular form of a "theatre of the real." I have indeed made some works that could be classified with the genre label "site-specific," for example, a spatial installation in a hospice in Athens or a work in a school in Berlin. In the vast majority of cases, however, I choose the theatre space as the platform and framework for my productions. However, and this could be another reason why I am standing here in front of you today, in recent years I have repeatedly expressed the thought that these theatre works are basically also "site-specific." They deal very concretely with the situation of the theatre. In addition to the themes and material they deal with, all my works are always about theatre as a concrete, constructed space and as a concrete, special form of the present with its special characteristics, possibilities and rules. They are always also about theatre as an institution, as a context, as a set of expectations, agreements and presuppositions, in short, about a special form of framing reality.

I think what makes the genre "site-specific" so interesting is its artistic perspective: It confronts a real, already existing space with a theatrical perspective. As a result, many social, ideological, legal and political constructions and fictions that permeate spaces and buildings suddenly become visible. Their supposed unambiguities suddenly become ambiguous and take on an aesthetic form.

For me, site-specific is not simply a genre description that refers to art in public space or in other real spaces. Rather, it can be understood as a very particular way of looking at reality, examining seemingly immutable conventions for their components, for their construction. It means, and I will return to this again and again in the course of this lecture, to look at reality as something that is potentially fake or the product of propaganda.

3

Let us perhaps try it out directly: If, for example, we look at this university classroom as a site-specific spatial installation or as a ready-made, then we don't just
see a generic neutral, rectangular room of which there are hundreds of thousands
in this world. Instead, we suddenly notice certain features that qua habit seem
quite normal and unambiguous to us, but which can now at least be identified as
remarkable under the particular theatrical gaze: for example, that this space is of
a very ordinary, rather sober aesthetic that is possibly meant to be understood as
"neutral" but actually is not; that the particular row-seating presupposes an essentially very unnatural disciplinarity of the people who are supposed to sit on
these chairs and that education is apparently thought of together with a hierarch-
ization of the gaze; we notice banalities that are nonetheless remarkable, such as
that I stand and talk and you sit and listen. I look at you and you look at me. It is a
situation created by both the space and the context: the university. And this context brings with it some preconditions while at the same time fabricating them,
not least with the help of this concrete space: for example, that you are the students and I am the guest who is paid to speak here. The space organizes a hierarchy and a social order, a kind of site-specific software that we take for granted,
which is why we mostly block it out and adopt a relatively uncritical view of
reality as a simple matter of facts.

We can see all this if we leave our naturalized, accustomed everyday gaze for
a moment and adopt an aesthetic perspective. Let's call it the *site-specific gaze*.
The *site-specific gaze* opens our perception to the constructedness of space and
our behavior in it. It opens our perception to the way reality is formed. If the here
and now were a site-specific performance installation in which we find ourselves,
then we would begin to take a more distanced view and wonder about all the supposedly self-evident things here. That would ultimately be the prerequisite for us
to play with them.

4

As a theatre-maker, I am always concerned with the following questions: What
does it mean to be seen by other people? What does it do to me that I am being
watched by other people? How does it affect the way I create a certain identity, a
certain image of myself? How does it affect my reality, my view of the world? And
how does it affect the way I look back? These are questions that are, to a certain
extent, inherent to the logic of theatre, but which I think can also be applied to
reality.

I would argue—it is a crude assertion—that reality is grounded in the fact that
we are constantly observing each other. To briefly put on the site-specific glasses
again: This is actually exactly what we are doing right now. You are observing me
and I am observing you. However, this mutual observation does not take place on
the same level, but—as we have just seen—within a hierarchical order that as-
signs each of us a place from which we make our observations of other people—
and thus of the world. I think the way we perceive reality cannot be separated

from the social "place" from which we do so, namely the socio-political role in which our bodies find themselves. Bodies are ultimately receivers and transmitters of reality. For this reason, I would argue, what we call "reality" is to some extent indistinguishable from "social reality." This is basically what we mean when we say that reality is a construct. A construct, but one that is so convincing in its appearance and in its permanent repetition that we are often inclined to naturalize it, to take it for granted, to believe it and forget its constructedness, like this room here where we are right now. It is, you might say, the point at which reality becomes *realistic*. It is the point where reality and propaganda intersect in the assertion of the authentic. But where the non-fictional, the real(istic), the authentic appears as a figure of thought and a model of perception, the fake is not far away. After all, only what we accept as real can be faked.

5

Most of my works have a non-fictional or documentary component. In most of them, the biographies of the performers or actors are central source material. At the same time, many of my projects have titles like: *Imitation of Life, F for Fake, Propaganda Piece, How to Win Friends and Influence People*. These titles indicate that there is a potential ambiguity in what the audience perceives, even if the material presented or used on stage has a documentary or non-fictional *look*. Roughly speaking, I use non-fictional material, but I invite the audience to be cautious. I do this because I believe that documentary or non-fictional claims should be approached with a certain amount of care. Because the document, in its unbroken gesture of showing or representing reality, harbors a structure that could be described as authoritarian.

A classic non-fictional assertion such as the one I started with this morning: "Good morning. My name is Boris Nikitin," is probably the simplest and, at the same time, the most fundamental documentary assertion of all. It says that this body belongs to Boris Nikitin, that this body *is* Boris Nikitin. I assume that none of you has doubted this assertion. Why should you? However, it is quite conceivable that I am not Boris Nikitin at all, but Boris's assistant, for example. And even if you now open your internet search engine and look for images of Boris Nikitin, you will basically not be able to be sure until the end of this seminar whether this body is really Boris Nikitin. You will have to trust that Kai Tuchmann—who is, after all, the director of this course and who has announced a Boris Nikitin—has not deceived you. But in the end: How can you know if perhaps even Kai Tuchmann has not been deceived?

One could continue this Kleistian game endlessly, but at least we can state that it is an assertion that is not necessarily true, but which, in conjunction with a certain meshwork of conditions, leads us to believe it. As early as 1890, William James wrote in *The Principles of Psychology:* "As a rule, we believe as much as we can. We would believe anything if we only could."

We do believe. That's how we organize our daily lives. And I think that's also the "nature" of documentary assertion: we tend to believe in it because it's embedded in a set of conditions we are used to organizing our lives with. But I would say that every non-fictional description of reality is potentially fake. And by potentially, I mean that reality has the capacity not to be the way it is. That it can be changed, which is why reality, if one follows this thought to the end, is per se always political and thus the object and subject of conflict.

6

This brings us to documentary theatre as an art form that deals with documentary content as non-fictional art. What distinguishes fiction from the documentary? To put it simply: In fiction, the recipients are aware of the constructed nature of the story, so that the category of credibility may play a role, but not that of belief. The recipients can be disappointed, but they cannot be deceived. There are exceptions, but they confirm the rule. In the case of documentary, on the other hand, an ultimately unspoken agreement conveys that it is a representation of real, factual events, especially real people, or documents concerning them. We are in the realm of information. As already indicated, it is not only the content that plays a role here, but also the context or paratext, i.e. the framework in which the content appears, including the necessary authority that lends legitimacy to the documentary character or stands up for it (the publisher, the theatre management, the party, the collective agreement, Kai Tuchmann). In contrast to the fictional, it plays a central role here that we believe and trust (or not) these authorities who assure us that everything is correct.

Many productions of documentary theatre appear with the claim that the production describes or represents an existing reality—in other words, that it is not a fiction. We are all aware of the importance of this distinction as a convention. Now I often say, somewhat polemically, that documentary and propaganda are ultimately structurally the same, both claiming to describe reality in a non-fictional way. Both, I would argue, therefore have an inherent manipulative potential. A manipulative potential, by the way, that is also inherent in a seminar like ours, since a seminar is also a non-fictional event. Basically, everything I say here can also be understood as propaganda. Assuming this was a site-specific performance, its title could be, for example, "How to convince students".

The reason I say this is not merely to make fun at the meta-level, but the same reason I choose these titles for my works that contain documentary, non-fictional, biographical material and present it as such: We cannot take away anyone's responsibility to decide what they will do with what they see or hear. By referring to potential deception, I am referring to everyone's responsibility to be prudent with the information he or she takes in. And likewise with the freedom to make a decision at all.

7

As far as the documentary as a genre is concerned, as I said at the beginning, I am skeptical about certain notions of the document *as document*. Many documentarists counter my skepticism by saying that the very montage of the material indicates that it cannot be understood as an undisturbed or uninterrupted representation of reality. This may be true in theory, but I think it can also be argued that in practice, it is precisely the montage that transforms the raw documentary material into a political realism that is potentially manipulative, that is, potentially persuasive. We know this practice from election campaigns, from education and from advertising, but we also encounter it in the theatre or cinema.

Ultimately, however, the crucial question is: What authority is attributed to the document as such and what is this authority used for? In the case of many artists working in the field of documentary theatre, most of whom I wouldn't assume to be authoritarian, it can be deduced from the way they work with documents that they don't doubt the authority of the document as such. Rather, they *use* it. Documentary theatre often appears with the claim that it is promoting enlightenment and pointing out grievances. This pedagogical—one could also say political—claim is often a decisive factor behind the work itself: For example, to show the suffering of refugees, or the humanitarian and political misery in certain regions of the world, the lives of homeless people, the everyday practices of cleaners, scientists or other people in their respective contexts.

In the context of this claim, the documentary material takes on the function of authentication. It makes what is reported credible and reinforces the message. One example in theatre practice is the staged, montaged reading or speaking of excerpts of documented speeches, writings, articles—a procedure used again and again in German-language documentary theatre, in which the mere fact of the document brings with it an increased aesthetic effectiveness. Another example is the use of contemporary witnesses who, as performers, represent their own biography live on stage and thus at the same time bear witness to the events that took place in their lives (or, if they are not live on stage, do so in recorded videos). In contrast to trained actors, you could call them "real" people. I don't mean that sarcastically, since it's the genuineness of their identity that distinguishes them from the characters who are usually traditionally seen on stage representing a fictional role. The real people in documentary plays are not to be confused with amateurs, i.e. actors without professional training who also embody fictional roles. The function of real people on stage is the opposite: They do not represent another character, but themselves. They vouch for the non-fictional reality of their statements and thus for the subject matter being negotiated on stage. They are witnesses.

8

Documentary is generally described as a genre that reports on events that take place or have taken place in (contemporary) reality. It is a form of non-fictional description of reality. The problem of documentary in this context is the impossibility of grasping what "reality" (or the present) exactly is. "Reality" cannot be separated from the modes of its perception, its representation, rhetoric and depiction. It cannot be conclusively grasped, is always assertion and interpretation. The dilemma of documentarists arises when they try to represent reality and get necessarily thrown back on their ideas of "reality"—on their subjective, selective presuppositions and on the collective norms that shape their gaze. Every representation of reality reproduces its own premises. But what are premises and norms but collectively accepted fictions, which create the illusion of reality through repetition?

The problem of using documents and/or witnesses in theatre to "prove" authentic content is what I have just called the reproduction of one's own premises. It is a side effect of documentary theatre. I sometimes call it the *stowaway*. The stowaway is what secretly flies along and gets off at the destination, while the documentarist tries to capture and depict reality. It is the unquestioned norms and attributions that travel along with this reality without being the center of interest. Often these stowaways are linked to questions and attributions of gender, race, class. Often these are clichés that are reproduced unseen in the act of documentation, while the latter focuses on its actual subject.

An example—from a European point of view—is found in documentary representations of crises in certain countries in Africa. Usually, the results are documentary works—theatrical as well as cinematic—that try to draw attention to the misfortune of other people and to the dysfunctional political systems that produce this misfortune. The stowaway here is the fading out of a reality beyond the crisis and thus the reproduction of a cliché, a prejudice that has ultimately shaped the image of this continent for centuries: that chaos reigns there and that this chaos has a dark skin color. In a sense, the documentary, in many cases, reduces reality to what is necessary for its mission.

In short, it curtails reality, and with this, it often reduces real people to the identity category relevant to the documentary so that they may vouch as witnesses for a very specific reality in a "realistic way": refugee, warlord, victim, perpetrator, man, woman.

9

I come from a background that is critical of representation on stage, especially the representation of identity. This is, in a way, the propagandistic imprint of my own education, the commonly formed discourse within a mutually understanding peer group, which I myself am a part of.

One of the essential questions here over many years has been: How are men and women represented on stage while a story is being told? While many plays try to analyze the world and criticize society, their productions often include clichéd representations of women and men. The reproduction of these clichés are the stowaways of these dramas.

This has a lot to do with European literature and the canon. While there are some interesting major female roles, they tend to be exceptions that confirm the rule. Most dramas are about protagonists who can be identified as male. This has primarily to do with the ways plays have been produced. Much of the dramatic literature performed on stages was written by men and is more than 100 years old. Consequently, it often reproduces gender roles that appear very traditional from a contemporary perspective.

This distribution of roles, identities, attributes and the status that these accord is, so to speak, a site-specific ideological and social feature of the concretely built environment of the "stage." However, this is not only about roles. It has implications for the entire profession of acting. The question is: Who plays the good roles, who plays the small roles? There is a clear division based on hierarchy between men and women, and again between men and women, on the one hand, and people who do not identify as either men or a women, on the other. Even though there has been some movement in these institutions in recent years, theatre is still very patriarchal structure. This has to do with literature, with how actors are trained, how many female, male, trans or non-binary directors we have, how many artistic directors we have. In Europe, eighty percent of theatres are run by men.

The question of gender is one thing. The other question is the category that in English is called race. In German-speaking theatre, practically all the people on stage have one skin color: They are all white. The theatre is interestingly much more conservative in this respect than the society within which this institution exists. If you go out on the street in Germany or Switzerland, not to mention France or England, you will find a more diverse population than on the stages that are supposed to represent the world.

Nowadays, theatre is gradually starting to become more diverse. But until today, most drama schools still refer to the expectations of an audience that is itself predominantly white and, so the argument goes, wants to see mainly white protagonists on stage for identification. This creates a circular reproduction of norms that assert themselves as seemingly incontrovertible reality. Drama schools have a certain typology of actors and actresses according to the theatre market. They practice type-casting. So it is as much about what is performed on stage as it is about what happens inside the institution—and ultimately in the bodies and brains that inhabit the institution itself. Memorizing a text is a physical act that affects the body and the brain. Repeating a text fifty times a day because you have to memorize it changes something in the brain: a person who is only supposed to internalize the role of the housekeeper of color, or the girl who is in love with the hero but he doesn't love her, so she has to kill herself... If those are the only roles they memorize as actresses, and there is no other content or identity on offer, then it's a political problem.

10

The more recent documentary theatre in the German-speaking world must be seen in the context of developments in the independent theatre scene in the 1990s. Until then, the independent scene was dominated by the production of dramatic plays, albeit in a non-institutional setting, under precarious conditions and often in connection with amateur theatre. With the emergence of postdramatic theatre, new aesthetic practices emerged that emancipated themselves from the dramatic and from acting as the playing of fictional characters. One of these postdramatic forms was the emerging *performance theatre*—a theatre that was not dedicated to the playing of characters but to "performance," i.e. a self-presentation on stage in which one's own real body and real biography were the material presented on the stage. One part of this postdramatic theatre was documentary theatre, which often approached reality journalistically—and sometimes converged with performance theatre.

But in both forms—and in many others—it was not just about different material. Rather, it was about the broader question of how the traditional system of representation itself, which had grown over decades, could be changed—on stage, but also backstage.

One approach was to acknowledge the fact that we have a problem with theatre literature. How can it be changed? One strategy was to say we need to tell new stories. We have to go outside and see how we live, for example, by doing interviews, by focusing on the lives of people who have never been represented on stage, by taking a closer look at everyday realities that were invisible until then.

Another way was to bring down the system of professionalism that mainly privileged the trained white actor who was assigned the big roles. In the 1990s, there was a feminist movement in performance, whose protagonists said: our lives are not represented on stage because there is no literature to represent them—so we have to go on stage and do it ourselves. It was a new aesthetic of progressive, self-empowering dilettantism. To change the dominant narratives on big stages, it was necessary to change the way you work, the way you collaborate, it was necessary to break the dominance of the director. Suddenly there were collectives telling their own stories in a different way than we were used to in "professional theatre".

Now I would argue that unlike performance theatre, which has embraced feminist, queer, postcolonial, non-ableist etc., influences, theories and practices and has begun to dare to take a progressive approach to reality, documentary theatre remained aesthetically conservative. This was ultimately a conservatism inscribed in the nature of the genre. While performance theatre derives its ideological as well as aesthetic power precisely from the fact that it attempts to transform reality and identity at the same time in the act of its representation, documentary remains, to a certain extent, aesthetically attached to the reality it documents. Since the directors/writers are interested in showing and criticizing reality "as it is," they must submit to a pre-existing aesthetic grammar. Therefore, documentary theatre tends to transport pre-existing social norms into the present as stowaways, because many documentary artists are more oriented towards the classical critique of power. The gesture of pointing to social or political conflicts is more important to them than deconstructing historically developed techniques of representation.

Another problem of the documentary and its tendency towards realism is the role of the witness. In the testimony play, this "realistic" staging of the people on

stage ("real people") serves above all to reconcile these people and their testimonies with the challenges of a stage situation. It is about giving the testimonies
dignity, credibility. This documentary realism also becomes the inevitable form
by which these people represent themselves on stage. It leads to a very limited
portrait of these people, since the way they present themselves is limited. This
has to do with the fact that their lack of stage experience means that they are not
as "strong" as the apparatus around them, which is basically alien to them. They
are "weaker" than the context that frames them, not least because its means of
production are not in their hands. Often, however, it is precisely this "weakness,"
the inexperience, that in turn makes them appear "real." Here, authenticity is not
an essence, but the product of a disparity between them and the surrounding
frame. In a sense, it only emerges on stage, as a lack—if you met the same people
on the street or in the theatre foyer, they would hardly stand out as "real."

A criticism of documentary artists who work with experts, witnesses, special-
ists or lay people could consequently be that they primarily work with people
who are weaker than themselves. There is an asymmetry in the distribution of
power, in the knowledge of the apparatus. The authentic is not an expression of
an emancipated personality—which the authentic could be—but the aesthetic
manifestation of this asymmetry.

Part of this form is that these real people on the stage, in their function as witnesses, *must necessarily be themselves*. They are enticed to represent themselves
on stage under their own civilian name in order to provide legitimacy to a construction of reality. They then become fixed to this self. It is here, above all, where
one can observe the clear connection between the documentary and the juridical.
It is a form of self-being that is not a possibility, but an inevitability. The witnesses
must be themselves, because otherwise the whole construct of testimony and thus
of the documentary would collapse. This leads to the almost surreal circumstance
that the people who enter the stage as themselves are, in a sense, made into their
own doubles, forced to reproduce their civilian selves—this legal construction—
with each performance, in an endless loop. But unlike the actress, these witnesses
cannot simply discard their role after leaving the stage.

In summary, we find in documentary a number of problems and challenges
that arise from the representation of the real and the original. One final challenge
could be added to this, which may at first glance seem somewhat trivial, but which
can be identified as an expression of a structure: the lack of irony that can be observed in many of these works. A lack of irony, however, that is not simply an
aesthetic feature, but—I maintain—is itself an expression of a tendency towards
the authoritarian that must produce unambiguities.

One question that has preoccupied me in this context for many years—and
with this I will end this first part—is whether there is perhaps a way to combine
the documentary and the ironic and to develop from this a form of queer documentary—a documentary that is committed to reality, but without automatically
representing its grammar; a documentary that works with the biographies of the
performers without nailing them down to specific identities. By irony, I don't

mean what some critics define as a postmodern "anything goes," but the breaking down of an unambiguous realism into ambiguities. What could a form of documentary look like that integrates this ambiguity? How can a reality be represented that at the same time contains within itself the possibility of not being what it is? Can a representation integrate its own modification while it is still taking place? It seems to me that this is a genuine question of theatre, because transformation requires an element that cannot be represented by purely pictorial means; that actually cannot be represented at all, but can only take place: time.

One of the attempts to bring these questions together is my performance piece *Hamlet*. We will deal with it after the break.

PART TWO—HAMLET

Julia*n/Hamlet

My father died a couple of weeks ago.
I don't actually want to talk about it on the stage because it's so private.

He couldn't do much anymore at the end.
He had difficulties with, like, motor skills.
But he was still really good at sensual and cognitive things.
And he could turn his head. Like this: -

Julia*n/Hamlet moves their head slowly

He had thought about getting help to die.
He wanted to be poisoned. He would have gone to Switzerland to do it.
But in the end his body just took over itself.

When he died he was in a hospital in Braunschweig.
I was with my mother and my sister.
He was hardly present any more, was breathing heavily.
I let a bit of music play from my laptop.
We were, like, all bent over him like in a painting and held his hands
but he barely reacted to it.
Then the nurse took a cotton bud with some water and wiped it across his lips.
He made a couple of abstract movements breathing quickly.

And then he was dead.

Seeing how this body carried that out by itself, as if at the end it was demanding
its own rights—that was kind of impressive.
That moved me.
So, I'm just, like, standing there and staring at this body, which is lying there like
a statue and its face looks like a mask.
And then all of a sudden it's all kind of strange.
I notice how my brain is busy synchronizing the image of this lifeless body with
the memory of a living person that had just been there.
But it's not possible.
There is only noise.

walks to the side, drinks water out of a bottle
then goes back to center stage

A year ago I shaved my hair off.
Up until then I had had very long, light-brown hair.
Sometimes I wore it down and sometimes tied up, with different clasps in it.
I got a lot of compliments for it. Which I quite liked.
And then one day I completely shaved off my hair.
And then my eyebrows.
I think it is interesting to remove these attributes and to pixelate my exterior self.
As a form of self-manipulation.
And the erotic dimensions of it fascinate me, I don't really know why, it's just so naked and round.
And what I like about it is challenging what's considered healthy.
But that's not so easy.
You have to train it.

11

Hamlet is a solo piece with performer and musician Julia*n Meding[2], performed together with a baroque music ensemble. The piece came out in Basel in September 2016.

For this work, Julia*n Meding and I have tried to create a person on stage who is in the zone between fiction and reality, between a documentary-biographical "I" and the "I" of the Shakespearean character. In other words, a person who is Julia*n and Hamlet at the same time.

I have said in the beginning that I sometimes call my plays site-specific, even if they are set in the theatre itself. They are site-specific, because I want to explore the conventions of theatre and make them perceptible. One of these conventions is that theatre is a place of observation and its consequence: evidence.

You could say that theatre is a machine that creates visibility. This fact is already implied in the Greek term *theatron*. The theatre is a visual apparatus. On a stage, people expose themselves to the gaze of others. They let themselves be looked at, evaluated, sometimes criticized. This results in a vulnerability that is also inscribed in this apparatus. Visibility is vulnerability. *Hamlet* is in many ways about precisely this blending of these two qualities. It is about the theatre as a place where the audience observes the performer Julia*n, while Julia*n reflects

---

2 Although Julia*n now identifies as non-binary, audience members are likely to perceive the body on stage as male. Julia*n began to identify as non-binary only four years after the premiere. For the conception of the evening and during rehearsals, we assumed the character Julia*n/Hamlet to be a male-connoted person who would also be identified by the audience as a "he" —albeit in an unusual, interesting interpretation of "heness". Since Hamlet is always also Julia*n and Julia*n is always also Hamlet in the performance, the linguistic representation of their gender identity in this lecture is aligned with Julia*n's later decision. It is a change made retrospectively.

and mirrors back this situation of being observed. The play with this situation and the resulting theatrical present is the material of this performance.

12

As you know of course, Shakespeare's "Hamlet" is itself a play that is self-reflexive in many ways; a quality that is most clearly visible in the famous mousetrap scene, in which the play within the play refers to the mechanisms of the whole drama. A crucial role in Shakespeare's dramaturgy is thereby played by the question of whether the protagonist Hamlet is suffering from a mental illness or whether he is only pretending and, to a certain extent, appropriating the attributes of "sick" and "unpredictable" in order to subvert the governing rules of the court. It is the great "reality question" of this drama, with which it simultaneously demonstrates its own consciousness as a play—that is, as a genre in which actors on a stage pretend to be someone else and thus invite the watching audience to participate in a game about appearance and reality.

This blending between "real" and "acted" and the indistinguishability of these two attributes resulting from the dramaturgy were the key conceptual point for our show, which is documentary and non-documentary at the same time.

[Nikitin shows an excerpt from the play.]

In this scene, Julia *n/Hamlet talks about the death of their father. In audience discussions after the play, audience members have often said that they found this scene uncomfortable. Not necessarily because they felt the description of Julia*n's father's dying to be too intimate—for some it was—but because Julia*n speaks this text in such an supercilious and distanced way. Many feel this stilted, arrogant form is inappropriate for a documentary-biographical text dealing with the real death of a real person. In fact, I feel the same way. It is important to mention in this context that the very first sentence Julia*n speaks after entering the stage at the beginning of the play is similar to the sentence I started my lecture with this morning. This first sentence is: "Good evening. My name is Julia*n Meding".

So the piece begins with the performer introducing themselves with their real name. The audience can deduce this from the fact that this name is identical to the one with which the performer is listed in the credits in the program booklet. This booklet with the non-fictional credits has a certain structural similarity to a passport or ID. A document records the presence of a person and constitutes them in the legal sense. It testifies to their identity. Of course, a program booklet is not a legal document, but since it works with legally authenticated facts and identities—the names of the people and institutions involved—it cannot be detached from the juridical either.

This brief digression is important because in many documentary theatre productions and autobiographical performances of the last 20 years, this presenting of oneself under one's real name is always a decisive dramaturgical moment. It is a sign that the people on stage are beginning to present *themselves*. In a classical performance of *Hamlet*, it is clear that the person on stage is not Hamlet, but an actor or actress portraying Hamlet. Therefore, the question of whether we "believe" this character hardly ever arises seriously, only whether we find them credible. On the other hand, the moment a real person begins to say things about themselves—or about others—under their real name on a stage, a different frame of reference is opened up.

So there are good reasons, in the sense of the documentary convention that is initiated by such an introduction, to assume that what Julia*n Meding tells about themselves in the piece is indeed autobiographical, or that it could at least—potentially—be autobiographical.

In our *Hamlet*, this question of identity—legal, poetic, documentary and non-documentary identity—continues in other moments that reinforce the audience's perception that what this person on stage is saying is true. For example, the moment we just saw in which Julia*n said, "I shaved my hair," and then reported that they also shaved their eyebrows right away. The audience, who have already been looking at this person for about 15 minutes and wondering what it is about their face—apart from the obvious wet-shaven baldness—that irritates them so much realize at that moment that what Julia*n has just told them is actually true. It's not a mask, it's not just a text. For good empirical reasons, the audience assumes that hardly any actors and actresses would shave their hair and eyebrows just for the stage—then to have to walk around like that in private. So the performance is really about Julia*n. However, not enclosed in a documented, legitimized, juridical identity, but as a physical presence, a body in time.

In a way, *Hamlet* is more about performance art than theatre: Julia*n really brings their whole physicality into the play as a theme. The moment when they mention shaving their eyebrows is very important. If up to this point the audience was still undecided about the possible biographical character of the play, at this moment at the latest a seemingly inescapable truth emerges through the physical evidence, which seems to underpin the non-fictional character of the whole evening. The shaved hair and eyebrows are the ingredients—one could also speak of circumstantial evidence—that construct Julia*n as a credible witness.

According to the conventions of the documentary, it also seems plausible that Julia*n's father actually died a few weeks before the premiere of the performance and became the verbatim material that Julia*n and I decided to integrate. It somehow happens to fit in with the fact that Shakespeare's *Hamlet* begins with the protagonist's dead father. It complements the idea of a double body that is both Julia*n and Hamlet. And, I can say this much, in fact, many audience members thought Julian*s father had died, even friends who are quite close to Julia*n and had not seen him over the preceding weeks owing to the play's rehearsal schedule.

But it is simpler than that. The story of the dead father is my story. It was my father who died a few weeks before the premiere.

13

As I mentioned this morning, most of my plays are about the people on stage. *Hamlet* is a play about Julia*n. Julia*n is not a classically trained actor, but a musician and performer. *Hamlet* is the third project we've worked on together, but it's the first solo. The show is very much about them—at the same time it's about Hamlet.

When you see Julia*n in this play as a performer entering the stage and speaking to the audience in this special, kind of annoying way, it's hard not to wonder: What's wrong with this person? Why are they pretending? Why are they acting so strangely? Are they really like that or are they just faking? These are also the questions people usually ask about Hamlet: Why does he act so strangely? Is he really like that or is he just pretending?

You could say *Hamlet* is a documentary piece about a person who leaves you wondering if they are really like that or just pretending. It is a documentary work about the construction of identity and reality and about the (im)possibility of a reliable representation of the world. It is a documentary work about the impossibility of the documentary.

Hamlet is both. It is documentary and non-documentary at the same time. The character on stage is Julia*n and Hamlet at the same time. The character is non-Julia*n and non-Hamlet at the same time. The person on stage *is* and *is not* at the same time.

14

To put it a bit more directly and also presumptuously (because what is art without presumption?): *Hamlet* is a proposal of an alternative documentary theatre. Most of the texts in the play are biographical, some are based on my biography, others are connected to Julia* n's biography, but they are all one hundred percent connected to Julia*n's body, which functions as a document in this play itself. The play is an attempt to merge Julia*n and Hamlet into each other, inventing a character that is on the one hand, real, but in any case, ambivalent. The play is an attempt to create a queer version of the documentary. With this, I don't mean a documentary about a queer person, but a form of documentary that is itself queer in its structure.

Even though the evening is unquestionably marked by queer experience in terms of its mindset—I am gay and Julia*n identifies as non-binary—I have held back on the term "queer" in any public descriptions of the piece, for example, in announcement texts. We do not explicitly take up queer discourses in the play, it does not engage in any kind of "queer critique" of society, nor is it about a politicized minority perspective. In their explicit verbalization, queer discourses are often very academic, as is their vocabulary, which sometimes has an exclusivity that I found unproductive for *Hamlet*. One quickly pigeonholes oneself into an identity, which can be right and necessary as a strategy for political activism, but quickly becomes constricting for theatre.

Hamlet is rather an evening about dying, about the vulnerable and transient body, about the construction of reality and identity: "Universal" themes that are also at the center of Shakespeare's *Hamlet*. The only difference is that now a queer person has appropriated this Hamlet. It is precisely this act of appropriation that constitutes all queerness here.

Perhaps this could be a definition of a queer form of documentary: A form of documentation that does not depict reality, but appropriates it in order to participate in and act upon the definition of what "reality" or a "collective norm" is. This has nothing to do with sexuality at first, but a lot to do with the production of self-images and the world images that grow out of them.

15

In terms of the discussion about the montage of materials that we had earlier, I would say: My approach is that I mostly try to stage the documents as part of a larger artistic composition and less to show the documents in the sense of evidence. As you could see, Julia*n has a special way of presenting his alter ego on stage—a particular way of moving on stage, a particular way of speaking, which on the one hand has something aggressive about it, but also something ironic, unserious. Even if the content is sometimes documentary, its form of expression by Julia*n is anything but sober. To a certain extent, the document enters a kind of feverish state. All this, in turn, contrasts very strongly with the autobiographical, documentary quality of the text. It contrasts with the realism of the documentary. This double, opposing movement is important in both opening up the connection between the civilian person Julia*n Meding and the stage person Julia*n/Hamlet.

This *being and not being at the same time* is central. It is a possible formula for sovereignty—for the possibility of deciding one's own being and its suspension.

16

In most cases, I am interested in working with performers who have knowledge and experience of the stage, but without having been professionally trained and exposed to the ideological influence that most drama schools maintain to this day.

I try to work with the knowledge of the performers, with their biography, and with the knowledge I have as a director, plus the possibilities of the theatre. I attempt to create something that is more than just the sum of our working constellation. As an artist, I am basically not so much interested in referring to an already existing reality but rather in fabricating a new one—a potential reality, a reality imbued with a heightened atmosphere of the potential, of the possible. A reality that is not fictional, not an "as if," but really real, even if it could only exist within the framework of two hours in the setting of a stage (which is itself, of course, a real setting). This possible reality makes much use of documentary grammar, of the documentary aesthetic, and of an aesthetic of the real. But it shifts it at the same time. This shift is possible with emancipated, sovereign performers, performers who can make decisions, who also have the ability to say "no." To this day, I find it amazing how few truly emancipated, professionally trained actors there are; it seems that the system that produces them actually prevents actors from emancipating themselves and achieving sovereignty—which, I suspect, must have micro-political institutional reasons.

In work with Julia*n, it was always about finding out how to become „strong" on stage. Part of being strong, especially in this play, meant learning how to reject the audience; being able to say "no" and: "I don't need your approval." Julia*n performs in a way that doesn't make people immediately like them. On the contrary. Many viewers report that they dislike this character in the first 30-40 minutes, even find them repulsive in some cases. We lose part of the audience in this first part of the play. The other part stays, either out of curiosity about what happens next with this person, or because they find the repulsiveness attractive at the same time.

After a while, however—this was also part of our bet—the audience that we have not lost begins to get used to this person, they spend time with them and gradually begin to recognize themselves in them—in their anger, in their querulous behavior, in their vulnerability. They realize that this person talks about death, they talk about illness, and about how the body becomes vulnerable. In the end, the audience realizes in a way that it is about them.

So probably the most crucial aspect in *Hamlet* is: Time. Documents can be very static. But you can counteract that stasis by creating a place where the person on stage has the ability to transform. *Hamlet* is not about facts that you put into a montage. Instead, it's very much about the transformation of Julia*n, it's very much about the relationship between them and the audience. Julia*n is alone on stage for 90 minutes. You watch this person and spend 90 minutes with them in the theatre space. That's what's theatrical about it: the transformation you experience while sharing space and time with—or against—each other. This possibility of transformation, of change, is an essential aspect of this play. It means creating an experience in which reality has the capacity to not be already fixed, to change, to be contingent. Or to put it a little less abstractly: in my experience, the tension of a theatre evening lies in its unpredictability.

17

My initial question when I started working on documentary theatre and with documentary materials about 12 years ago was: how can I liberate the documentary from the legal context from which it comes?

It is the document that ultimately makes us legal persons. Attached to these legal documents are certain markers of our identity, such as our birthday, our name that is given and repeated to us, our gender, the political and social classification of our bodies. The legal document of the passport links us to "our" nationality and associates us with an ethnic background.

Ultimately, this kind of legal documentation classifies our lives into certain categories, and these categories themselves influence our lives, our self-perception, our external perception, our world. These categories are real—in the sense that they are effective. They are connected to the law.

My wish is to see what a form of documentary theatre could be that has broken away from this juridical, representational context and does not force the people on stage—and thus also in the auditorium, because that is what it is all about—into a self-being, into a product of representative violence, but enables them as complex existences and contradictory forms of being.

HAMLET

Boris Nikitin

TEXT Boris Nikitin and Julia*n Meding

https://tinyurl.com/Nikitin-Hamlet

ENGLISH TRANSLATION FROM THE GERMAN Dora Kapusta

WITH Julia*n Meding
DIRCTOR Boris Niktin
SONGS Julia*n Meding and Uzrukki Schmidt

PREMIERE September 24, 2016, Kaserne Basel, Switzerland
AUTHOR RIGHTS Verlag schaefersphilippen, Köln, 2016

PROLOGUE

Julia*n comes on stage, wearing a wolf mask

Good evening.
My name is Julia*n Meding.
I am a musician and performance artist.

Some information before we begin:

yells

This is not theatre.
This is not a performance.
This not a concert.
This is not real life.
This is not reality.
And it's not the first act either.

First Song.
Julia*n stops singing in the middle of the song, walks in front of the audience.
The music stops.
Julia*n takes off the mask. We see a young person, their hair completely shaved,
watching at the audience. Julia*n silently walks the boundary of the stage.

I

Tonight I am standing here in front of you on the stage.
It is about bodies.
And reality.
About something that's tipping over.
We are here in the theatre. You can see and hear everything that I do.
Everything that I divulge to you, is a matter of public record.
You can appropriate it. You can take it home with you.
You can try to identify with me and my story. And with this body.

walks, observes

But, on the other hand, this is also a safe place.
Because this here is not reality.
Rather, it is an artificial situation.
Because there's always the possibility of fiction.

walks, observes

So, when I show you my body, for example,
when I tell you the story of my childhood,
or of my problems
then it is all ripped from everyday life and from real life.
It is no longer verifiable.
And that is why I can make myself completely public here
and put myself up for discussion.
Because these things split off from my real body
and from the real identities that I create out there in everyday life
and enter into a relationship with this space.

walks, observes

Everything becomes material.
For example, what if I now told you that I'm not Julia*n Meding at all,
but actually Julia*n Schmidt. Or Urzukki Schmidt.
And if I tell you that I'm attracted to people who wear raincoats.
Or that I have a clinical anxiety disorder,
which is why I always wear camouflage when I'm out in town.
You see, my examples would have to be less spectacular.
If I tell you that I don't ingest any warm meals, only raw food, because I think that
the energy of the plants stays better conserved.
Or that I have 10 pairs of running shoes at home, of which I never wear any pair
more than once in 10 days.
Then you can put that down to this person here.
You can tie it to this body.
That is my offer.
Interpreting things into this body that is moving in front of you.

walks, observes

But when this body leaves the stage it will no longer be the same one.
This body only exists on the stage.
It will not be there before or afterward.
It is, so to speak, a phantom.

As I already said, I am a musician.
And I have brought a few songs with me.

Second song.
*In the middle of the song Julia*n drops the microphone stand on the floor. The*
music stops.
*Julia*n looks at the audience, observes it.*

II

There is a village there that I come from.
It's called Rütten. It is located between Braunschweig and Hannover
and it is surrounded by countryside and a network of country roads.

There are two neighboring villages.
On the one side is Wasbüttel, and on the other side is Warnbüttel.
There's a restaurant in Warnbüttel, where there's schnitzel with potatoes and
schnitzel with croquettes.
There's also a gas station with a car wash and a vacuum.
And there's "Carpet Centre."

walks, observes

Rütten is built around a village green. It's actually like a square or a hexagon,
made up of streets with houses on both sides. And in the middle there used to be
pasture land. There used to be quite a few farms, and they used to be able to put
the cows out to graze.
Now there's one of those housing developments.
It's all built-up.
There's those typical housing development houses with clinker and red bricks.
And everything is, like, around a front yard, with a hedge or a fence.
And everything looks very clean.
And I must say that I find this artifice kind of interesting. It's really kind of wicked
to walk around in there at night.

When my parents first moved there, they tried to assimilate.
But then they began to distance themselves from it.
I don't know, they probably wanted to keep up their self-image of being teachers
and part of the educated middle class.

Julia*n observes the audience.

My father died a couple of weeks ago.
I don't actually want to talk about it on the stage because it's so private.

He couldn't do much anymore at the end.
He had difficulties with, like, motor skills.
But he was still really good at sensual and cognitive things.
And he could turn his head. Like this:

Julia*n moves their head slowly

He had thought about getting help to die.
He wanted to be poisoned. He would have gone to Switzerland to do it.
But at the end his body just took over itself.

When he died he was in a hospital in Braunschweig.
I was with my mother and my sister.
He was hardly present any more, was breathing heavily.
I let a bit of music play from my laptop.
We were, like, all bent over him as in a painting and held his hands
but he barely reacted to it.

Then the nurse took a cotton bud with some water and wiped it across his lips.
He made a couple of abstract movements, breathing quickly.

Then he was dead.

Julia*n observes the audience.

Seeing how this body carried that out by itself, as if, at the end, it was demanding
its own rights—that was kind of impressive.
That moved me.
So, I'm just, like, standing there and staring at this body, which is lying there like
a statue and its face looks like a mask.
And then all of a sudden it's all kind of strange.
I notice how my brain is busy synchronizing the image of this lifeless body with
the memory of a living person that had still been valid only a moment earlier.
But it's not possible.
There is only noise.

Since then I haven't been able to localize that person in my head anymore.
It has become a memory without a body or place that I could fix him to.
It is everywhere.
And I think that that is the reason why some people suddenly think they're seeing
ghosts.
Because the memory of the person is so strong but that person isn't there any-
more.
You know that that person, that body isn't at home sleeping. Or in the hospital in
bed. Or here on the stage.
They have just become an image.

*Julia*n walks to the side, drinks water out of a bottle, then goes back to
center stage.*

A year ago I shaved my hair off.
Up until then I had very long, light-brown hair.
Sometimes I wore it down and sometimes tied up, with different clasps in it.
I got a lot of compliments for it. Which I quite liked.
And then one day I completely shaved off my hair.
And then my eyebrows.
I think it is interesting to remove these attributes and to pixelate my exterior self.
As a form of self-manipulation.
And the erotic dimensions of it fascinate me, I don't really know why, it's just so naked and round.
And what I like about it is challenging to what's considered healthy.
But that's not so easy.
You have to train it.

walks to the left and gets a chair and a guitar. Brings them to the center.

I prepared a few songs for this evening.
After all, I am a musician and I come up with music and texts.
And for some reason I had the feeling that this song fits really well here.
Maybe because it has something to do with the text here that came before.
And it's called: "Everything's so nice."

Third song.
Julia*n breaks off the song, drops the guitar. Stands up from the chair.

III

Near my village there's a forest.
Well, I have always thought that it was a forest. I always went there as a kid and ran around and went off the paths and kind of ran around the groves and stuff.
But one day I realized that it's not a forest at all. It's a FOREST PLANTATION.
And that they were carrying out forestry operations there.
And that the trees are actually only there so that at some day somebody can saw them down and turn them into wood.
And that's not a proper forest at all.

Julia*n observes the audience.

I didn't just bring songs with me, but also experiences from my biography.
And I have no idea how you see it, but for me it is an ambivalent but also interesting matter. Making yourself public in a context like this. And just talking about things and stuff.
But, of course, there's also risk involved.

I think it has to do with this invisible line, here at the front, between this side of the space and the other side...

And a story that I think is kind of fitting, it goes like this:

A while ago I was in a clinic.
It wasn't so long ago,
I wasn't doing so well.
Physically or mentally.
I had to stay there for a while and I was surrounded there by all kinds of bodies.
And they were moaning. Some loud and some quiet.

Some of them couldn't control their functions anymore—They vomited on their blankets or on their mattresses or pissed their beds.
And diagonally across from me there was someone who always held a teddy bear tight in her arms, and she reminded me of my gran. And she always said to the nursing staff that she wanted to die. And she always grinned: Like this.

And I, I wasn't allowed to leave my bed. That means I needed support dealing with my excrement. And I don't know either. I found it kind of difficult.
Because it kind of felt like a loss of control.
But then there was, like, a moment, when I kind of noticed that everything was shifting, and that somehow some pressure had been released somewhere.

And I thought:
Fuck it! I don't fucking care!
It's a kind of utopian place.
It's closed and detached.
Nobody has to have control of themselves or pull themselves together.
Everyone is sick and that's okay. And it doesn't matter who is who.

> Julia*n observes the audience for some time.
> Moves around.

One day I noticed that I actually enjoyed subjecting myself to the gaze of others and letting myself be objectified.
Because it stretches the norm.
Of course, it's not that easy, sometimes it's quite hard.
But it lets me "participate."
And become visible.
And when I am standing on the stage then I try to use that.
Of course it does something to me, but also with the person who is looking at me, too.

Julia*n observes the audience.
Walks around.
Sits on the chair in the middle of the stage.

I just ask myself to what extent my actuality has anything to do
with my activity.
I don't know if you have it too, this need for activity.
Yeah of course, everybody wants recognition, otherwise they just die out.
But that's also connected to the activity that I have—with my body, with my
thinking, my speech, my gaze.
The word for the potency of activity, for the degree of influence
is: power.
Those who can influence reality have power.
Those who can't influence it don't have power.
That's all there is to it.

So, I don't know, it's a very banal example, but e.g.
a model.
He takes a new suit from the clothes hanger and puts it on.
Or then he shaves his hair off.
That's a form of power.
And it produces: Happiness.

And if I lose my abilities, and lose them more and more, if I notice that I don't have
any influence on reality at all anymore.
As if my powers didn't even exist anymore.
Reality is indifferent toward me, for reality it's not even relevant if I'm there. Or
not.
Then I notice: I WON'T BE ABLE TO BARE IT.
This feeling of impotence and powerlessness, as if your own body is at a standstill,
as if it weren't there anymore and time is passing without you.
I CAN'T STAND IT.

That's depression. But it's nothing clinical.

And the question is: how do I deal with this powerlessness?
I have to interrupt it.
Somehow create a gap, a distance.
There are two forms of interruption.
The one is: I destroy something.
I take a stone, throw it through a window, the window shatters and then there is
a moment of happiness because I notice: I am relevant. I influence reality and it
changes.
I have done something. I have worked. That's a good feeling. A feeling of power.

That's something that I want to keep. And that's why I might throw another stone. And notice how I'm feeling a bit more secure again, in my body and in my skin, because I have the feeling that the world does give a shit about me.
Because I can change it. It's possible for me to throw stones.
Or to blow something up.

The other possibility is: I direct the stone toward myself.

Now how does this feeling of impotence come about?
It's quite simple: When there are enough people who tell you that you are stupid, then you also think that you are actually stupid.
That's reality: Repetition.
It's like a knife and you use it to scratch it into your brain bit by bit.

And when people give you the feeling that you're not worth anything
THEN YOU ARE ACTUALLY NOT WORTH ANYTHING.
Because, that you're not daft and that you are worth something, you haven't learned that. Unfortunately, nobody taught you.
Bad luck.

That's why you wanted to get rid of it, to destroy it, to plunge it in, to extinguish it in a physical or mental intervention.
And finally to not be scared of the pain anymore.
And the injuries.
And then to jump.

Julia*n takes the guitar and starts playing the fourth song. It's a happy song. During the song, a baroque ensemble enters the stage and starts accompanying Julia*n.
Julia*n goes to the microphone and makes an announcement.

Hi everyone. Welcome to the theatre, to this piece with the title "Hamlet".
Here on this stage, in this space.
This is not the official intermission of this evening. And this is not the second act. And at this point of the official intermission, I also don't want to forget to introduce our musicians, who constitute the award-winning ensemble "The Musical Garden."
It's a baroque ensemble by the way.
Yes, dear audience, I hope that you're all doing well. You all have reason to.

Julia*n goes back to the guitar and finishes the song together with the ensemble.
Stares at the audience for some time, sitting on the chair.

IV

A low, atmospheric sound is emerging.
Julia*n puts the guitar on their lap and changes their attitude. Gets a bit softer.

Reality has somehow flipped over.
That's the impression Hamlet is confronted with.
The impression is that the world has turned upside down.
On the one hand, into something threatening and grotesque—it's flipped over—
and yet, at the same time, it's been asserting all along that this is not the case.

That's his conflict, all the time.

And he's trying to make his position clear and communicate that something is
not okay here.
That something is somehow wrong.
The whole system has flipped into injustice.
The legislature is, in a sense, no longer in the right.
And that puts him in a borderline state emotionally, because somehow that has
to be seen.

But it doesn't work. It's not seen or heard at first.
And then he gets louder.
The confrontation becomes stronger and stronger and it becomes clearer and
clearer that this experience of injustice nonetheless remains.
And that's why he becomes louder and louder, and then at some point it's no
longer possible to overhear him.
And the reaction of this system is then to pathologize him.
"You're crazy," they say, "that's why it's like this." "Everything is fine here...You,
however, are acting kind of weird and saying strange things".

And the thing is that he is indeed destabilized. So one can say, "Yes, that is clear
to see, you are unstable, so you are crazy and therefore everything you say is
wrong. And that's why we don't need to listen to you now."
It's a kind of incapacitation. Because otherwise he could become a problem.

Therefore, he changes the strategy.
He appropriates the attributions "insane" and "sick." He affirms them and starts
to work with them. He starts to understand them as material and to play with
them—according to his rules.

Only: Nobody can know when he does this or when he started with it.
It's unpredictable.
And that's what I find kind of interesting.

scratches the strings of the guitar, making a metallic noise

I feel that this system is violent.
I think it's totally obvious that it's like that. But I have the impression that this reality is working all the time to legitimize itself and to constantly send out the message that everything is right and that everything is okay. And I think it needs that. Because otherwise it would collapse immediately.

The string players of the baroque ensemble are starting to create ambient sounds.

In my life I have often felt that I am on the receiving end of stuff that's just not visible.
And that's the reason why I needed a really long time to be sure that it exists at all.
Whether I am just imagining it or if what I experience as a form of violence actually exists.
If there is really an external cause, or whether it is after all a problem that I create for myself, or if the problem is the way that I deal with it.

So, I can't be categorized.

But that's what I'm supposed to be, and so it's my risk to take or my problem to overcome.
Or to cope with.
And it's so totally clear that that's the way it is and that's why I can't bring that in or that's why I can't criticize that.

But I am getting closer to that!
It is my hope that I can develop a gaze that is so precise that I can notice things that are happening and distinguish and name them.
And then maybe I can organize and show solidarity or stay in spaces where I feel safe.

For a long time, I thought that I was falling out of everything, that there were no such spaces for me.
Where I can show everything about me and publish myself.
And where we can give ourselves new names.

*Julia*n stands up, walks towards the audience.*

We have the right to have secrets.
But I would actually really like it if we didn't need them.
If we could pull the things we're ashamed of more toward the outside.

The secret is there: I am done.

Often I was so overwhelmed by the expectations that I had of myself, that I thought:

I can't do this anymore, I won't manage, I don't function anymore!

And then you withdraw. You go to your room. You're totally screwed by something. You do the reproductive work on yourself at home.

But if you expose it again and that would be a huge risk for you,

then that would strengthen the whole thing.

I have felt somehow exposed to it, for a very long time, even since I was very little.

Nevertheless, I was always confronted with being looked at.

And the question is whether you say: "Stop. I have a right to be viewed as normal".

Or that you say: "Yes," and "Fuck you and your system of values".

But you can't do that the whole time, because it's too hard.

And I wouldn't do it just now because I would be scared of the consequences.

For example, now, here, here and now on the stage, I wouldn't say: "Fuck you and your authoritarian expectations, fuck you and your emancipatory aspirations, fuck you—....."

I wouldn't want to say that here.

Julia*n gets louder.

Maybe we will be able to experience a moment of solidarity with each other tonight.

Is this space here tonight suitable for that?

The more I think about it, the more I realize that this here is maybe one of the last possible spaces where we can achieve this moment of creating solidarity.

Because we all have the need to live out our propensities!

starts moving strangely and jumping, the strings are getting louder

What we are missing is solidarity! WHAT WE ARE MISSING IS SOLIDARITY!

Because we all have the need to live out our propensities!

And in reality we all do it too. But we don't talk about it.

We are ashamed and go home. And why?

starts screaming

I'M JUST ABOUT TO START DOING IT!

TO TURN MY DEFICITS OUTWARDS AND CLAIM SOLIDARITY!

AND THIS EVENING YOU HAVE THE CHANCE TO PRODUCE SOLIDARITY AS WELL AND AT THE SAME TIME RECEIVE SOLIDARITY FROM THIS COMMUNITY

THAT WE ARE TONIGHT AND THAT YOU HAVE PROCURED BY PURCHASING AN ENTRY TICKET.
OR MAYBE BY PURCHASING A REDUCED-PRICE ENTRY TICKET!

BECAUSE THIS ENTRY TICKET IS A CONTRACT!
IT'S THE ENTRY TICKET TO AN EVENT, THE ENTRY TICKET TO ENTERTAIN-MENT, BUT IT CAN BE ALSO THE ENTRY TICKET TO A NEW FORM OF COMMUNITY THAT WILL CONVERGE HERE TONIGHT.
WE DON'T NEED ANY SECRETS! WE DON'T NEED ANY PRIVACY!
WHAT WE ARE MISSING IS SOLIDARITY!

Julia*n exhales.
Grabs the microphone, goes to the video camera and looks into the lens.
Julia*n's face is now projected on the big screen at the back of the stage.
The strings continue the ambient sounds. Julia*n takes the microphone and talks slowly. Very, very slowly.

V

It is my
hope
to develop a
gaze

that is so
precise
that I notice the things
that happen

and can differentiate between
them
and name
them.

And that I can spend
times in spaces
in which I am safe.

But what kind of spaces are they?
Spatial spaces?
Temporal spaces?
Cognitive spaces?

Being able to evade
the permanent demand
for consistency.

10 am: to be.
10 pm: not to be.
Not having to
be.
Not having to be
me.

Not having to live.
Being able to live.
2 pm: both.
Living and dying
at the same time.

Julia*n walks towards the screen. Some old family videos are shown, a child's birthday party, people swimming in the sea. Julia*n makes some stretching movements in front of the screen.
He lies on the floor and continues with the movements. The ensemble starts a piece—something between "Le Sacre du printemps" and "Jaws." They are continuously increasing the volume of the piece. Julia*n stands up, takes the microphone, starts to count the acts:

This is not the third act. This is not the fourth act. This is not the fifth act. This is not the sixth act. This is not the seventh act. This is not the eighth act. This is not the ninth act. This is not the tenth act. This is not the eleventh act. This is not the twelfth act. This is not the thirteenth act. This is not the fourteenth act. This is not the fifteenth act. This is not the sixteenth act. This is not the seventeenth act…

The ensemble keeps on increasing in volume, while Julia*n is counting and counting dozens of acts, slowly getting louder with the music.

This is not the 90th
act.
And this is not the 91st
act.
And this is not the 92nd
act.
And this is not the 93rd
act.

Julia*n continues counting, they are all getting louder, reaching a kind of climax, Julia*n starts yelling the acts

AND THIS IS NOT THE 108th
ACT
AND THIS IS NOT THE 109th
ACT

    yells

AND NOW:
CONCENTRATION AND RELAXATION!
CONCENTRATION AND RELAXATION!
HEY YO, YOU THERE! RELAX YOUR NECK, RELAX YOUR NECK!
RELAX YOUR FOREARM! RELAX YOUR UPPER ARM!
CONCENTRATION AND RELAXATION!
CONCENTRATION AND RELAXATION!

Julia*n drops to the floor, exhausted and somewhat dramatic.
Julia*n lies in front of the screen. The ensemble keeps playing. The screen shows the entrance of a courtyard. A person appears in the video. He is walking strangely. Then another one. The ensemble stops playing.

The video takes us into a building. A person in a wheelchair. The camera follows a staircase. A waiting room, a TV is on, people in wheelchairs are watching. Some are sleeping.
The strings start playing a continuous high tone.

VI

Julia*n starts speaking very slowly into the microphone, lying on the floor, while the video shows what now becomes visible as a kind of a hospice. People in beds, long corridors, elderly people, people smiling into the camera.

You are
only half awake, I think.
Half awake
at the most.

And what
you are looking for
is a kind of revival.
An awakening
not as a linear process,
but as an invasion.

A waking up, where you
see the world with different
eyes for the first time.
With eyes that you never had before.

That's what I mean by awakening.

You are getting more and more tired.
I don't just mean the corporeal exhaustion
of everyday life.
Rather that total exhaustion,
that sets in bit by bit,
when you're somehow not running synchronously
with time.

When the world,
the way it presents itself,
and the world,
the way that you experience it,
aren't running synchronously.

And you think:
Now I would have to throw a stone through a window
to interrupt it.

But there's no window here.
And this isn't the third act. And not the fourth act either.
And not the fifth act. And not the sixth act.

   starts singing gently

Ich würde gerne ausgehn
Doch ich muss noch meine Haare föhnen

Sie sind fest, wie Beton
Und ich singe diesen Song

   the cello starts playing

Ich würde dich gerne sehen
Doch ich muss vor dem Spiegel stehen

Und ganz genau hinsehen
Das kannst du sicher gut verstehen

The harpsichord and the other strings start playing as well.

Ich würde gerne aufstehen
Doch ich muss schon wieder schlafen gehen
Um ausgeruht auszusehen
Das kannst du sicher gut verstehen[i]

The video freezes, Julia*n stops singing, getting up, walking to the front of the stage.
There Julia*n takes a mask (it's in the likeness of the Emperor from Star Wars).
Stares at the audience for a while.
The baroque ensemble suddenly stops playing.

The king is dead.
Long live the queen.

The king is dead.
Long live the queen.

Julia*n takes the microphone.

There are a lot of people who say
that the crises of today are based on the fact that the fathers are somehow absent.
That's the biggest bullshit.

The king is dead. Long life the queen.

Yes. That's how it is.
Some play, others watch.

walks to the back of the stage, addressing the ensemble

I have thought about making an experimental video film. And you could make the music.

So there is this tower that is standing, like, alone on this field.
And it is being watched over by ravens.
And nobody can leave the tower, because otherwise they will be attacked by the ravens.
And there are two people who live in this tower and they are, like, together.
And they, you know, can't leave the tower but it's not so bad because they kind of have everything that they need.
And so there are quite a lot of books in the tower. And, like, sofas.

And they also have something to eat because there is this garden around the tower.
And there is stuff to drink.
And they lie on the sofas. They hold each other in their arms. And read the books.
And they, like, look out the window.
And the ravens fly around the tower.
And then one night one of them wakes up.
And notices that they are alone in the bed.
And the other person isn't there.
And they go down into the kitchen and fetch a bottle of beer.
And then they see the other person talking to the ravens.
And, like, summon them.
And tell them that they're not allowed to let anybody leave the tower.
And then you sort of think about what happens.
But then what happens?
Nothing.
And on the next day you see how they are both lying together on the sofas again.
Holding each other in their arms. And reading the books.
And the ravens are, like, flying around the tower.
And I thought that would be so nice because that could mean that the person thinks:
Oh well, that's pretty crazy. The other person, like, trapped me here.
But on the other hand I have everything I need.
And it's a pretty flattering compliment that they went out of their way to enchant ravens to keep me trapped in this place.

stares at the audience, then again at the ensemble

Award-winning baroque ensemble.
Hello, award-winning baroque ensemble.

crowned with awards
crowned with awards

crowned
crowned
crowned

Julia*n takes of the mask. Walks to the microphone stand.
Sings the last song titled "Drowned Body".

Drowned Body

Ich bin
Eine Wasserleiche
In deiner
Gerichtsmedizin

Ich liege
Auf deinem
Seziertisch
Die Wände sind alle
So clean

Die Fliesen
Schauen ein bisschen
Aus wie
In deinem Bad

Du wirst ein
Bisschen brauchen
Glaub ich
Denn meine Knochen
Sind ziemlich hart

Du schaust
In meine Augen
Doch mein Geheimnis
Verrate ich dir nicht

Du kannst es
Gern probieren
Doch ich glaube ich
Behalte es für mich

Ich bin
Eine Wasserleiche
Und ich wurde
Aus dem Fluss gefischt

Ich schwamm so
Darin herum und jetzt liege ich
Etwas hart
Auf deinem Seziertisch[ii]

Julia*n/Hamlet leaves the stage.

The End

---

i I'd love to go out
But I have to dry my hair
It's as hard as concrete
And I'm singing this song.

I'd love to see you
But I have to stand in front of the mirror
And look very carefully
I'm sure you understand.

I'd love to get up
But I have to get back to sleep
So I will look rested
I'm sure you understand

ii I am
A drowned body
In your forensic lab

I lie
On your
Autopsy table
The walls are all
So clean

The tiles
Looks a little
Like
In your bathroom

You will need
Some time
I think
My bones
Are quite hard

You look
Into my eyes
But I won't tell you
My secret
You can try
If you want
But I think I'll
Keep it for myself

I am
A drowned body
And I was fished
From the river

I swam about
In it and now I lie
Quite hard
On your autopsy table

Practice of Theatre—Rehearsal of Life

Lee Kyung-Sung

I would like to begin by introducing myself a little bit and also by introducing my personal connection to the Central Academy. My name is Kyung-Sung Lee, I am from Korea, and I am a theatre-maker, director and founder of the Korean creative group *Creative VaQi*. Unfortunately, I cannot speak Chinese, so I have to speak in English and use an interpreter. I am very happy to be invited to this kind of big and interesting ... not conference, but space where we can exchange our experiences and thoughts regarding theatre and art. I am really happy to be part of this, and my thanks goes to Kai Tuchmann. This theatre and art connected me and Kai Tuchmann as friends, and our friendship was also initiated by just this kind of platform for exchanging experiences and thoughts on theatre and art. Very wonderful things happen in a theatre-makers life. I also have an interesting personal connection to the Central Academy.

The Dream of Sancho at the Central Academy of Drama in Beijing, Dongcheng
© Create VaQi

When I had just graduated and founded a theatre company with my colleagues from the university, my first international tour brought me to the Central Academy. The piece was called *Dream of Sancho,* and it was based on Cervantes' novel.

We reinterpreted the text and made an outdoor performance, projecting a video on the outdoor wall of the Central Academy of Drama. I found a flyer from this time in storage, but that was a decade ago, and since then my work and aesthetic of making theatre have shifted a lot. Yet my first work did contain many creative seeds that blossomed in the future. Above all, at this time, what I needed to experience was an audience from a different culture.

Today, I will share how my company works and how I communicate with the society and culture I am from. I think the form of theatre always comes from a specific social or cultural context, because you always create a dialogue with the culture of the society you are from. I have been creating works not only in the theatre but also in the public space, outside of the theatre. Shifting my venue and platform helped me to create tension between art and life outside the theatre. I cannot go deep into each piece. But I will briefly introduce my findings and my strategy to deal with the places I was in.

Invitation 1 (2007) © Creative VaQi

Invitation was my first outdoor, site-specific creation after my graduation. When I was a student, I had two problems with the theatre I was learning from my professors. First, theatre, for me, was not powerful or real enough to capture life. The theatre on stage looked so fake to me. Even though the scene might be wonderful, you can see how it is constructed and made up from the side. To me, this was not strong enough to capture life. Secondly, as a director, I was not satisfied by constantly reinterpreting the text of the writer. As a director, I wanted to be the first interpreter of the world by myself. In the fine arts, the artist sees the world and creates. But as a theatre director, you always have to read a writer's text, and then through the text, you see the world. But I wanted to encounter the world through my own eyes. So, I started to look outside of the theatre. Outside I found more real life, actual life, I would say. As a young artist who had just graduated from university, no organizations offered me a venue. I had to find venues that were free of charge.

Invitation 2 (2007) © Creative VaQi

This was a very simple performance. At a crossing, you wait while the red light is on, and you cross during the green light. I wanted to create a meeting point in the middle, where people could recognize each other, so I opened a kind of wine party in the middle. When the red light is on, the curtain is closed, so you cannot really see who is waiting on the other side. I wanted to create an expectation: who am I going to meet when the green light comes on.

While I was preparing the wine party, I lived in that area, but I had to move to a different place, which was two kilometers away. I called one small truck to carry my furniture, but the truck was a bit too small. One couch was left behind, and I had to carry it together with my friend.

At the same crossing—I remember—the light was red. Because the couch was very heavy, I and my friend had to put the sofa down and we sat on it to wait for the signal. And that was a very special moment for me, because a couch is normally associated with a private space like a living room or your house, but when this intimate object is positioned in a public space, you are sitting in this private space—this was a very poetic moment. I found this was a clash between these two spaces. I started to think about where would be the most interesting area to put this couch and play with it, and I thought about the square, which is regarded as the most public realm in the city. At that time, there was a big debate about Gwanghwamun Square in Seoul City. The former mayor wanted to renovate the whole structure of the square: basically, the plan was to create a plaza in the middle with roads on both sides and the pedestrian walkways on the outside edges. The plan was to isolate the square in the middle of the highway. So many architects advised the mayor that if you want to make the square function, you have to connect the square with the walkways. But the mayor did not take the advice, and many people thought he wanted to prevent the people from gathering.

As you know, we had a massive kind of revolution, called the *Candle Revolution*, two years ago, to impeach the president. And actually, we made it work. Now we have a new president. During that time, people just walked on the highway and debated and covered all the roads.

Anyway, after the renovation, the square was transformed into a very nice looking park, but there were more than 600 surveillance cameras, and it was factually under the control of the authorities. There was only one way to exist in this public space. You could not be in the space and act autonomously—you always had to follow the public norms of behavior. Every time we tried to do something a little bit unusual, the police came and stopped us. This is a picture from our workshop.

Let Us Move Your Sofa (2010) © Creative VaQi

One thing I tried for the first time in this workshop was to answer these questions: How can we create an artwork together, not by one genius director or writer? How can we create texture and performance in a more ... I don't want to say democratic, but in a more equal way?

Map from *Let Us Move Your Sofa* (2010) © Creative VaQi

That was the first time I tried out this way of creating theatre that can be called a devised theatre. And so I invited not only actors but also an architect, and a chore-ographer, and a video artist. And for three months, we did a workshop and research on this area. Together, we all created a map based on our research of this space. The map was an exciting device for us to reflect on and represent the space.

We usually regard maps as a very neutral and objective way of representing the world. But actually, a map is a space onto which people project their subject-ive ways of representing the world.

For example, if you see the map of China from the 15ᵗʰ century, you can see how China has portrayed itself as the prominent center of the world and all other countries around it seem to be very small. By this, you can see how China regard-ed itself. For us, the square was not the green, well-established park; to us, it was more gloomy. On the map, we pointed out each spot where a performance was happening. And all those performances were happening at the same time. And out of this came the dramaturgical strategy for how we summed up the structure: We asked the audience to come to a certain point at six o'clock, gave them this map, and asked them to come back after one hour of walking. The audience could choose their own order of visit. We intended to create an individual experience in this space, not a mob or group experience. We aimed to establish an individual experience in this one way by pushing the limits of public space. But as you see, no one can experience the whole performance, because everything happens at the same time, and nobody sees the performance in the same order. So everybody will have their own experience and narrative of this performance. We called this an "open structure." But I have to say that the structure, this experiment failed in a way, because we set up an area that was too large to cover in one hour. For the audience, the area was too big to walk around. For some audiences, when they visited a place, everything was already finished. Some audiences were even just walking around the whole time and saw nothing. They came to us and com-plained. To them, it was not an "open structure" but a non-structure. To create an open structure, we had to be denser.

Kai forwarded me your questions that you came up with after he introduced me to your class, and one question was about the connection between internet space and public space.

Within the project *Let Us Move Your Sofa*, we created a character that we called "Shadow."

The public space was too bright, and everything was too positive—but we thought there is also negative energy and a dark side of the city. So this character observed all these dark sides of the city. She wandered around this very polished city.

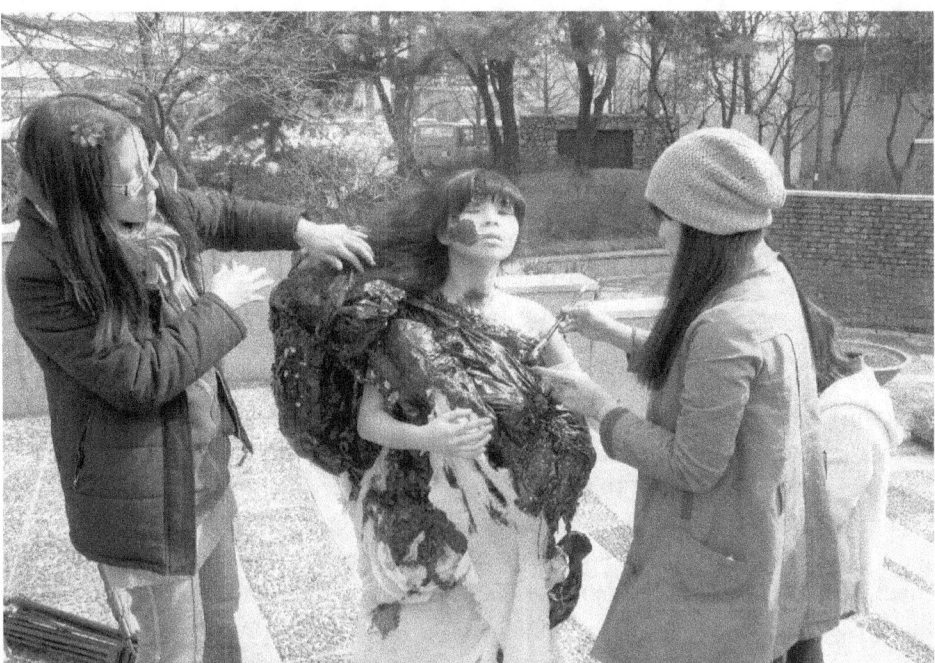

Making "Shadow" during the process of making *Let Us Move Your Sofa* (2010)
© Creative VaQi

2010 was the year Korean people started to use smartphones, and all the people took photos of this character and put them on the internet. This character was the top news on several websites. The actress who played her was very shocked and surprised about this. That was not our intention. We didn't expect these kinds of things to happen. We didn't expect that this wide use of smartphones would in-fluence our performance. Before our project, we asked the most significant media outlet in Korea if we could use the billboard at their building, but it was too ex-pensive for us. But when the character of the shadow became a huge internet phenomenon, they used the same billboard to display news about our perform-ance for free. That was a very ironic moment. Through this performance, we realized that although it looks "nice" in our public space, there are a lot of invisible restrictions. The performance can make these restrictions visible.

The next piece: After doing this big project in the public realm, I wanted to find out how we can bring the world outside the theatre to the stage. What kind of tension, what sort of aesthetic, what kind of strategy had to be found to do this? One day I read an article in the newspaper about a teenager that had murdered his parents to receive compensation money from the parents' insurance. The shocking point was that the teenager said he wanted to use the compensation money to buy himself a good car and a good house on the south side of the Han river. Maybe some of you know that Seoul is divided by the Han river, and the south side is called Gangnam and is relatively rich while Gangbuk, the north side, is economically poor. In this sense, the social structure in Seoul is very polarized. He was from a very poor area. This murder is about personal corruption, but we found it related to our social structure and could be considered as a symptom. Through the performance in the theatre, we aimed to make a connection to this murderer. Am I connected to the murderer? We felt connected to this tragedy. I wanted to make this connection visible on stage. So for our research period, our whole company visited the neighborhood where the murder happened, and we met the families, the friends of the teenager, and the policemen who arrested the murderer. We wanted to see what was happening in Gangbuk. We wanted to find out why a boy would do something like this. There are some interesting things that we found out during our visit. First, that neighborhood, even though it was economically poor, was still a very warm community. It was not like Gangnam, where everything is cold, and people just go for the money. Maybe in Chinese culture you also have this: In front of a house, we used to have a table where you sit together, eat together, talk together—like a meeting point. Seoul also used to have this but it all disappeared. But in this neighborhood, I still found a lot of these meeting points. But Korean society does not appreciate these values. We regard a town that allows such gatherings as underdeveloped. And the teenager who killed his parents had this habit of despising his own neighborhood. Additionally, this area was suffering from gentrification. The whole environment surrounding the teenager influenced his values and perspective on life. After the research period, we tried to transform our process and findings into a form of performance. We took a video the a subway. Geographically, it is an interesting thing: If you take the subway in this impoverished area and go just one station and cross one bridge, you already are in Gangnam. By this one bridge, you enter a very different world, and we were playing with this reality.

The actresses are like flight attendants in the airplane who give you tips on behaving in the different world after crossing the bridge: "Welcome to Gangnam/ You have to be reminded/The gravity here is different/You will be floating/ Please hold your credit cards/A kind of ghost appears/You have to take care of yourself in this area/At Gangnam station there are a lot of luxury shops."

When we were preparing this performance we were very poor, we didn't have much money. But during the rehearsal, one big advertising agency called me. Do you remember the performance that I did at the road crossing? This advertising agency asked me: "Can you create an advertisement using the crossroad concept advertising our pizza?" They would give us triple the amount of money we had during this time. I brought this issue to our team and asked them: "What do you think? Shall we do it or not?" Half of the company said: "Of course, let us take the money, we can spend it on our process and put it in our theatre"; the other half said: "Our initial goal, why we did the performance, was to create a meeting point, an encounter of strangers, and advertising a pizza does not make any sense to us and betrays our ideas." And me, I thought we could do it: "Let's get some money!" That was my opinion. But in the end, we decided not to do it. Discussing this question raised a lot of issues connected to the topic of our work.

Copyright © 2011 Creative VaQi All rights Reserved

The History of Gangnam, Spec-Tackle Epic of Ours (2011) © Creative VaQi

In order to confront an issue and to make something out of it, it is essential to be there, at the site, and to spend time there, so we try to visit and see what it is really like at a place—and in a way, this relates to an ethical perspective I will talk about later. To make a performance out of a social theme, I think the ethical issue is fundamental—and one way to approach it is to visit the place where it happened.

In 2014, I came back to the square again. A festival asked me to do an opening performance, and I decided to do something at the square where I had done *Let Us Move Your Sofa* four years ago. But now, four years later, that public space, Gwanghwamun Square, was totally changed. In 2010, Gwanghwamun Square was a very ordinary space, where people go to work or spend time after work. But on the 16th of April 2014, as some of you might know, a big ferry named Sewol sank. Most of the 300 dead passengers were high school students going on a field trip, and they drowned there, and the whole system failed to rescue them. A huge protest started to happen, initiated by the victims' families, and Gwanghwamun Square was the central spot where they gathered. It was a challenging place. There were hundreds of photos of students who had not been found, crying families, angry people. It was hard to be in that space as a human—as a part of this community. Also, because people started to protest in that area, the authorities began to strictly enforce regulations in this public space to arrest people and stop the protest. So I had to find a different strategy compared to my work in 2010. In 2010, if you even slightly avoided following the expected behavior, you could be easily seen. But in 2014, with everyone raising their voices, to exist as artists in this place you had to approach it differently. Also, you cannot let the police arrest your performer; you have to be smart about that. I looked up the public law. Korean public law states that one-person protest is allowed. But if you are two people, protest is not allowed. There has to be a distance of 20 meters between one person and another person if you want to be acknowledged as an individual. I started to play with that public law. In the middle of the square, I set up a 25-hour, one-man performative protest. So I got not only artists but also citizens, students, protesters, housewives. Everyone back then had something to say. I gave them just one rule: please do not use any written letters or placards. I gave them this restriction because I wanted to differentiate this space from the realm of public protest. I wanted to shift our practice to the artistic realm. I didn't want them to appear like political protesters. Starting at twelve o'clock, it lasted for 24 hours. I also broadcast it on Facebook and YouTube so people in other spaces could watch it. In the last hour, all 24 people gathered at 20-metre intervals, so they would still be regarded as individuals, and they performed for one hour. After 24 hours, this last hour created a space of being together without violating public law.

25 Hours—To My Era (2014) © Seoul Marginal Theatre Festival

She is a performer. She looks at the opposite side of the square, where a lot of people are protesting. She tries to make a connection. The people behind her are hired by the authorities to disturb the protest about the ferry. This area is where our red couch was positioned. In 2017 I repeated this format as the opening performance of the Seoul Marginal Theatre Festival, which I curated.

So as I have shown you: Reality always shifts from moment to moment, and it is always influenced by what is happening in society. If we want to reflect reality and if we want to react to it, the form always has to shift. You cannot keep the same format because social reality constantly shifts. So after 2016, the whole of society was in a very gloomy mood because of this tragic Sewol ferry incident, and I started to think about what theatre could do. What is its function? Do we have to do something now? Or do we just stay calm and wait? And we had a difficult time confronting ourselves as theatre practitioners with these incidents. We say, or we learn, that theatre is a space where we understand each other or approach humanity from diverse perspectives. Then how do we represent the pain of the other in the language of theatre performance? That was our question, and at that time, many performances were made based on the Sewol ferry disaster. That made it more difficult for me because most of the performances approached it by having characters on stage telling the story of people who lost their families in the disaster, using the strategy of identification. It was really weird to see an actor acting the pain of one of these families. It created more distance from the actual pain and even distorted it. When she [pointing to the translator] is in pain, I can consolidate her. But I cannot be her. I cannot fully understand her. She is the Other, and I am me. You can try to understand and do your best to understand her pain, but you cannot fully confront her pain. But when you see someone acting pain in a conventional mode of representation, I feel this is too naïve. It is like saying: I can understand the pain fully. So I think we have to find a different approach if we want to do something. We thought of the concept of the witness because we are living at the same time as these incidents. Somehow we are witnesses of these events in our society. As a witness, even at a crime scene, you have to speak out about what you saw or what you heard. You have to speak this out.

First, over a period of two months, we met five mothers that had lost their children in this incident. We asked about their memories and their feelings. We started to write the interviews into a script. We did not interpret it but decided to convey their words. So our role was to disseminate the stories that we heard. One actress did a ritual. She could memorize the whole 304 names that died during the disaster, and then she spoke out these names for forty minutes. In a way, it was a very long time, and it could be a boring time just standing on the stage speaking out names one by one. But through this monotony, we touched some-thing, and the spectators started to imagine each dead person's life, how these people have disappeared from this world, and how the utterance of these people's names makes the scale of the disaster apparent. But what I want to share with you is that, when we made this performance of the Sewol disaster, about these other people's pain, we felt we could not just stay in the rehearsal room and prac-tice theatre. Somehow we felt we needed to engage more with the actual protest. Somehow we felt a bit uncomfortable. So during the rehearsal process of three months we went out one person-protesting. Like this:

During the rehearsal process of *Talking of Her* (2016) © Creative VaQi

These are pictures of people whose bodies are still missing. That is just in front of the President's official residence. What does it mean to act? What is the difference between acting as an artist and acting as a member of a social group? I think the roles are a little bit different. At that time, we felt that acting only as artists was not enough, so we also acted in the social realm. I had an interesting debate with my mother after the premiere of the show. She is always my first audience. The morning after the show, which was called *Talking of Her*, I asked my mother how she felt about what she had seen. She said something interesting, which I did not accept at that time. She said she could see the effort to act socially to reach the pain of the others and deal with social issues. But she also said: "You spent too much energy acting in the social realm, but the energy you put into the art realm was not enough to create an interesting form." That was a very tricky point. I do not define myself as a social activist but as an artist. But: An artist that deals with social issues and an artist as a member of the society. Then, given my identity as an artist, how can I embrace social issues? We definitely felt that dealing with that issue by walking into the rehearsal room was naïve. That's why we went out and participated in the social movement. And what happened was that we spent too much emotional energy in the social realm, which was inevitable. This became a tricky question and a dilemma.

After finishing this project, after dealing with all these social issues, we started to think: Why are all these issues originating in our time? Why are they all coming out now? And tracing it back, we faced the reality of our society, which is divided into North and South. This division for more than 50 years actually created all these social restrictions. While dealing with all the social issues, we realized that we cannot avoid this big issue: the reunification or the division of the Korean peninsula.

But this issue was too big, so I did not know where to start. As we did before, we decided to experience it physically, bodily, so we planned a very long walking trip. There is a division line from the west sea to the east sea. The whole company decided to walk along this line.

We went to the gate between North and South Korea, where President Moon and Kim Jong-un met recently. We had just seen the images in the media. But when we actually visited it, it was a completely different experience. It is facing North Korea. You can see the land over there, but physically you cannot go there. We walked from west to east, so you cannot walk to your left. That is a very strange feeling. We also met a soldier who is part of the border guard during our trip, and we interviewed him about his everyday life.

We made a theatre piece out of this experience that was supported by Doosan Art Center. It is called *Walking Holiday*. Not "working"—but "walking" holiday. In this piece, we filmed miniatures with a camera to bring the experience of our walking into the theatre.

Projecting miniatures in *Walking Holiday* 1 (2017) © Doosan Art Center

We had to find a strategy to engage the audience in a dialogue about our experiences. These miniatures were also related to our experience of looking at North Korea. You always had to look far away, so North Korea always appeared small. Also in the Dora Observatory, North Korea is always displayed as something very small.

Walking-Holiday 2 (2017) © Doosan Art Center

This was an overview of my ten-year journey through reality and theatre. I think because life and reality are complex and not easy, theatre, as a form that seeks to reflect reality, should also not be too simple or neat. A lot of theatre is too beautiful. When it is too beautiful, it distorts reality. Sometimes when I meet theatre practitioners, or even some masters of this profession, I feel uncomfortable. Life is always bigger than the theatre. We are not making theatre to make good theatre. We are making theatre for many reasons, but we are trying to become good people. It is strange to say that. To make good theatre, these practitioners are always talking about and looking at the theatre. But I think we have to see life outside the theatre to make good theatre—because life is always bigger than theatre. When you are really in this industry, sometimes this relationship is missing.

As I mentioned before, I believe each society has a different context and history, and the form has to be applied differently. These days many people talk about universality. I am asking myself if it is possible to create universal content. I think our contemporary communication cannot be universal. It can only happen in a very specific context. But if you work in the art world, you see many people trying to create universal content, which you can communicate everywhere in the world. I am not saying this is impossible. But nowadays, I am asking myself, what is the universal and specificity in cultural communication? This was my talk, and now I would like to receive any thoughts or questions from your side.

XU LI (STUDENT): You mentioned that your mom did not like your art piece because she thought it was not artistic enough. My first question is, why did she think it is not artistic enough? Was she speaking in a technical sense, or how did she mean this? My second question is about your statement that if theatre is too beautiful, it distorts reality. Do you completely reject the beauty of theatre? Or do you just don't care about this aspect at all?

LEE: These are good questions and not easy to answer. When I had the dialogue with my mother, I finally agreed with her that we did not spend enough time creating a form. We were just too simple and loose. On the stage, we were just reciting what we had written down from our interviews. For some audiences, it was not an artistic experience. This was her point, because she said we could also hear these things on the radio or TV. If audiences confront the body on stage, there should be more than the voice. You are not giving your opinion by only conveying the perspectives of others. You are just staying neutral. I love making beautiful things as an artist. But what I mean by being careful of creating beautiful images is that I try not to manipulate the audience's perception through beautiful images. That erases a lot of other contexts. For example, once I made a performance called *The Conversation*, which included an old lady who had been my nanny. In one scene, she was cleaning the theatre. As a theatre director, you always have to take care of aspects like timing and rhythm, and you try to shape a scene according to a good rhythm. But once she started cleaning the stage, she had to finish it, because this was her habit and technique of cleaning. So as a director I could not stop her and tell her: "Time is over, please just do the front floor." It must be boring for the audience. But somehow, that is more connected to her life and makes sure that it is about her reality.

GAO FENG (STUDENT): It is a very technical question. Once you have done an interview, how do you make use of it? I mean, do you just put it on stage one-to-one?

LEE: It depends on whom I interview. These days, I am working on another performance, called *Love Story*, that is based on the Kaesong industrial complex located in North Korea. Many North Koreans and South Korean workers worked there together and shared deep friendships and even love in the past decades. But now it is closed because of the political situation between North and South. So I interviewed the South Korean workers who worked there for a long time. I've got a lot of information from them. But I did not feel that I could use these interviews in the performance because they talk in such general terms—this time, I have not found a strategy for using them. I am a little bit lost.

TUCHMANN: I just want to jump in on this topic of interviews. I would be interested in how you structure your interviews. Are they open or structured? What is your method?

LEE: It depends on whom we interview. For example, when we questioned the mothers who lost their children, we needed to be more cautious. We visited their houses, where they feel more comfortable. We call them "interviews," but they are not official interviews. We just spend time there. The mothers always got very lively when they talked about their daughters, their children. They did not use the past tense. They always spoke as if their daughters were still alive. We tried to spend time with them in their everyday space.

TUCHMANN: I remember that last semester when we had the anthropologist Matthew Gutmann in our seminar, and he said this sentence: "I do not *interview* people. I *talk* to people." Is this approach characteristic of your concept of an interview?

LEE: Sometimes I think it is good to set up an official interview. It is about shifting the form of the interview. But it can be helpful in trying to approach someone's story. After visiting the ordinary spaces, we also invited the mothers to the rehearsal room to set up a more official encounter. And here, an ethical issue comes out. How many interviews, how much research on this person makes it enough to talk about it on stage? It is always very difficult. You always have a certain amount of time to approach an issue or to meet people. And then you have to make something out of it.

It is always tricky to decide. "Ok, we met ten times and now we will make something out of it." It is very tricky to decide how this relationship should continue after the performance as well. Once I had a chance to talk to a German theatre group, *Rimini Protokoll*. They also do a lot of work with nonprofessional actors. And I asked one of the directors, how do you maintain relationships after performances, since you are dealing with people's lives on stage. The director said: "I don't maintain the relationship. I've worked with 8000 people. It is impossible to maintain relationships. I just give them the chance to gain some distance from their lives and reflect on their lives on stage." I felt a little bit too *kalt*[1] after listening to that. It is not a simple issue. After working with nonprofessional people, time passes, you slowly lose connection with them. A year after the performance, you call them every month. After two, three years, you start to contact them once a year. It's challenging to maintain relationships, but somehow I feel guilty. The human relationships created through the process of making theatre leaves a complicated feeling on my mind.

LI YINAN: I saw your piece *The Conversation* live. It is about the generation gap, and it also talks about your frustration at failing to communicate with your

---

1   German for "cold."

nanny. So, I am curious about her reaction to using her story and using her as an actress?

LEE: Basically, she enjoyed spending time with young people. Because in her own life, it was the first time that many people had focused on her story. She also enjoyed touring the piece around the world with us. One critic wrote about the creators who were using her in this performance, that they should have let her know in advance what interpretations and reactions would be triggered by her performance. Although she enjoyed performing on stage, she is not an expert in performance art. She does not know what her performance evokes, what kind of reactions or feelings will be produced. So the critic said the creative team should have told her about possible audience reactions. But we, as a creative team, always saw her enjoying performing, and we thought this is enough. But after reading this critic's opinion, in a way I agree, we kind of used her. Not used her, I mean, we should have informed her more about the side-effects of the performance, because she was watched as "the Other" on stage. But basically, she liked it. After telling her story on stage, she felt that something had been released inside her.

GAO YINFU (STUDENT): My question is about the 25-hour performance. Everybody seems to be protesting against different things. Did you make a decision, and if so, how, about who would participate in this performance? Also, some of the performers were interacting with people passing by. Were there limitations about how freely the performers could interact with pedestrians?

LEE: First of all I released an article about the project and asked citizens to apply. We received all kinds of applications. I did not select. It happened to be 24. I met every person one by one. For three days, I had meetings and we talked and shared the concept and issues each participant had, and then we had two workshops all together. We visited the site and got to know each other. During the performance I did not intervene or control the interaction between performers and strangers. So, I was not a director during this time, I was more like a creative producer.

TUCHMANN: On our way to the Academy this morning, you told me that reading Hans-Thies Lehmann's *Postdramatic Theatre* meant a lot to you, because this book provided you with a language to speak about your work. Could you tell us a little bit about the words and the concepts in this book that have been especially important to you?

LEE: When I was thinking of the *Dream of Sancho* as a very young artist who had just graduated from a very conventional theatre school, my goal was to create a very dramatic performance but without using too much text. I wanted to create a universal performative language that dealt with all kinds of aesthetic approaches. But after this work, I was not sure about the structure of the drama, if it is the best way to capture our reality these days. I tried many different ways of making theatre, from different materials. This is how it was from the beginning of my career for three years: sometimes I made physical theatre; sometimes I made theatre based on using objects like soil or chairs; sometimes I also did theatre outside. At that time, one critic critiqued me, saying: "He does not know what he is experimenting." I remember this sentence well. At that time, I was trying to find my artistic language. I read the book *Postdramatic Theatre* in 2011. It was the English version, and through the book, I realized that what I was going through was connected to the process of art history in the 20th century. The function of pedagogy has been important, but now these concepts are changing, and new questions are emerging about how we create communication with new factors and strategies. In Lehmann's book, I found different approaches to answering this question. That theory gave me confidence because it gave me a context where I could find a form. So I could keep focusing on my experiment. But also I have to confess that it was not easy to read or to understand.

LOVE STORY

Lee Kyung-Sung and Creative VaQi

The performers Woo Bum-Jin, Na Kyung-Min, and Sung Soo-Yeon of the Creative VaQi wrote their own texts and created their own characters based on their research and imagination.

https://tinyurl.com/Lee -LoveStory

ENGLISH TRANSLATION FROM THE KOREAN Colin Marshall, Emily Bettencourt, Julie Lee

SUPERVISION Alyssa Kim
This text was translated in Advanced Stylistic Practice Class, LTI Korea Translation Academy.

WITH Woo Bum-Jin, Na Kyung-Min, and Sung Soo-Yeon
DIRECTOR Lee Kyung-Sung
DRAMATURG Jun Kang-Hee
ASSISTANT DIRECTOR Hyun Ye-Sol

Throughout the creative process, the assistant director archived the words and materials found by the actors, then the dramaturg brought a new perspective and set of interpretations to bear on the texts to create the final structure. Finally, it was only possible to complete the performance thanks to the work of the space, sound, and lighting designers.

PREMIERE November 6, 2018, at Doosan Art Center Seoul, South Korea, as a new work by the winner of the 5th Doosan Yonkang Art Award (Lee Kyung-Sung)
COMISSIONED BY Doosan Art Center

The setting is the actors' workroom. Each of the three actors has their own table. Gyeongmin's table, stage right, is a folding ping-pong table, and Suyeon's table in front of the blackboard has a laptop connected to a screen. Beomjin works at a piano, stage left. Upstage there are a blackboard and a video screen, and above that are the South and North Korean flags. There are photos attached to the walls.

As the audience enters, the actors are onstage, doing their respective work. Suyeon writes "imagining" on the blackboard. Then she begins to search on her laptop. (North Korea. North-South relations. Inter-Korean summit. Handshake.) When she searches "handshake," the three actors shake each other's hands.

Suyeon continues searching.
(North Korean woman. Kaesong Industrial Complex. How to get to Kaesong Industrial Complex.)
After she searches "how to get to Kaesong Industrial Complex," she reads an interview script.

SUYEON: Which checkpoints do you have to pass through to get to Kaesong from your house in Seoul?

GYEONGMIN: There's an army checkpoint at the end of Unification Bridge. You get the first inspection there, and then you go on to the Dorasan entrance office. If you go by car, you get a vehicle inspection at the CIQ and have to write down your personal information, and before you go to the UN checkpoint, everyone gathers at one place. There, the cars going in at a designated time slot all line up and the number of people get confirmed, and then you leave the army checkpoint guided by a UN vehicle driven by UN military police. When you get 100 meters from the Military Demarcation Line, the UN vehicle returns. A North Korean car takes you from there on. Following that car, you pass a Northern checkpoint and arrive at the Northern CIQ. There they check the number of cars and people again. After that, you follow another car from Northern customs, and at the last intersection there's an army checkpoint. You pass it in single file and enter the complex.

SUYEON: It sounds very complicated.

GYEONGMIN: Getting through it all takes about an hour.

BEOMJIN: It's not that far. About seven kilometers. But it takes a little more than an hour.

SUYEON: What if you don't have your own car?

GYEONGMIN: They do a headcount at the army checkpoint. While the people coming by car are going through the CIQ at the Dorasan entrance office, the people on foot go through a process like customs at the airport. When you are done with the procedure, an escort vehicle picks you up and you stand by at the last army checkpoint. There's another headcount, and the rest is the same.

BEOMJIN: It's just like taking your passport and visa when you go abroad. From the Unification Bridge onward, you have to show your South Korean passport. When you get your pass scanned at the Southern CIQ, it goes into the system, and you also get it scanned in the North to enter. They used to do this all by hand, but now it's automatic.

GYEONGMIN: Everything was done by hand at first. So it took much longer.

SUYEON: It must've felt very different, the first time you passed through.

GYEONGMIN: It feels different every time.

BEOMJIN: (*breathes deeply*) The air is so fresh there. When I come back to Seoul, I can notice the air pollution right away. The Kaesong Industrial Complex is like a country in itself. Getting in and out of there is just like getting in and out of a country.

SUYEON: I definitely want to visit the place at least once.

SUYEON (*recorded voice*): When I go somewhere, if it's outside, I always look for cats that might be living there. I really love cats. I look for places near grass, with food waste bins close by and a couple of cars parked. This is the back parking lot of a factory. There's a sign on the wall that says Se something Corporation. Cats like this kind of place. I take the can of food I brought and call for a cat.

SUYEON: Meow Meow.

SUYEON (*recorded voice*): The air is nice. I can see the far-off mountains clearly. It might be nice to sit out here and drink a can of beer. I decide to keep looking for cats on my way to the convenience store. I go into an alley. A narrow alley between two factories, not quite wide enough to be called a street. I like this kind of place. Cats like this kind of place too.

SUYEON: Meow?

SUYEON (*recorded voice*): It seems like a good place for doing things secretly.
I suddenly remember hearing that women in North Korea aren't allowed to smoke or drink in front of people. I look down as I walk. I want to find a cigarette butt with lip gloss on the end. No, it's fine even if there's no lip gloss. I hope that some female North Korean worker smoked cigarettes here in secret, mocking the people who said she couldn't.

That secret smoker's footsteps, stealthy, looking around, holding her breath, like a cat, like she could run away at any moment.

I walk along the alley. I think of things that are better suited to alleys than large streets. Things that are often pushed aside in favor of more important issues. People who silently watch others make decisions. Emotions kept hidden in one corner of the heart, in case it ruins one's relationships with others.

SUYEON: (*sighing*) Ahh...

SUYEON (*recorded voice*): I remember what one Kaesong worker said about seeing a cat fleeing through the window of the bathroom. I look carefully at the small windows of the buildings as I walk. I peek in through one of the windows. There's a poster on the opposite wall. I can see a slogan that says "Normalize at Any Cost."

Normal. Abnormal.

North-South Summit Meeting.

I look at a picture. Among the twenty-four people in the picture, only one is a biological woman.

There's a blue ping-pong table under the poster. They say that the Kaesong workers gathered in twos and threes during their break times to play ping-pong. As a rule, North Koreans and South Koreans couldn't enjoy sports together, but once they got to know each other, they could play ping-pong, at least. I'm no good at ping-pong. I would just stand and watch the good players send the ball back and forth.

I think about a cat watching a toy in my hand and jumping back and forth.

A cat I saw every time I took a walk in the neighborhood park near the theatre. I called that cat Neighborhood. The cat that lives here—what do people call it?

Since it's the Kaesong Industrial Complex... Industry? Industry.

SUYEON: Meow.

SUYEON (*recorded voice*): What kinds of sights would Industry see in this alley?
Many feet all walking to the same place. Someone sighing deeply. The hands that petted her. The eyes that glanced at her. A small pebble that was thrown at her. People saying the word "unification."

I imagine a person who might have stood and looked at the cat. She slowly crouches down. She extends her right hand, slowly. She shows the back of her hand to the cat. The cat looks at the hand approaching her. The cat thinks about whether it's a friend's hand or a foe's. The cat hesitates for a moment and then disappears around the corner to the back of the building.

It's noisy behind the building. Out flows the sound of machines operating inside. The wind that comes from the fan vents is hot and smoky.

I imagine someone who might have leaned against this wall. The sound of machinery is unexpectedly comforting. She would have stood here, tired of people's sharp words and cold gazes.

What would she have thought about this place? Did she talk to herself, inaudible words muffled by the sound of machines?

I call the cat as I walk.

SUYEON: Industry Industry

SUYEON (*recorded voice*): As I walk, I imagine someone calling the cat Industry.

SUYEON: Industry Industry

SUYEON (*recorded voice*): When I see a traffic sign, I remember drawing a poster of the North and South when I was young. The South was always blue, and the North was always red.

Every year there was a competition to write letters to North Korean kids. The title of the letter I wrote in third grade was "To My Nameless Friend," in fourth grade it was "To my Friend in North Korea," and in fifth grade it was "To the North Korean Friend I Want to Meet." To the North Korean friend I want to meet. To the North Korean friend I want to meet.

SUYEON: To the North Korean friend I want to meet. To the North Korean friend I want to meet. To the North Korean friend I want to meet.

SUYEON (*recorded voice*): At some point, I arrive in front of the convenience store. It's called CU, Kaesong Industrial Complex Branch #2. The employee is North Korean.

The first North Korean I've met in North Korea.

What kind of person is she?

I slowly open the glass door and go into the store.

The video shows images of the Kaesong Industrial Complex.

GYEONGMIN: I'm actor Na Gyeongmin. Since I'm in the acting business, it's my job to mainly deal with fictional characters created by writers. But this time, we set out to make a play about the Kaesong Industrial Complex or more specifically, the real people who worked at Kaesong. But the thing is, even as South-North relations have abruptly gone into reconciliation mode, we weren't allowed into Kaesong. Moreover, we had no way of meeting any North Koreans who worked there. So we started to imagine. Using everything available to us, we tried imagining the North Korean workers of Kaesong.

He writes "Choi Song-Ah" on the chalkboard.

The character I've created is a young man who drives the Kaesong commuter bus. You know, once you're assigned to a manufacturing process, you don't really get to leave that place. I thought it'd be nice if he had a job that took him to places and allowed him to meet lots of people. I also wanted him to be someone who'd faced a great deal of change.

The North Korean Kaesong workers' wages came from the country. North Korea, that is. The company didn't pay them directly. Apparently the workers called what the Southern corporations provided in lieu of a salary, "labor service supplies." Choco pie, coffee mix, stuff like that. So I pictured a young North Korean man who grew up eating choco pies from a young age thanks to his parents who also worked at Kaesong. A young man who'd been raised welcoming the waves of capitalism in the world's only communist country under the socialist system, you know?

Choi Song-Ah. Male. Late twenties. There's a small mountain right next to the complex. Janam Mountain. It's more of a hill. Almost all the mountains in North Korea are barren, but apparently Kaesong used to be known for its pine trees. Which means Janam Mountain must've been packed with pine at one point. His mother had loved that pine hill. So she named him "song" for pine and "ah" for hill. Song-Ah, Song-Ah. He enters the military at 17 like all the other North Korean men. But he has a small accident and finishes his military service early. I didn't want my character to be in the army for too long. Afterwards, he attends the Kaesong College of Arts and dreams of becoming an actor. Because he loves the works of Anton Chekhov, he wants to study in Russia after finishing college. "Mother loves me, loves me not, loves me, loves me not. I shall show them the people's Treplev!" My colleagues said my character studying theatre seems too contrived. But I told them, "Rather than imagining a world I don't know anything about, I'm trying to meet the character through the world I know well." Anyway, Choi Song-Ah ends up not studying abroad. Why? Because he starts working for Kaesong on behalf of his parents under a policy order. He ends up working as a bus driver because of his army driving experience. His leg is slightly uncomfortable from his accident in the army, but otherwise he has no problem walking or going on with his daily life. It's a bit of discomfort that only he can feel.

Gyeongmin touches his own knee.

He takes a lot of pride in his job of transporting nearly 50,000 Kaesong residents to the Industrial Complex via the commuter bus. He grows secretly close with a Southern worker who teaches him repair skills. They play ping-pong together, share some ginseng wine, and the Southerner shows him photos of his family vacation to Jeju Island. He lets Song-Ah drive his car and puts his hand on the steering wheel. In this way, they grow really close. Song-Ah sees his co-worker's sister in vacation photos. He asks half-jokingly, "Um, is your sister married?" The Southerner chuckles and says, "I'll introduce you if you're interested, comrade!" From that day on, Choi Song-Ah dreams of reunification.

I'm sure all actors do this, but we pour in a lot of effort to get close to our characters. For Song-Ah, I eat choco pies in my spare time. Why did I want to imagine a young North Korean man working with South Koreans at the Kaesong Industrial Complex?

He eats a choco pie.

He wears jeans. They should have some oil stains. You know how they say North Koreans don't really wear jeans because they're American? Apparently North Koreans don't understand why people wear ripped jeans. But because denim is so durable, some men have started wearing jeans to go fishing or do hard labor. Choi Song-Ah also likes the pair he tried on and keeps wearing them. They're fine even when he goes under the bus for maintenance and scrapes them on the ground or against metal parts. "Go on now, I've fixed you well."

BEOMJIN: What about the top?

GYEONGMIN: Top? Jacket? He wears the kind of jumper that industrial workers here in the South also wear. You see, there were no uniforms for drivers. Since he started working at Kaesong, Song-Ah likes wearing the jumper he got as a gift from a Southerner. He basically never takes it off unless it's summer. He didn't accept the gift at first because of his pride. "I don't need this sort of thing." "I have lots of jackets at home." But the Southerner leaves it behind in the breakroom, saying, "Ah, I have two of these, so I'd better throw this one away." Only then does Song-Ah take it and even stitches his name into it in case some other driver might take it. Choi. Song. Ah.

Gyeongmin takes out his nametag and puts it on his jacket. He puts on a glove.

He always wears gloves, and his palms are grimy. He doesn't really ever take the gloves off because his Southern co-worker is missing a pinky finger on his right hand. Since *he* doesn't take his gloves off, Song-Ah doesn't take his off either. When Song-Ah saw his co-worker washing his hands with only four fingers on one side, he said, "Are you a crip, too?" But he only learns later that he hurt the other guy's feelings. Likewise, the Southerner learns only later that there is no word for "the disabled" in North Korea—only "cripple."

He takes off the glove.

I can't really picture his face. Have you ever met a North Korean, by any chance? I've only met two in person; they were both defectors and women. So I tried turning to films for North Korean male faces. Kang Dong-Won in *Secret Reunion*. Hyun Bin in *Confidential Assignment*. Jung Woo-Sung in *Steel Rain*. Kim Soo-Hyun in *Secretly, Greatly*. Who should it be? What kind of expression? Choi Song-Ah likes driving cars and fixing things, and is satisfied working at Kaesong. He's curious about the world, and his eyes are wide open because there's so much he wants to learn about. And he rolls his eyes well. Apparently not fulfilling your military service or being discharged midway is really shameful in North Korea. He's a bit cautious because he has to hide his leg injury. He always smiles with his mouth wide open. But he was told that he'd get in trouble with the North Korean administrators if he were that friendly with the Southerners, so he's since made a habit of keeping his mouth shut when smiling.

I wanted to ask Choi Song-Ah the following questions:

What does the North Korean radio station play?

Has anyone died from an accident on the commuter bus?

How did you change after working with Southerners?

How did you feel when your workplace was suddenly shut down?

What will happen to us following this sudden disjuncture?

After the last question, Gyeongmin takes out the glove from his pocket and looks at it in his hand. He pulls on the glove.

As for me, I worked part-time at the Shinwon Eben Esel factory in Gwangju, Gyeonggi Province. For about half a year? My job was simple, just unloading containers of clothes made in foreign factories and shelving them in our factory. Apparently, clothing-factories moved around a lot because the labor costs were high and kept rising. First China, then the Philippines when China got too expensive, then Malaysia, then Indonesia, then finally Kaesong, North Korea. They built an aggressive number of factories because Kaesong has ridiculously cheap labor and uniform wages. Shinwon did, I mean. Even if they make it in North Korea, it's still "Made in Korea." I unloaded boxes of clothes with that tag. (*Spreads the fingers of his right hand*) I used to cut myself here a lot. On the hangers. And we'd ship off the fabric and buttons and zippers and other subsidiary materials in the empty containers. The fabric from our country will become a garment after North Korean workers cut and sew it; it'll pass through the hands of a day laborer like me en route to department stores, where someone will buy it. Someone. The same for school uniforms, Cuckoo rice cookers, glue sticks.

He returns to the table and holds up a book.

This book is called *The People of the Kaesong Industrial Complex*. It features interviews with South Koreans who worked at Kaesong, including what it was like on the day of the bombardment of Yeonpyeong, what kinds of conflicts came from their different understanding of labor and wages, how they felt when the complex was shut down then started up again. In this book, I found conversations that Choi Song-Ah might've had with his Southern co-workers. Beomjin, could you hand me the text?

"Why are you so desperate to make money?"

<u>"We gotta make money to feed ourselves, no?"</u>

"We eat just fine without doing all that."

<u>"We try to make more money to live a better life."</u>

"I don't get that at all. Is that capitalism?"

<u>"I don't understand you either."</u>

"Is this your car?"

<u>"Yes, it is."</u>

"No way. I don't believe you. Prove it."

<u>"I'm not even done with the monthly installments."</u>

"And what's that?"

<u>"It's a thing. In the South."</u>

"Tell me... Are all the Southern cars in Kaesong?"

<u>"Hahahahaha."</u>

"The photos from your trip to Jeju Island. Show me those again."

Gyeongmin closes the book and holds up a notebook.

I tried writing a story about things that could've happened on February 10, 2016. That was the day that the Kaesong Industrial Complex was shut down by the South Korean government.
    "Go on now, I've fixed you well."
    Shutting the hood of a repaired car, Choi Song-Ah picked up his toolbox.
    "Where did everyone go?" He walked to the back of the lot and saw people gathered in small groups, whispering to each other.

"What's going on?"

<u>"The Southerners will be deported right away.</u>

<u>They have to leave the tools, the parts, everything—and go back to the</u>

<u>South."</u>

"What are you talking about?"

"They pulled this fucking shit about three years ago,
and they're doing it again."

He dragged his bad leg to the office. Many had already gathered, but they were all keeping quiet. The manager started to speak, breaking the heavy silence.

"Starting tomorrow, we North Koreans won't be coming here to work,
so everyone make sure to take all your belongings with you."

Right then, the workers started moving quickly. It's not that there were lockers or any special place for storing personal items. But from various corners, people started pulling out the Southern items they hadn't been able to take home due to the exit search. The manager must've understood, because he pretended not to see anything that day. Choi Song-Ah rushed out as well. He, too, had hidden something.

Gyeongmin brings a blanket from off-stage.

He tried imagining where he'd be, carrying three cartons of Ryongbong cigarettes that he'd exchanged for ration tickets and saved up, as well as two bottles of Kaesong wild ginseng wine, all wrapped in cloth. *Maybe?* He rushed to the breakroom with the ping-pong table. *Of course.* His co-worker was blankly watching the Northerners clock out for the last time through the window. Choi Song-Ah approached him. "Comrade, take this. Ah, you begged me for ginseng wine. And cut back on those cigarettes, will ya?"

Receiving the cloth-wrapped gifts, he looks at Choi Song-Ah, and places his own toolbox at Song-Ah's feet.

"This is yours, comrade. Have it."

"No thanks."

"Anyway, we might never see each other again.
Why don't we call each other brother?"

"...I have something to ask you."

"Go ahead, brother."

"How are we getting last month's overtime incentive?"

"I'll give it to you instead. Is this enough?"

"No thanks."

"I'll get it for myself later."

"Give it to me in dollars, then."

<u>"How about betting on a final round of ping-pong?"</u>

"With a busted leg like this, no bet for me."

<u>"What about it! Look at my finger!"</u>

"If I win, send me on a trip to Jeju!"

<u>"And Baekdu Mountain for me?"</u>

The two face each other at the ping-pong table. With Choi Song-Ah's serve, their never-ending rally begins...

Ping-pong ping-pong ping-pong ping-pong ping-pong.......

Beomjin plays The One Left in My Heart *on the piano and sings. When the song ends, he writes "Ri Ye-Mae" on the blackboard.*

BEOMJIN: <u>1. Ri Ye-Mae's view</u>

February 2015. Ri Ye-Mae first arrived for work. In a few years, how would he remember this day? Maybe other than his bumbling, he wouldn't remember anything. Even though it was February but snowed heavily, and even though early that morning a young woman worker was run over and killed by a bus, he wouldn't remember. He was like that. Always clumsy at first. And he could never remember his firsts: The first day he'd been placed in a unit in Musan, North Hamkyeong Province, the first day he'd gone as a laborer to Krasnodar, Russia, the first day he'd met his wife, his wedding day, and even the day his mother died. He couldn't remember any of it. He needed to pass through the tunnel called adjustment to see the surroundings more clearly.

Even though he had seen the Kaesong Industrial Complex a few times from afar before, heard about it from the people in the area, and been trained at the National People's Committee over the past few weeks, going into the complex was another matter entirely. Going to work together with his wife in a bus driven by his neighbor Song-Ah must have been some comfort. Everyone who'd arrived for their first day of work gathered at the entrance. Then they moved to the support center in the middle of the complex and received training all morning from the people of the Reconnaissance Bureau. But there was no way Ri Ye-Mae would remember or understand what he was taught.

When the training ended, the people from the Southern companies came to get the workers assigned to them. Ri Ye-Mae was assigned together with five other workers to a logistics company called Y, but he had no sense of what the company did. Two Southerners took them to a van.

"Hello. Nice to meet you. Before we go to the office and eat, we'll first take a ride around the complex and explain to you what's where. Since we're a logistics and sales company, we have to know where everything in the complex is. We'll explain as we go, so pay close attention."

The van set off. But Ri Ye-Mae couldn't possibly remember what was said. Looking at the factories out the window, he thought only this:

"What does this company do that we have to know every place in the complex?"

"How come all the buildings and roads here look the same?"

"How am I going to remember all this?"

"Oh, why am I so unlucky?"

2. Introduction

While studying the Kaesong Industrial Complex, we always had to use our imagination. One day the director told us to try writing a story. So he's making us do all the work now? But how? Well, I had to give it a try. What kind of story will I imagine? What kind of character will I picture? In the end I had these questions: "What kind of people am I drawn to? What kind of people do I feel for?" And the answer, to put it my own words, was, "people who can't do things that well." That is, people who don't pan out, the people who worked at the Complex and wanted to do their best but couldn't pull it off. I thought I had to tell their story. I didn't want to make them just naïve or nice or innocent; I wanted them to be the ones who make me uncomfortable. Out of what I then scribbled down came the previous scene.

3. North Korea

North Korea, Korean people, unification. If I think back on my sentiments about these words, I go back to 1991, my third year of elementary school. I remember that my teacher back then was a man, born in 1933, who talked about the Korean War with hot anger and about unification with hotter love for the people. It influenced me, of course. That spring, the North-South unified table tennis team won the women's team competition in the world championships. I remember watching it on TV. My memories and feelings about that time are buried at the very bottom of all things.

4. What kind of person is Ri Ye-Mae?

I'll start with his appearance. He is 164 centimeters tall, shorter than average because of the hardships he endured while growing up. But his body is strong-looking. With a thick torso like Maradona's, developed back muscles, and sturdy calves, it would be a good body for weightlifting.

His eyes. His gaze. His field of vision is narrow, like he's wearing blinders, so his face is also tilted forward. And he can't focus or concentrate well, so his gaze doesn't stay at one place for long but moves around.

His nose. He is dense and unaware of his surroundings, and on top of that his sense of smell is poor. One side of his nose is always blocked due to sinusitis and rhinitis, so in order to breathe more easily his mouth is always open. Possibly out of a lack of consideration for people around him, he spits and blows his nose everywhere. (*Blows nose.*)

His mouth. Uncouth and hot-tempered, he has had to repress his temper since he was young. So his upper lip is always tense, and it covers his upper teeth. But he is also simple and honest, so when he is happy or angry, he ends up smiling or getting pissed off, showing his upper teeth. (*A happy expression, then an angry expression.*)

His hands. Worker's hands. Large, thick, and stubby. They have many small scars and calluses as well. He often does manual labor, so his hands always look as if they're clenched around eggs, and because he's dense and insensitive, his fingers always look like they're stuck together.

Honest and unafraid, he thrusts his chest confidently forward. Having performed manual labor for a long time, he stands with a straight back. Because his back muscles are tighter than his abdominal muscles, his hips are open, and so his feet are turned outward. His center of gravity is toward the front of his feet, which suits his straightforward and aggressive personality.

5. Q&A: What would it be like to meet someone like him?

SUYEON: What do you think it would be like to really meet someone like Ri Ye-Mae?

BEOMJIN: Honestly, I think I'd be uncomfortable enough to keep my distance.

SUYEON: Have you met someone like him?

BEOMJIN: Hasn't everyone met someone like him one time or another? I've met a lot of people like him while trying to earn a living. One time I did demolition. It was hard work. And on top of that, all the dust and sweat and noise. One older guy I worked with was friendly and good-natured, but he would start yelling at the drop of a hat. One time there was a fire-hose spigot sticking out of a building. They're really expensive. So the guy gave me a sledgehammer and said, (*sweetly*) "Hit it softly!" I hit it very softly. *Tap, tap.* Then he suddenly shouted, (*abruptly*) "Shit, are you kidding me? Are you kidding me?" Taken aback, I said, "You told me to hit it softly!" He said, "Give it here!" He took the sledgehammer and started hitting the spigot really hard. We had different definitions of "softly." And when we finished work, he was back to saying, (*sweetly*) "Good job." Ri Ye-Mae has that side to him.

6. What happens to Ri Ye-Mae?

What happens to Ri Ye-Mae? I haven't written that yet. Though I did think of a plot.

Ri Ye-Mae isn't a good worker. He's slow to learn and makes a lot of mistakes. And he doesn't get along well with others. What's more, because the company does sales and distribution, Northerners and Southerners get along better than they do at the other companies. But that's not the case for Ri Ye-Mae. Even when everybody else gets together to play table tennis or volleyball, he can't. He's not good at sports.

They say that at the Kaesong Industrial Complex, Northerners and Southerners secretly exchange gifts and necessities. Suppose a Northerner says "gloves." A few days later, a Southerner will buy gloves and leave them in a place only the two of them know about, and the Northerner will pick them up. But to Ri Ye-Mae, that's unthinkable. Time passes this way, and then comes the year 2016. Ri Ye-Mae has a son who looks just like him. The son demands soccer shoes as a combined birthday and Lunar New Year present. "I want them! I want them!" Like his father, he isn't good at sports, but he wants to play in an important match on February 12th no matter what. Ri Ye-Mae generously promises to buy the shoes. "I'll get 'em for you!" But his wife won't hear that kind of nonsense. Suyeon! Gyeongmin!

Suyeon and Gyeongmin read aloud, with Suyeon reading the wife's lines.

"What? Idiot? You call your husband an idiot?"

"Well, what else do you say to an idiot? And not so loud. You'll wake up Seong-Geun."

Ri Ye-Mae is on his feet, shouting, and his wife berates him while still lying down, with her eyes still closed.

"I mean, why would you make a promise you can't even keep? Now Seong-Geun is thinking only of his birthday."

"I'll keep it! I told Manager Park all about it! He said he'll bring back some Nikes next time he goes to the South!"

His wife snorts.

"Oh, bullshit. You think I don't know you? It's obvious you couldn't bring it up at all. What's so hard about talking to them, making friends with them... all the comrades you work with get along with the Southerners, play table tennis with them, and exchange gifts with them."

"You know I can't play table tennis. Don't worry. I'll get the shoes for sure."

It's February 10th. His son's soccer game is the day after tomorrow, but Ri Ye-Mae still hasn't said anything to any Southerner. Nervously smoking a cigarette outside, he spots a Southern employee looking around with a black bag and heading toward the doghouse. At that moment, Ri Ye-Mae knows what it is. "Soccer shoes!" In truth, a Northern co-worker has been bragging about them for a while. What's more, their sons are friends. Ri Ye-Mae hides. Ri Ye-Mae silently watches the Southerner tossing the black bag into the doghouse. Before he knows it, he's heading for the doghouse himself, and soon he is leaving the place with the bag in hand. He runs to the bathroom and hides the shoes in a ceiling service duct.

There is a commotion, Ri Ye-Mae is suspected which leads to a fight, but he ends up with the shoes. But he can't take them home with him. The next day comes the bad news. The Kaesong Industrial Complex has been shut down due to a reckless decision by that Park Geun-hye and her cronies, so he has been told not to come in for work. Ri Ye-Mae runs the ten kilometers to the complex. "Soccer shoes, soccer shoes!" But the entrance is firmly guarded by soldiers, and nobody is going inside. Ri Ye-Mae wanders the area around the complex. He hangs around the barbed-wire fence that surrounds the complex, not knowing what to do. "Soccer shoes, soccer shoes, soccer shoes..."

Calisthenics. Music plays and images are projected.
The actors move to the music.

SUYEON: Did everyone really do this in the North? It's way harder than our National Calisthenics.

BEOMJIN: I saw a video of the factory workers doing the calisthenics. More or less, anyway. But their hearts weren't in it, and it wasn't exercise at all. Just like how we used to do it in school.

GYEONGMIN: I thought the calisthenics would be robotic because it's a communist county, but there are a lot of wavy dance movements.

BEOMJIN: What would happen to you if you were to do the exact same movements to the exact same music at the exact same time all your life?

SUYEON: You'd become a good dancer.

GYEONGMIN: You'd definitely become a good dancer. And wouldn't an individual learn through their body that they're a member of the country?

SUYEON: Even having learned that automatically, I think they could still wonder one day, all of a sudden, "Why am I doing this?"

GYEONGMIN: Still, wouldn't it give you a strong sense of belonging? That would grow into a love of the country, and that love of the country would grow into nationalism.

BEOMJIN: Like what we call getting a shot of patriotism about being Korean.

SUYEON: Which must be a hairsbreadth different from love of the country.

BEOMJIN: By what criterion?

SUYEON: The criterion in your heart. So I've prepared a short test that can show our feelings about our country. Shall we give it a try? (*Gives papers to Gyeongmin and Beomjin.*) Let's have some music.

The patriot test. "Arirang" plays as background music.
The actors hold the papers and read the questions.

SUYEON: I feel touched by the music playing now.

GYEONGMIN: When I travel, I always pack kimchi, *gochujang*, and other Korean foods.

BEOMJIN: I feel inexplicably happy when I see another Korean abroad.

SUYEON: When I watch an international sports competition like the Olympics or the World Cup, I often scream and cry.

GYEONGMIN: I watch Korea-Japan sports matches no matter what.

BEOMJIN: Honestly, I kind of dislike Japan.

SUYEON: I think that Dokdo is, without a doubt, Korean territory.

GYEONGMIN: I think the Japanese government must issue an official apology and reparations for the comfort women issue.

BEOMJIN: I know about the atrocities Korean soldiers committed in Vietnam.

SUYEON: It's not because I'm from here, but I think there's something special about our history.

GYEONGMIN: I think it's a great shame that ancient Goguryeo's territory doesn't belong to us now.

BEOMJIN: I'm proud that our country has retained Confucian customs and manners.

SUYEON: I'm proud of our country's inventions, like Hangeul, the sundial, and the rain gauge.

GYEONGMIN: I can sing all four verses of the national anthem. (*The actors sing the national anthem.*)

BEOMJIN: I think Samsung has a lot of problems, but I'm proud of the fact that it's a globally recognized company.

SUYEON: I truly wish for just one thing. When can we see our friends on the other side of this divided land?
(1) I think the fact that we are one people is reason enough to reunify.
(2) There are economic and military reasons to reunify.
(3) I think that even if we don't reunify, we can find another way to coexist.

GYEONGMIN: If an opportunity arises, I will emigrate.

BEOMJIN: ("Arirang" *crescendos*) When I hear this song, I cry. (*The test ends.*)

GYEONGMIN: How would the characters we've created answer? How patriotic are they?

BEOMJIN: Ri Ye-Mae's patriotism is moderate. It used to be average, but while working in Russia, he experienced capitalism, and his sense of patriotism became moderate. And Song-Ah's?

GYEONGMIN: Out of 100 patriotism points, 97? Out of 100 nationalism points, 99? He is satisfied working at the Kaesong Industrial Complex, and has no complaints about Chairman Kim Jong-un or the system. The younger you are, the more you accept everything you're told. Suyeon, how about your character?

SUYEON: One point.

BEOMJIN: Out of 100?

SUYEON: No, out of 1000. At first, I vaguely believed that Northerners were very patriotic. You know about the episodes of collective protest at the Kaesong Industrial Complex when the Southerners thoughtlessly tore up calendars with Kim Il-sung's face on them. But do you suppose everyone felt the same way and reacted the same way? There must be some who didn't.

BEOMJIN: Then how did you approach your character?

SUYEON: Basically, I wanted to picture Northern women laborers in the Kaesong Industrial Complex, but it wasn't easy. So I first imagined the stereotypical Northern woman. Steadfast, strong, but feminine, bright, who says things like, "Cheer up, comrade. You can do it. Lift up your spirits." Like the main character of that Northern movie we watched, *Comrade Kim Goes Flying*. I wrote down all the modifiers that came up when I searched for "North Korean women." They were similar to my stereotypical ideas of North Korean women. I must have been influenced by the media. A nice, kind-hearted, affectionate, tenacious, pure, uncomplicated, obedient, devoted, tough woman warrior with strong convictions, but one who dreams of romance, awfully confident but who still wants to be a man's only woman — with big eyes and fair skin. If that's the society's typical image of women, maybe it's also the image forced onto them. How hard it must be for those who don't want to comply with those images... More than half of the 55,000 workers at the Kaesong Industrial Complex were women, and it must have been very difficult for some of them. When I started thinking this way, it connected with what has happened to me recently. For about a year now, I've been absorbed in certain thoughts.

Why me?

Why me?

There are some people who have just begun to voice their opinions, and I wonder if there is a way to stop their voices and words from being swept away by other people's louder voices and words. And I thought it would be meaningful to ponder this issue with the character I've created. Basically, I approached my character by reflecting my reality.

GYEONGMIN: Tell us your character's name.

Suyeon writes "Kim Bbul" on the blackboard.

SUYEON: <u>Kim Bbul.</u>

Bbul, like "horn." You know that the Northerners and Southerners who met at the Kaesong Industrial Complex made the same joke back and forth: "Oh, we all thought Northerners had horns growing on their heads." "Oh, we all thought Southerners had horns growing on their heads."

I wanted to create a character that seemed angry to Northerners as well as Southerners. On the surface she looks normal, but somewhere in her heart, she has horns growing inside her. An angry person, someone who doesn't get along. What we would call an outsider. Kim Bbul was a bit of an outsider to begin with, but since working at the Kaesong Industrial Complex, she has started to grow horns.

Kim Bbul works at a convenience store in the Kaesong Industrial Complex. CU, Kaesong Industrial Complex Branch #2. There's a CU store here, right across from the Doosan Art Center. I hear there are three in the Kaesong Industrial Complex, including the one in the Support Center. In all three, the managers are Southerners, the employees working at the register were Northerners, and only Southerners could shop there.

Apart from cigarettes, the best-selling item at CUs in the South is banana milk. (*Hands a banana milk to Beomjin.*) At the CUs of the Kaesong Industrial Complex, Coca-Cola sells the best. (*Hands a Coca-Cola to Gyeongmin.*) What Kim Bbul likes best isn't banana milk or Coca Cola, but beer. (*Grabs a beer.*) Cheers! (*Toasts with Gyeongmin and Beomjin.*) But she absolutely can't drink where people can see.

Kim Bbul worked for a long time as a seamstress, sewing women's underwear at a factory that makes underwear and children's clothing, but she came to work at CU when the second one opened in the complex. At first, Kim Bbul was thrilled to get out of the underwear factory. Given the nature of its products, the factory was rife with dirty jokes. Her shift leader was a bit rude and took his jokes too far. The other workers laughed at his jokes, but she couldn't.

"Comrade Kim Bbul's is so flat-chested. What will she do if she gets married?"

To that, she just stayed silent.

"It's a joke. Why so serious? Can't take a joke?"

To that, another silence. She didn't even laugh. Awkwardness hung in the room. As this sort of thing kept happening, she became the odd one out. But she did the job well. While she worked without saying a word, "Comrade Kim Bbul has such a plain face. So she has to work hard, because there's nothing else she can do for the country."

The others joined in the laughter. As if it's funny. As if it's embarrassing. As if they're making fun of her. (*Gradually, a blank expression.*) Over her four years working in the factory, Kim Bbul gradually became clumsy and sullen. She couldn't look people in the eye. She developed a habit of biting the inside of her mouth until it bled.

But now, working at the convenience store, Kim Bbul sincerely wishes she could go back to the underwear factory. There she spent so much more time looking at underwear than people at the factory, but here she has to interact with people all the time. Her Northern co-workers. And the Southern customers. It's hard for Kim Bbul to interact with anyone, Southern, Northern, Eastern, Western. She feels more at ease with sewing machines and fabric. To someone like Kim Bbul, a convenience store is a difficult place to work.

Kim Bbul often stares vacantly out the window at work. At times like those, she doesn't hear when people call her.

"Comrade Kim Bbul! Comrade Kim Bbul! Comrade Kim Bbul!"

"Oh, yes?"

"Ah, come on."

"I'm sorry. So sorry."

Even if she gets chided, she soon goes blank again.

What Kim Bbul sees through the window is a choco pie wrapper being tossed by the wind.

A white volleyball flies up over the wall and lands on the other side. Industry the cat, cautiously prowling around. People saying the word "unification."

A group of Northerners and Southerners gathered under a parasol in front of the store, talking heatedly about unification. Amid it all, one person is smiling without saying a word. It's a Southern worker, a woman. That worker is a smoker who sometimes comes into the store to buy cigarettes, and she has become a subject of talk among the Northerners, both men and women.

"A lady comrade smoking... could you even imagine it in our country?"

Someone speaks harshly: "What trash. Who would want her? She would bring disgrace on the family."

Kim Bbul doesn't agree with them. Partly because she can't join the conversation, and partly because, after Industry the cat, that worker is the only living being in the Kaesong Industrial Complex she likes.

The worker, who was sitting quietly, walks over to a spot away from everyone else and lights a cigarette. Kim Bbul watches her intently. The worker stares at Kim Bbul. Their eyes meet. They nod at each other. She stretches and points to the bathroom. It's a signal that she's put it behind the toilet. "It" is music. The worker, who has exchanged pleasantries with Kim Bbul now and again, secretly shares with her music she likes. Kim Bbul sometimes leaves her impressions of it. (*Peeling off a sticky note.*) "The melody was a little sad this time." Picking up the device in the bathroom, Kim Bbul looks around and stealthily ducks into an alley behind the building. She puts the earphones in, covers them with her hair, and plays the music. (*Plays the music.*) Kim Bbul has never heard this kind of music in her life. Her heart fills with energy different from anger. She can't be discovered listening to music. But when she focuses on it, her body keeps moving to the rhythm. She's never seen anyone performing this kind of music. As she listens to the music, she imagines how the people playing it must look. (*Removes earphones.*)

Now Kim Bbul's heart starts to pound. It beats in time with the music. It has never, ever beaten this fast before.

Kim Bbul's Challenge. Chapter one: Kim Bbul and the Cat

"Industry! Industry!"

After looking for Industry in every free moment all day long, Kim Bbul found her. A group of people had surrounded her. Industry stood in a corner, looking quite angry. Her ears were folded back. With her brow furrowed, she was hissing and mewling. Snickering, the people were throwing pebbles at her. Right then, a pebble thrown by someone struck her in the eye. It was Kim Bbul's former manager from the underwear factory. Kim Bbul started to tremble almost as reflex. Her heart also beat faster. She couldn't just leave Industry crying there. She clenched her fists and walked toward her old manager.

When I wrote the next part, I wrote it like this, hoping that Kim Bbul wouldn't endure any consequences.

Kim Bbul looked askance at him and spoke. "Don't do that. You know how miserable that poor thing is."

I didn't like it. It felt like the character had collapsed. I rewrote it.

Kim Bbul spoke to him as if making a joke. "If you keep that up, she might attack. Aren't you scared?"

That didn't do it for me either. I rewrote it again.

Kim Bbul spoke to him softly. "Tormenting a cat. And you don't even have the guts to say anything to your supervisor comrade. Subservient to the strong and overbearing to the weak. You're good at turning a blind eye to injustice. It's really pathetic."

GYEONGMIN: Suyeon, could there really be such a person in the North? Do you think there is?

SUYEON: I thought about it for a long time, and I think there is.
I've never handled a situation like that one directly. I'm too scared. But in any society, in any era, there are people who have their doubts about what is taken as given and who bring about change by starting with small things. Even in North Korea, however conservative society is, they must be somewhere.
We see the North from so far away, we only know what happens on the main streets, not in the alleys.
Hmm... I think there is such a person. It would be good if there is one, even if what they do doesn't look like anything special.

Chapter two: Kim Bbul and the Fart

A man walked up and stood near Kim Bbul, who was outside the convenience store getting some fresh air. Kim Bbul was quite afraid of this man, whom she'd occasionally seen when she went out walking. But so as not to show her fear, she did her best to put on a calm face. Noticing the young woman in the vicinity, the man turned his head to glance at Kim Bbul, then looked away, and lit a smoke.
Kim Bbul looked sideways at the man smoking. She imagined snatching the cigarette out of his hand and smoking it like crazy. Then, as if he'd felt her gaze, the man turned and looked at her. The two met eyes. Kim Bbul hurriedly looked away. Suddenly the man, who had been smoking so casually, farted.
The man was acting nothing was out of the ordinary. He might not have heard the sound of his own fart, or he might have forgotten about the person next to him. He smoked a little more, then spat.
Kim Bbul thought for a moment.

"Do I feel bad because I just heard something so gross, or do I feel upset because he's acting as if I'm not here? Anyway, it must be nice to be him. Whether someone is next to him or not, he lets out what's inside him just like that. What a relief that must be!"

After a bit of hesitation, Kim Bbul squeezed out a fart. Pfft! The man looked at Kim Bbul. Kim Bbul also looked at the man. A moment passed in silence. Kim Bbul hastily turned and, heading back to the store, looked back at the man and farted once more. Then she quickly opened the door and went back inside.

How far can you go in imagining these things? The Kaesong Industrial Complex isn't a fictional place like Hogwarts. The people who worked there were real people. Can we imagine things like this when we haven't even met any of them? Sometimes when you imagine things, it can make you fall in love with someone, or it can make you misunderstand them. Maybe because I felt uneasy about it, the story I wrote kept turning into fantasy.

There was a scene where Industry the cat eats a marble given to him by the spirit of Songak Mountain and turns into a human, and I even added a plot in which Kim Bbul actually starts to grow horns as she takes on one challenge after another. The story I have now is not like that, but it is still close to fantasy.

Fantasy. The kind of story where wishes impossible in reality come true.

Maybe the Kaesong Industrial Complex could have been that kind of place. A place where the people who thought they could never be or live together ate together, exercised together, talked together, and cared for each other. Through my protagonist, I also decided to realize a wish of mine that seemed impossible in reality.

Chapter three: Kim Bbul and the Sheet of Paper

Kim Bbul who had been slowly transformed made a big decision. She decided to do something at the Kaesong Industrial Complex, something she had never imagined of doing. In that miraculous space where a small unification took place every day, she made a decision to hope for another miracle.

The day before she carries it out, Kim Bbul finds Industry the cat. She slowly holds out her hand to her.

Now Industry, who has become pretty friendly with Kim Bbul, comes up to her without hesitation and rubs her hand with her head.

"Industry, I don't think we'll be able to meet again. Before you get close to a person, think carefully about whether that someone is going to treat you nicely or is going to catch and eat you. But even if you can't tell, it's not your fault. Please stay well."

That night on the way home from work, Kim Bbul rips a leaflet off of a wall.

Then she thinks of one sentence that implies everything she wants to say.

Suyeon writes *"Guarantee women's smoking rights!"*

She thinks about how good it would be to hold that sheet while standing some-where in the Kaesong Industrial Complex. She thinks of the best spot to stand among all the streets she has walked along in the complex. She decides to stand under the giant letters that spell out "IN SERVICE OF THE PEOPLE." Holding that sheet of paper, with a cigarette in her mouth.

Kim Bbul thinks for a moment.

"What will happen to me tomorrow? How long can I stand here like this? Will I be dragged off to the Aoji coal mine? Either way, it's fine. I hope tomor-row comes quickly."

She can't stop herself from grinning and every so often laughter bubbles out.

Early the next morning, Kim Bbul receives notice that, due to the suspen-sion of all activities at the Kaesong Industrial Complex, the people no longer need come to work.

The North Korean national anthem starts playing.Standing, the actors listen to the anthem. When it ends, Suyeon writes on the chalkboard:"To my North Korean friend, whom I want to meet."
Gyeongmin walks to center stage with a mic stand and reads the letter.

GYEONGMIN: To my North Korean friend, whom I want to meet.

Comrade! In the long hours I spent imagining you for this project, I had mul-tiple dreams about meeting you. Even in sleep, I couldn't let go of the imag-inative thread. In my dreams, your face was my face. Not Kang Dong-Won's or Hyun Bin's. Probably because I'm an actor, I think I was used to the process of you, my imagined comrade, ultimately becoming me, and my becoming you.

Thinking about the feelings you might've felt when the Kaesong Industrial Complex was shut down, I recalled the disjunctures I've witnessed or experi-enced myself. I can't compare my experiences, of course. Because your world and my world are different. Because we ultimately can't know. Even if I were to live in your world. So it seemed foolish to speculate about someone else's feelings. All I can say for sure is that life would be very different. For me, as for anyone else.

You know, there are societal moments we simply can't avoid. Systems we can't escape. Decisions we can't make for ourselves. It's the same for reunifi-cation as well as capitalism. How can I remain steadfast in such systems? Working on this project, I wanted to find the answer and tell you. I couldn't find it. If I did, it would've been extremely idealistic. Like writing a letter to a North Korean friend, like a homework assignment from elementary school. One of my creative writing professors once told me, "Don't kill off your char-acters so easily. The characters you kill will haunt you." I think she said that because a lot of inexperienced creatives would kill their protagonists willy-nilly if they couldn't think of a conclusion. In creating you, my comrade in North Korea, I instinctively wrote you to be satisfied with your life, to have a happy ending no matter what obstacles you faced. Reconciliation, peace, re-unification, happiness. Even if those are the most obvious, clichéd conclusions.

In discussing this project, my team said the process of imagining you could be a process of steadily accumulating misconceptions. Comrade, I hope that my misunderstanding of you will serve as a step towards understanding you better. Even if this statement itself is overly idealistic.

Sincerely,
Na Gyeongmin
November 2018

The actors exit.
The ending sound plays.
In a video, Choi Song-Ah, Ri Yemae, and Kim Bbul appear in succession, look at the audience, then fade away.

The End

III
POSTSCRIPT

Shame and Power.

A Critical Conversation on the Postdramatic Condition

Lee Kyung-Sung, Boris Nikitin, Wen Hui, Zhao Chuan, and Kai Tuchmann

TUCHMANN: We are meeting today online, roughly two and a half years after your residence at the Dramaturgy Faculty at Beijing's Central Academy of Drama. I am delighted that you could make time for the conversation we are about to have, which will provide an opportunity for you to articulate changes and shifts in your aesthetics that might have occurred since our encounter in Beijing. In addition, I want to use the conversation to let you reflect on some assumptions of mine that are underlying the publication project. These assumptions are mainly connected to—what I consider—the commonality of your aesthetics and to the notion of dramaturgy. I want to start with my understanding of what your different artistic approaches have in common.

   The most significant commonality in your approaches towards making theatre is that your theatres claim a specific relationship with events in the real world. Your works want the audience to see and understand that reality is never something natural, never something given, but rather something that is made up, something that has grown historically. The remarkable thing now is that your approaches don't stop at this point. All of your theatre is doing much more than "just" depicting reality as a construction, because you are all paying nuanced attention to the life of individuals and to the rich cosmos of detail. Your theatrical performances thus have developed dramaturgies that enable an audience to constantly swing back and forth between historical and individual perspectives, between the demystification of history and the poetic realness of the individual.

   I would be happy to open this conversation by having you all comment on this understanding of mine.

ZHAO: I like what you said about the poetic realness of individuals. I think this is somehow quite connected to my work in recent years. In China, people always say I would be anti-something, I oppose something, or I would be very critical. I am always driven by the effort to overcome these attitudes. A crucial part of my work with *Grass Stage* consists in seeking future possibilities, but this is no easy thing. Life is harsh for many people. For my work on *World Factory*, I collaborated with migrant workers who work in factories in Shenzhen; most of them were never exposed to the world of the theatre. When the production is done, it seems like that all that we talked about in the theatre is also over. Their life continues in factories without much change. How to deal with this? This is the question that keeps me occupied. Professionals often say, okay, you did what you did, you made your theatre piece, and raised the question. That's it. But for my work in the past 15 or 16 years with *Grass Stage*, it all comes down to the issue of how to continue with its collaborators and members; what could we bring to them? In *Grass Stage*, we are not connected to each other like on most commercial productions. Actors are not material for the director. We treat each other as equal partners. Somehow in the past few years, I started to think that maybe what *Grass Stage* could bring to its collaborators and members is to show them the possibility of being brave. We cannot change anything with the kind of theatre we are doing. By working with us, our members don't really earn money or get famous, or achieve a professional career. After it is all over, they simply return to the factory or wherever they were before. So, maybe through their experiences with *Grass Stage*, like touring, meeting people in other cities, or even overseas, those individuals would find ways to be braver. Hopefully, they become more experienced in confronting the harshness of reality.

WEN: I understand what Zhao Chuan means. I think for us, for the *Living Dance Studio*, it is quite a similar situation. A lot of our members, like Li Xinmin or Zou Xueping, are confronted with the exact issue of keeping on after the performance, because the impact that our work can make on society is very small, and so are their prospects within the performing arts world.

LEE: Zhao Chuan, I remember you once said that there is always a discussion after presenting your work and that this discussion is often stronger than the performance. Do you think of that discussion as a part of your theatre, or do you consider it instead as a part of life, as something connected to the world outside of theatre? How do you define the relationship between theatre and the discussion that follows the performance?

ZHAO: Yes, right. From the beginning of *Grass Stage*, we were always doing this kind of talk after the show. After quite a while, I realized that this had become a tradition for us. Our audience even started to expect this post-show discussion. So, over time, these post-show discussions became a part of our theatre. In the beginning, I did not plan for this kind of development, but I simply recognized that this practice was something important to the theatre we're doing. Nowadays, I do regard it as a part of my theatre. I have a Chinese term for it— *yanhou juchang*—which literally translates as "theatre after the performance". This *yanhou juchang* has become an essential feature of this theatre we are making. Theatre and real life meet here and respond to each other.

NIKITIN: I would like to take up what Zhao Chuan said before about the question of how to be brave. If I understood you correctly, you have connected it to your project *World Factory* and how far this project can help the performers to become bold, braver in society. I think it's pretty interesting to use the word "brave" in this context. I relate to it very much because I believe what Kai called "the poetic realness of the individual" could be translated into the word "bravery." It has something to do with an individual who denies the prevailing collective reality. This denial could be described as a poetic act: you bring something into existence, of which you don't yet know what it might lead to afterward. That needs a certain bravery, and it also means being, for a moment, less ashamed. It's very much about shame, and it's interesting that this, what one calls postdramatic in the sense of a specific dramaturgical technology, could also be understood as an attempt to deconstruct the construction of shame. Shame is a form of collective violence that designates to the individual where it belongs, who it is, what it is supposed to do and what it has to be, and therefore what it has to represent every day to keep reality stable. The artistic practice of deconstruction, as I understand it, is not just an intellectual game of talking in a sophisticated way about reality. Instead, I realized that I have possibilities for action only by deconstructing reality, and these possibilities are grounded in a confrontation with shame. To confront shame needs a lot of bravery because stepping out of the prevailing concept of reality is always a risk. I think this is why the whole idea of postdramatic dramaturgy is related to technologies of becoming very personal on stage. When you, Zhao Chuan, talked about the members of *Grass Stage* and how they can become braver, it also means how to be very individual.

ZHAO: Yeah, thanks for expanding this rough idea I just formulated. I like the word that you mentioned: "shame." The mainstream culture we live in, is permanently making you feel ashamed. For example, during an official presentation, all the people you see on the stage or television are beautiful—and they speak Mandarin in a certain trained way. Most Chinese, we are not able to speak this kind of Mandarin; we immediately feel ashamed once confronted with such official presentations. Now, "being shamed" has also become a strategy of consumerism to target the middle class and produce their desires of being wealthy and healthy. So eventually, a lot of people feel ashamed about their bodies, appearance, and income. When we are making theatre, we are constantly dealing with this issue of shame. One way to deal with it is to encourage people to perform in front of others with their real appearance, their own story and creativity. Standing on the stage with dignity is very powerful. Another way to deal with this issue is being a part of a collectivity. Especially for the migrant workers I worked with for the past several years. It is interesting to see them becoming a part of the theatre collective of *Grass Stage*. The ideal of collectivity that is promoted by our state is just fake. It's all about obeying a given authority. Some of the workers are not well educated. Mostly, their life is very narrow without many choices. Through theatre activities, they learn to take notes, deal with people other than themselves, socialize, or confront issues together. It's very real for us to make theatre.

NIKITIN: I guess that a collective that has no space for the individual will always be this fake collective that you talk about, because it cannot avoid becoming an oppressive system in which the individual cannot think of itself other than being a part of this collective. Such a collective is a political force. It's also a legal force. To step out of it for a moment, and to dare to be individual for a moment, is maybe only possible in the realm of the arts or in the realm of activism. If you're a factory worker, you're so designated, told who you are, where you are, and how you have to behave that you don't even have the idea of emancipation. That's exactly where your theatre, Zhao Chuan, comes into play, by suddenly confronting workers with performance and the possibility of having access to a different kind of identity. This is quite a Brechtian approach.

ZHAO: Theatre as we practice it is a collective work. It happens collective efforts. But when our members come to the workshop, they give their own stories. It all starts with a collection of individual stories, but in the end we have something that we all have in common: our production. It's our stories, so people don't feel isolated anymore. The workers gain their strength when they feel that there are many of them. They experience being allowed to share, being able to communicate. They are not beaten up for being individual. In the reality of the world factory situation, they are powerless and have no bargaining rights. There are just big companies and big managements. Not seeing one's own experience as a lonely personal one but looking at it from the perspective of "many" will make people stronger.

NIKITIN: You are right. Individuality alone cannot be the starting point for a political change. If you're alone, then you're powerless. But you also stay alone if you don't start to talk about yourself. I think it is a question of how to use the terms "individual" and "collective" because these terms are very close to each other. I think that being individual has a lot to do with having dignity. It doesn't mean being alone.

TUCHMANN: I want to try to pause the conversation between Boris and Zhao Chuan here, because I want to invite Kyung-Sung and Wen Hui into the discourse. I mean, there has been a lot of talk about the role of the individual and how to empower the individual. Are there any thoughts that you want to share on that?

WEN: I have a question for Zhao Chuan because I share a similar work environment. I often have similar things to struggle with. I very much liked your *World Factory*, but I want to know if you are still in contact with these workers.

ZHAO: I remember that when you came to the show in 2014, we just started working on the history of industrial mass production and the current situation of labor. We always work very slowly, and we had just started trying to unpack this issue with the production of *World Factory* then. Under the same title, we did many different productions until 2017. We traveled with those productions. But also from 2015 onwards, we started to collaborate intensively with migrant workers, most of them from Foxconn. Between 2015 and 2018, we often went to Shenzhen every month to meet the workers. We had a small team of four people, Wu Meng, Wu Jiamin, Gao Zipeng, and I, who continuously worked on this project. Shenzhen is quite far away from Shanghai, so we usually spent five to eight days there per month and workshopped with the workers. The workshop participants continuously changed over time, but there were also some of them who stayed there throughout. They started their own theatre group called the North Gate Workers Theatre Group. They produce their own work, and they even received an award from a festival in Shenzhen. This was discontinued in early 2019 because the NGOs that backed this work were forced to disappear by the authorities. Nowadays, we still try to keep in loose contact with these workers. At the peak time, we were working in four different locations with the workers. Now, Wu Jiamin still frequently goes to the only NGO left to work with them.

WEN: I generally don't define my work. I am afraid of being bound by definitions. Regarding this flow of history that Kai has talked about in his introduction, I believe everyone looks at history from their own place and time. Of course, history is life. I always feel that history is like a building that you are in, and then suddenly somebody comes and knocks at the door. This person who knocks then becomes the key to the history of the person inside the building. Kai, I don't know if you remember: When we were in the early stages of rehearsing *Red* in Caochangdi, there was this day on which we did an improvisation, and suddenly you started reading *Capital* by Marx from the auditorium. And at that moment, I suddenly realized that everyone's relationship with history is different. I thought, look what Kai is doing there, and I realized that you also have a connection with the history of Marxism. I think my practice is to base the work on the personal situation, be it that of the dancers, or in your case, that of a dramaturg.

TUCHMANN: I immediately think of linking what you just said to the conversation that Boris and Zhao Chuan had about being brave about overcoming shame. Because I remember how much work on shame there was while doing these improvisations in *Red*, how many times the performers on the stage felt ashamed—for so many different reasons.

NIKITIN: It is also a question about artistic practice, in general. I remember, for example, when Kyung-Sung talked in Shanghai about his piece in the public space called *Let Us Move Your Sofa*. This work is a poetic practice that also relates to the question of shame, because to do funny and absurd things in public space means to break—or at least to shift—the norms of public expectations imposed on our bodies. There's an empowering aspect to it. Maybe bravery is a too big word for that, but in the end, it is about doing something, presenting it to an audience—and people will judge it. There's a moment in which you have to overcome your shame and embarrassment, and you have to activate a little bit of bravery. I don't know if you would agree.

LEE: Thank you for describing the work. It happened like 11 years ago. Its main intention was to create a subjective, individual experience in the public space of Gwanghwamun Square, because at that time the mayor wished to redesign that square into a very new, very fancy place in the middle of the city. This was utterly manipulating the experience of subjectivity in the city. I think this is pretty much related to the issue of shame because many people felt alienated in this new public space, which looked so neat and fancy.

To create a personal experience in this public space became the main artistic aim at that time. There is one loosely related thing that I want to talk about, rooted in my latest experience. I recently made the work *Brothers* with a North Korean refugee and a South Korean actor, who perform on the stage together. They were both born in the same year, in 1983, but their childhoods were totally different. I was trying to intertwine their personal experiences of the times and spaces they went through. But there was some conflict with the South Korean actor during the process because he was not willing to share his personal view or personal memories to the same extent as the North Korean refugee already had. I had been working with this actor for a long time. He became sick of being personal on the stage. I could not push him anymore to share his stories. This problem became reflected in the form of the theatre piece as well because, in the performance, the South Korean actor was mainly asking the North Korean refugee questions. These two individuals were not equally present on the stage: it was the actor who investigated the North Korean refugee on a stage in South Korea, which has a society in which violence and prejudice against North Korean refugees are common. To a certain extent, one could say that this form made visible how North Korean refugees are experiencing the reality of South Korean society. Still, we were not able to swing between the personal view and this historic structure. We were kind of stuck in one person's private experience. Also, one of the critics criticized this work as too emotional. He claimed that it is just consoling one individual and does not touch the fundamental, the social and political structure.

TUCHMANN: May I ask about this actor who refused to become personal on stage? Was he getting tired of repeating his story, or was he refusing to turn himself or herself into a document of history? Was he refusing to become a building block of your aesthetics? What exactly happened?

LEE: I think he's just such a person. I don't know exactly why. He thinks that being just one individual on stage somehow restricts his possibility of representing the world more diversely.

TUCHMANN: This refusal of "just being there" is interesting to me. There seems to be an emerging mistrust and disengagement with the personal story, with the "real thing" on stage. What do you think, why are people having difficulties nowadays in presenting and reading reality?

NIKITIN: I think I understand this actor's reaction. I have also seen such protests with actors I worked with who had problems telling their personal stories on stage. When you go on stage and are asked by a director or a writer to portray your personal life, you are usually not the one who has authorship, let alone the one who holds the means of production. It's a tricky situation. People who go on stage in these documentary formats are, after all, not only asked to portray themselves and their personal story, but to do so under their own name. It's not so easy to keep track of things as a performer. The distance to the material is missing. You have no control over the outcome. Some, therefore, feel exposed, become insecure, distrustful.

In my case, at some point, that was the reason I started writing the texts myself. That made it more playful and less difficult for the actors because they didn't have to cannibalize their personal lives with their own words. Another tool I often use in that context is to claim that everything is potentially fake— to subvert the sense of unambiguity, in the sense of "this is me" and "this is real" and "this is documentary." In this way, the biographical space can become a space of play. I think reality and identity are something complicated today. Many people are no longer willing to simply reproduce uncritically the narratives they have been told and taught for so long. At the same time, many people struggle to be visible and have a right to show their identity. It's just very ambivalent. And I think the theatre space is a very interesting space for these ambivalences.

ZHAO: I was impressed by your *Hamlet* I saw in Zurich back a few years ago. I experienced what you said: You constantly questioned the border between theatre and reality in your performance. I want to suggest something to Kyung-Sung about the situation with this South Korean actor and his confrontation with the person from North Korea. When working with my theatre collective, we welcome anyone who wants to join, and they can leave at any time. When some of them become very active in their participation, I usually have to accept most of the ideas they contribute. I have no other choice. I would not say: This is not so interesting, or this is not a good response, or this is not something I really want. But it is exactly from this limitation that the most interesting part of my work starts, which is all about searching and finding the connection between these different people's responses. For example, when this Korean actor doesn't want to present himself anymore, maybe we could just show this as it is—and to invite others to react to this. So if the reality is the refusal to talk about personal matters on stage when confronting a North Korean refugee, can we present how we try to work this out? When I started working on *World Factory*, quite a few of the members of *Grass Stage* had no interest in this theme or knew very little about industrial workers. So, in the beginning, we produced a lot of clichés about the workers, about the worker's community, and some very different ideologies came through the responses. I don't judge them. I rather try to find the connection between all these different attitudes. So maybe, this actor of Kyung-Sung's, who doesn't want to say anything about himself on stage, is also an interesting starting point.

TUCHMANN: This book project has two layers of inquiry. One is all about archiving your theatrical approaches. The second layer seeks to archive the work and the belief system of our dramaturgy faculty in Beijing. The understanding of dramaturgy that we teach in Beijing expands how we understand and make theatre. Therefore, I also want to ask you what dramaturgy actually means to you. How do you understand the concept of dramaturgy in relation to your practice? When did you encounter this term? I am particularly asking this question, because I feel that all your works share a very radical notion of dramaturgy. All of your projects had to be established against the market, against the ruling canon, against what was there when you started. So I just want to throw that idea of dramaturgy at you and let you play around with it. Feel free to comment on it, deny or support it.

NIKITIN: Actually, I hardly use the term dramaturgy. But it's interesting to think about it. A recurring motif for me is certainly the play with the real and the supposedly real. I'm interested in the simultaneity of these two levels—a theatre that oscillates between the documentary as something based on facts and as something that only looks like it's based on facts. I mix documentary forms with fiction, and with fiction, I mean the possibility of reinventing yourself. I think most of my works try to blur the idea of identity—even the identity of the pieces themselves. Some people would call them documentary, some would say they're not documentary at all. I would always claim that they are both at the same time. This could be called, if you like, a dramaturgy, from a conceptual point of view.

    If I look at it from the practical level, I would say that for me dramaturgy is the organization of the experience of time. You could call it composition. It's very much about how an audience is experiencing time or realizing that time is an experience at all. It's something that happens with your body; it's about aging, even if it is just the aging together that occurs in two hours. That said, the idea of dramaturgy would interest me at a technical level—to understand it as a craft. I think it allows us to be less ideological. But I'm not sure.

TUCHMANN: In China, the concept of dramaturgy is highly debated: We have all these discussions around its translation and whether this profession is applicable to the Chinese theatre market. Wen Hui and Zhao Chuan, could you talk us through your understanding of these discussions. I don't know about the debates in Korea, Kyung-Sung, so maybe you can tell us a little bit about them. I remember that there are new, young artists like Yi Danbi, who identify as dramaturgs. So there seems to be an increasing focus around dramaturgy in Korea as well.

LEE: Starting from the last decade, we have established a certain position for dramaturgs in the National Theatre and at big public theatres. I think the Korean theatre has adopted the German theatre system in that sense. In the theatre academies, though, we do not have any departments for dramaturgy. It is usually graduates in theatre studies who become dramaturgs. In the independent theatre scene, the role or position of dramaturg differs from these main theatres. I sometimes worked with a dramaturg, and it was very helpful, but I'm not sure if I always would like to tour with a dramaturg. I mean, dramaturgy is an important position, but at the same time, what the dramaturg does is interfering with the director's job. Further, I think dramaturgy is not really rooted deeply in the existing Korean theatre system: You can find dramaturgs being part of some productions, but they are not needed for others. I think dramaturgy means finding the relations between materials. What I mean by "finding the relations between the material" is, in other words, to deconstruct the center. Dramaturgy is directed against making theatre too neat, or too understandable, because the reality is much more complex. But having said that, it does not mean that I personally always need a dramaturg to create my work.

WEN: I think in my practice, the dramaturg is my interlocutor, who triggers discussions in a rehearsal. So this position is very important to me. Sometimes it is precisely the dialogue with a dramaturg that gives me space to breathe. I think Kai knows that quite well. I liked working with him very much. One of my favorite things working with Kai was how deeply he observed our improvisations, how he was reading any instance from the outside. I think we dancers are just doing what we do on the stage, and we try to live in the very instance—and Kai's reading really transformed and transported these instances into reflections, into new tasks, and even into new ways to explore. Also, Kai, you are the first person in my working history who is a professional dramaturg, because, in China, we haven't really had a concept of professional dramaturgy, but what we always had before were friends visiting rehearsals.

ZHAO: For me, it is a real luxury to have a dramaturg to work with. It's really a luxury to have support from this kind of "other" knowledge. And this is why I do understand the purpose of the faculty at the Central Academy and also Li Yinan's immense efforts to bring this concept of dramaturgy to China. Now actually, this concept has become very popular in China. I see many different productions that include dramaturgs in their casts. It seems to me, however, that they do quite different things, and some of my friends who are theatre makers suddenly started to call themselves dramaturgs. They began to work under this title even without having a director or scriptwriter in their production. So, somehow "dramaturg" becomes a very fashionable job and a powerful position. I find this is interesting. This deconstructs the concept of what dramaturgy actually is and what it is supposed to do, but also comes with new possibilities.

NIKITIN: I, by the way, try to avoid working with dramaturgs.

TUCHMANN: But this does not mean that your work has no dramaturgy—like you just explained. I assume there is a dramaturgy, even (and maybe sometimes because) there is no dramaturg around. Dramaturgy primarily concentrates on how a performance programs its relationship with an audience. So dramaturgy lives as something that is practiced and has been around much longer than the idea of directing.

NIKITIN: I wonder actually if this idea of dramaturgy is not deeply embedded in German conversations, because when I talk, for example, to French colleagues, they very often say that dramaturgy is a very German thing, in the sense that one attempts to separate dramaturgy as a discipline from a group's artistic practice or a director. I don't think that you can extract dramaturgy. Especially in contemporary theatre and performance, the dramaturgy is almost identical with aesthetics, the aesthetic framework, and the handwriting of the artist or the group. If you decide as an artist to work primarily with non-fictional material, or to make projects with groups of people who are not educated in acting, like factory workers, then that is a dramaturgical decision. And I think, nowadays, it has a lot to do with what artists are doing anyway.

TUCHMANN: My last question starts from this luxury position we are in now: We can look back at the people we were two and a half years ago, when we did the seminars together in Beijing. As professional theatre-makers, what are the most significant changes, ruptures, and continuities that you would say have occurred in these three and a half years? I do feel that there is a process of mainstreaming the postdramatic. In Germany, the postdramatic aesthetics goes more and more together with identity politics. It becomes a most favored aesthetic approach because it allows individual performers to put their case on stage. In China, there is quite a tendency towards happenings and performance art. You cannot go in a shopping mall without encountering performances, and more and more spaces are opened up for happenings: Deserts, beaches, factories, everywhere is site-specific performance. What started as a kind of an alternative, highly political enterprise, like the early *juchang* works of the 1980s, becomes entangled in mainstream and consumerism now.

How do you respond with your practices against these trends of mainstreaming the postdramatic, of mainstreaming *juchang*, of mainstreaming performance art? Is there something particular in your work that reacts to this trend and tendency?

ZHAO: Sometimes it's kind of sad, because when I start conversations or have to give talks, I introduce myself as a theatre-maker, but actually in China, it's very difficult for us to truly present work in theatres. I do not connect to the Chinese theatre circle. I think Wen Hui is maybe in a similar situation, or at least you understand this. So, I would not even say that we confront the mainstream. We're just not in the whole thing. In the last few years, and especially since the pandemic, expression is even more controlled. I am relating this to make this point—we could not even say we are against something, but rather that now something operates against us. So maybe, up to ten years ago, we were trying to push the boundaries; now we are pushed back. The red lines are moving towards us. In terms of practice, we are in a pretty difficult situation. In the past decade, the spaces for us to work have become more and more limited. On the one hand, this is due to the tightening of control; on the other hand, it is a result of commercialization: Everything costs money. The theatre scene in China is very vibrant. But it is a very different concept to what municipal theatre means in Europe. Theatre in Europe typically would respond to the current political situation, to urgent issues, more or less. But in China, theatre means something else. It is not daring to touch the real situation. People are afraid. You understand this very well.

At the moment, it's really about survival for us in China. When we started in the new millennium's first decade, I found spaces and possibilities to work. But now, sometimes I even think I should move out because there are so few possibilities left. It is quite a powerless feeling.

WEN: I absolutely agree with what Zhao Chuan said about the Chinese situation. I don't know very much about the situation of German-speaking theatre, but in China right now, it is difficult. Six, seven years ago, there was much more space. For example, our *Living Dance Studio* was based in a big space in Caochangdi. Kai, you lived there with us for a while. We had our own theatre and presentations there, and we basically did whatever we wanted to do. But now, the government managed to unite the forces of political control and capital, which gave it even more power. Among the people that are connecting them-selves with postdramatic theatre are a lot who are doing so because it is a popular thing to do right now. It is something that fits well into this new power structure of capital and control. It runs a risk of become mainstream. I often think this is not real; what we would need are expressions of political iden-tities. I know that five, six years ago, a piece like Zhao Chuan's *World Factory* could be performed in some theatres. I don't think that is possible today any-more.

ZHAO: Now it's impossible, no no.

WEN: It's impossible! Because you cannot find a place—not even a small space. I am literally talking about physical space here. One could not afford to rent a location these days. Of course, I saw some young artists—they have an oppor-tunity, they have the chance to perform at Wuzhen Festival, but I don't think they are able to do what they want to do completely. Because they get money—they go there, but they cannot do much in artistic terms.

TUCHMANN: Zhao Chuan used the word "powerless," and I really can sense this feeling of powerlessness that Zhao Chuan and you, Wen Hui, are describing. Do you have any strategies to cope with that situation?

ZHAO: It's really funny and also contradictory: In the beginning I talked about being brave, and now I'm talking about powerlessness. Quite a few years ago, we started to work a lot inside contemporary art museums. Some people criti-cized us for having "gone arty" instead of keeping our initial connection to so-ciety. But to us, appearing in the museums was the only way to get public spaces and get support. But since last year, even museums have become diffi-cult to cooperate with.

It's interesting to see the young generations born from the late '80s or '90s, who were born in an environment in which everything is expressed and done online. In recent years, they realized that the online space has become limited because it is even easier to control by the state. Now in almost every major city there are independent spaces operated by young people. You can go there to stay without paying for any accommodation if you have the right connec-tions. They even made a particular map for this loose network. Sometimes these spaces are connected to art, sometimes they are not. It's not like those alternatives spaces back to the '90s, which mostly were art spaces—facilitat-ing artistic presentations, gatherings, or exhibitions. These spaces established by the young people today are much more living spaces: People live there, doing art or not. Maybe three or four young people share a big apartment, with some spare rooms to host meetings and events. So it's all offline: Meetings, independent film showings, discussions, small activities; also, these places have become a kind of cheap accommodation for young people, who connect to those alternative circles. There's another boom that takes place offline, namely underground publishing. We've got our documentations of *World Factory* printed in two volumes.

So slowly, you can observe the establishing of new or other marginal channels. They are definitely not dealing with big audiences here. Now, we also started working on small productions that maybe can perform within two or three square meters. For audiences of up to twenty people, we don't need much promotion. Sometimes, promotion creates problems for us. These recent developments only happened in the last two years.

NIKITIN: It sounds a bit like if you were going back to the start; you started working, found places, did projects—and now you're thrown back to the beginning, like a board game. Only real. That's tough and sad.

ZHAO: It's so hard. It's like turning from the public space into private space for the sake of avoiding checks, controls, and repression.

WEN: It is even more difficult than before we started. Because when we started, we just decided not to sell any tickets, and by doing so, we could avoid some censorship, and we got rid of a lot of regulations. We had some space of our own; our friends knew about this situation and supported us. Eventually, we could perform. But now, every place costs a lot of money, and you also have to go through much more censorship.

ZHAO: In the '80s and '90s, they didn`t know what we were doing, and thus our work was negotiable.

NIKITIN: It really sounds like a question of technology, of social media, smartphones, etc. I mean, this whole idea of connecting and creating a network leads to networks of surveillance, observation and self-observation. I think that's the big difference between the '80s and now, because the '80s were obviously much more analog. So the idea of independence is more complicated today because we have internalized this idea of being connected in our bodies, so that it has become more difficult to think of the idea of an alternative space. That's why I'm so interested in what you just said about this new generation, who are trying to find these more analog spaces to escape.

In general, I think our connection to reality has changed a lot within the last ten years, primarily due to a technological shift. In China, it seems that this shift has translated into surveillance, censorship, and then manifested itself in a lack of physical spaces and means of production. While in Switzerland and in Germany, this shift translates itself into metastases of realities: There are extremely many possibilities, but because there are so many possibilities, again, reality becomes indifferent because you simply cannot handle that amount of realities and frames of reference. Of course, that also has to do with the internet, which uncritically gives in to this idea of globalization, which, in fact, does not exist. What we are doing now is that we are having this conversation between Germany, China, South Korea, and Switzerland. There is an illusion of borderlessness. But I mean, clearly, you two, Zhao Chuan and Wen Hui, are in a different legal system. That's a fact. And it is this technology that we are using right now for having this conversation that is blurring this fact.

ZHAO: Yeah, you're right. It's an illusion.

NIKITIN: If I went to China, I would probably experience the difference a bit more than in a Zoom meeting. Because everything becomes more physical then. I would not experience it as much as you, because I would still be a tourist, just coming and leaving again. So, the consequences for me would not be the same as for you, who experience the boundaries of the reality that has suddenly taken possibilities away from you.

ZHAO: I do agree with you. All these technological mediations of actual meetings between people are a kind of illusion. Technology hides the price that one pays when it weaves different lives together. On the other hand, this weaving together is also a very powerful practice. Just today, at these moments, I shared my project *World Factory* with you, and then I heard the remarks by you, Kyung-Sung, Kai, and Wen Hui, and then I feel that I am not alone. You know it is true. We need all this. We should learn from the virus—people need to meet each other. So now I call my kind of theatre practice "theatre of social contagion." It is important that the people meet, share, talk and have dialogue.

NIKITIN: I agree. It is. This conversation we're having right now is not an illusion. We're having a real discussion and are exchanging ideas, and that is important. But it's an illusion that we're sharing the same space. The illusion of "globalization." I mean, we actually live in different spaces and in different legal systems that shape our identities and bodies in different ways. We can't escape the fact that we have to deal with real space, and that real struggle always relates to the legal-political system that does something to your bodies and the bodies of the people around you. I think the dilemma we face is that the internet—and by that, I mean digital publics in particular—on the one hand create possibilities, but at the same time make us forget that we are physical bodies and experience the world with our bodies.

TUCHMANN: Wen Hui and Zhao Chuan talked about these new, harsher, more brutal circumstances in China. Are they related to the pandemic and how digital surveillance is used to observe people and take space away? I mean, can you comment on the question of if, and if so, how far the pandemic has contributed to this situation of powerlessness?

WEN: That's a good question. I don't think it is the pandemic that caused this situation. I think it is due to the politics that is constantly merging the powers of capitalism and political control.

ZHAO: I would think the pandemic actually contributed to this situation in the past year, because it allowed the introduction of new technologies to tighten the control of the people. Now the government does not need any reason for collecting your data—it can be perfectly done in the framework of preventing the spread of the pandemic. Some of those policies were not that easy to install before. Now, in the name of the war against the pandemic, everything is so easy.

LEE: One change that I can describe is that until 2018, Korean society experienced many incidents and social changes. The social reality of this time was very powerful. Many of the artists, including myself, struggled to find a strategy to reflect these events and social changes on stage, for example, the Sewol ferry disaster. But after those times, I feel like I'm much too focused on the use of art in society. I want to be more free from that these days. I want art to reflect society—but there has to be more than just dealing with issues on the stage. I want to find a different strategy to reflect on them. Where to start with this is one of my questions. Also, in the Korean theatre scene, "political correctness" was a big issue, and how one could represent queer or disabled people on stage. Many mainstream theatres were trying to bring these topics on stage, but when they take them and represent them on stage, it does not really reflect the people who are directly involved in these identity struggles. I mean, these pieces are raising the issues, but in a way, they simply distort the reality with a particular formula or convention of making theatre.

Sometimes they use the term postdramatic as a strategy to stage these topics, but in that sense, postdramatic theatre becomes like a genre.

NIKITIN: Sorry, did you just say it becomes a jungle?

LEE: Genre. G-E-N-R-E.

NIKITIN: Ah, because I sometimes think it also has become a jungle.

LEE: This is the Korean theatre reality as I am facing it now. I've also been presenting my work in several mainstream theatres, but now I'm trying to get away from those contexts and to explore how to position myself independently.

TUCHMANN: It was indeed very interesting—also partly saddening—to learn how your aesthetics and production contexts have changed over the last two and a half years. I want to thank you all for taking the time and making this conversation happen.

Biographies

Regine Dura works as a director, author, and dramaturg. After studying theatre/film and media, German, and literature and art education in Frankfurt/Main and video at the Berlin University of the Arts, she worked in Berlin and for the European Film Academy, Wim Wenders Produktion, and as a freelance curator and jury member. Since 2000, she has been working with the documentary theatre director Hans-Werner Kroesinger. She is responsible for play development/concept and text, e.g., for *Stolpersteine Staatstheater*, (Staatstheater Karlsruhe, 2015), with which they were invited to the Berlin Theatertreffen 2016. Since 2019, she is also co-director of productions including *Frontex Security*, *Burning Earth* (*Brennende Erde*, Schauspiel Leipzig, 2020), *Westwall* (Staatstheater Mainz, 2021), and *Room 600* (*Saal 600,* Staatstheater Nuremberg, 2021).

She has received various scholarships and residences, including a DEFA scholarship, the Research Grant of the Berlin Senate, scholarships from the Cultural Academy Tarabya (Istanbul) and Villa Kamogawa (Kyoto), and the #TakeCareResidency Hebbel am Ufer (Performing Arts Fund).

In 2021, she was awarded together with Hans-Werner Kroesinger the Poetikdozentur Landau for "new standards in documentary theatre".

Hans-Werner Kroesinger studied at the Institute for Applied Theatre Studies at the Justus Liebig University in Giessen with Andrzej Wirth and Hans-Thies Lehmann from 1983 to 1988. In 1987, while still a student, Kroesinger began working as an assistant director and dramaturg for Robert Wilson. He was involved in the productions of *Hamletmaschine* in New York and *The Forest* in Berlin. In 1989, he became Heiner Müller's artistic collaborator on the *Hamlet/Hamletmaschine* production at the Deutsches Theater Berlin. Since 1993, his productions have been staged at venues including the Berliner Ensemble, Maxim Gorki Theater Berlin, and the Hebbel am Ufer HAU in Berlin. He took part in documenta X in Kassel in 1997. Since 2000, he has collaborated regularly with Regine Dura.

Hans-Werner Kroesinger and Regine Dura are considered among the most important representatives of contemporary documentary theatre in Germany. Kroesinger's works have been invited to national and international festivals such as "Politik im freien Theater" (Hamburg 2003, Dresden 2009, Freiburg/Basel 2014), "Internationale Keuze" Rotterdam (2007), "Bitef" Belgrade (2014), "Mess" Sarajevo (2014), Steirischer Herbst 2016, the Berlin Theatertreffen (2016) and the Berlin Theatertreffen in China (2017).

In 2012, Kroesinger was a visiting professor in the Scenic Research program at the Ruhr University in Bochum, which has since been established as the Schlingensief Professorship.

Lee Kyung-Sung is a theatre-maker from Korea. He was born in Basel, Switzerland, in 1983 and moved to Korea in 1987. He majored in theatre directing at Choong-Ang University and performance practice and research at the Royal Central School of Speech and Drama, London. In 2008, he founded *Creative VaQi*. In 2010, he became the youngest winner of the prestigious East Asia New Conception Theatre Award for *Let Us Move Your Sofa* (2010) and also received the Doosan YonKang Artist Award for *Namsan Documenta* in 2014. He is a director with exceptional abilities utilizing a diverse range of sensory stage languages to convey the problems of modern society. His works engage in genre-deconstructing, multimedia experiments, and reducing dependence on text, maximizing the possibilities of the message's multisensory transmissibility with an exacting and critical mindset while actively countering such logocentrism by utilizing media, installation, and performance. His work was presented in numerous festivals worldwide, including Festival Tokyo in Japan, Black Box Theatre Festival in Hong-Kong, the Melbourne Live Arts Festival, and Theaterformen in Germany. He was invited as a guest artist by Kinosaki International Arts Center with his company *Creative VaQi* in 2018.

Since 2015, Kyung-Sung Lee has served as the 3rd artistic director of the Seoul Marginal Theatre Festival and has curated three editions of that festival. He is a professor at the Department of Acting at Sungkyunkwan University, Seoul.

Li Yinan is the professor of dramaturgy and theatre studies at the Central Academy of Drama, Beijing. Her research focuses on various aspects of new dramaturgy (including dramaturgy for documentary theatre, dance, and new media art). She teaches courses on New Dramaturgy and Documentary Theatre in the BA, MA, and PhD programs. She is also a theatre director. Her theatrical productions include *Have/Have not* (*You Mou*, 2015), *Home* (*Jia*, 2016), *In the Dream Land* (*Ying De Zun Leng*, 2017), *Water Margin* (*Shuihu*, 2017), and *The Black Temple* (*Heisi*, 2017). She is the Chinese translator of Hans-Thies Lehmann's *Postdramatisches Theater* (1999).

Boris Nikitin is a theatre director, author, and essayist, who was born in Basel as the son of Ukrainian-Slovakian-French-Jewish immigrants. Nikitin writes and directs in the international independent theatre scene as well as in established city theatres. He also curates festivals, talks, and symposiums.

Nikitin has been exploring the representation and production of identity and reality since 2007. His plays seek the boundary between illusion theatre and performance, between documentary, propaganda, and fake. In the process, they sometimes completely resolve the contradiction between offensive dilettantism and artistic virtuosity, between concept and grand theatrical gesture. Time and again, the plays are rewritings of classical material, as in *Woyzeck* (2007), *The Broken Jug* (*Der zerbrochne Krug,* 2010), or *Hamlet* (2016). "Like few others, Boris Nikitin is currently leading theatre to a critical point," according to a German professional journal. Recently, Nikitin has increasingly been dealing with the relationship between art and illness.

In 2017, Nikitin was awarded the J.M.R. Lenz Prize for Drama of the City of Jena for his oeuvre. In 2020, he received the Swiss Theatre Prize.

Kai Tuchmann works as a dramaturg, director, and academic. He holds a directing diploma from the Ernst Busch Drama Academy in Berlin. He is a guest professor at Beijing's Central Academy of Drama—where he, together with Li Yinan, has developed the curriculum of the first dramaturgy BA program in Asia. He has held research fellowships at The Graduate Center, CUNY (Fulbright), the Mellon School of Theater and Performance Research at Harvard University, and the Academy for Theatre and Digitality in Dortmund (Germany). Kai also teaches dramaturgy and theatre management at Zurich University of the Arts, Jawaharlal Nehru University New Delhi, and the Frankfurt University of Music and Performing Arts. In his research, Kai argues for an understanding of dramaturgy as a practice that expands the possibilities of theatre. As dramaturg, he has collaborated with Hans-Werner Kroesinger (*The Suppliants,* [*Die Schutzflehenden*], Mainfranken Theater Würzburg, 2012), Wen Hui (*RED* [*HONG*], 2015), and Zhao Chuan (*The Refuse* [*Feiwu*], 2015), and *The Gele Mountain* [*Geleshan*], 2018).

Kai's artistic works have examined the afterlife of the Cultural Revolution in present-day China, the effects of urbanization on the population of migrants in Europe and Asia, and the ontological status of embodiment vis-à-vis digital technology.

His stagings and dramaturgies have been invited to i Dance Hong Kong, Seoul Marginal Theatre Festival, Zürcher Theater Spektakel, Kunstfest Weimar, Festival d'Automne à Paris, Wuzhen Theatre Festival, Asia Society New York, and OCAT Shenzhen, among other events.

Wang Mengfan works as an independent theatre director and choreographer in Beijing. She studied art history and dance studies in China and Germany. Her first theatre project, *50/60-Old Ladies Dance Juchang* (*50/60-Ayimen De Wudao Juchang*), was created in Beijing in 2015. The work was premiered at the Beijing Nanluoguxiang Performing Arts Festival and presented at the VIE Festival in Bologna. At the 2017 Beijing Fringe Festival, she created her second dance theatre piece, *The Divine Sewing Machine* (*Shensheng Fengrenji*), which featured thirteen children.

She was selected as a "Dance Hopeful (*Hoffnungsträger*)" by the German dance magazine tanz in its 2018 yearbook. Her most recent production is *When My Cue Comes, Call Me, And I Will Answer* (*Gai Wo Shangchang Deshihou, Jiao Wo, Wo Hui Huida*) which premiered in 2019 at Wuzhen Theatre Festival. In 2021 she was awarded the Pro Helvetia Studio Residency, in the context of which she is collaborating with *Theater HORA* to reconsider how different bodies are choreographed as "problems" in the context of dance.

Wen Hui, who was born in Yunnan, is a dancer, choreographer, documentary filmmaker, and installation artist from China. Originally trained as a folk dancer, she attended the Choreography Department of the Beijing Dance Academy from 1985 to 1989 and was then a choreographer in the *Oriental Song and Dance Ensemble of China* (*Dongfang Gewutuan*). In the 1990s, she studied modern dance in the United States and Europe, including at Folkwang University in Essen and Pina Bausch's dance company in Wuppertal. In 1994, Wen Hui founded China's first independent dance theatre group, the *Living Dance Studio* (*Shenghuo Wudao Gongzuoshi*), together with filmmaker Wu Wenguang. With *Report on Body* (2004), she and her team won the ZKB Prize of the Zürcher Theater Spektakel. With the support of the Goethe-Institut, the *Living Dance Studio* produced the piece *RED* (*HONG*) in 2015, a reflection on the model opera as a cultural-political symbol and a part of the collective consciousness during the Chinese Cultural Revolution. Wen Hui has participated in numerous independent Chinese and international festivals. Her works are shown at theatres, museums, and art centers. She is presently working on *I am Sixty*, which premiered in autumn 2021. Wen Hui lives in Beijing.

Zhao Chuan, born in 1967, works across theatre, literature, film, and visual art. He creates alternative and socially engaged theatre and is the founder and artistic director of the Shanghai-based theatre collective *Grass Stage* (*Caotaiban*, established in 2005). As a theatre-maker and writer, he has created various theatre works across China together with *Grass Stage* for over a decade. However, they are often unable to present these works in conventional theatres.

The group encourages people from different backgrounds to consider human living conditions and historical issues and stimulate participators and audiences to respond to those issues through a creative process, rehearsals, performances, and post-talks. Given its strong interest in social practice, the group's theatre activities have often been considered too rough, ideological, marginal, and undefined by the mainstream. In recent years, *Grass Stage* has supported industry workers in making their own theatre pieces; through dialogues with young people from diverse backgrounds, the group has developed stage plays on youth issues in today's China.

His theatre works include *Wild Seeds* (*Zacao*, 2018–2019) and a trilogy (*Shehui Juchang Sanbuqu*) about contemporary Chinese society (2006–2017), comprising *World Factory* (*Shijie Gongchang*), *The Little Society* (*Xiao Shehui*), and *Madmen's Stories* (*Kuangren Gushi*). During the pandemic in 2020, *Grass Stage* started the new series *Theatre of Contagion* (*Renchuanren Juchang*).

Zhao Chuan has been awarded several international literature awards, including the Unita Prize for New Novelists (Taiwan, 2001). His publications include fiction, essays, and art criticism: *On Radical Art: the 80s Scene in Shanghai* (author, 2014), *The Body At Stake: Experiments in Chinese Contemporary Art and Theatre* (co-editor, author, 2013). He is also the producer of an independent documentary titled *Shanghai Youth* (2015). He has been involved in many international art residencies, collaboration projects, and teaching.

Zhuang Jiayun is a graduate of playwriting from the Central Academy of Theatre in Beijing. She received her PhD in Theater and Performance Studies from UCLA and held an Andrew Mellon Fellowship. She has worked as a concept developer and writer at CAMLab at Harvard University and as a dramaturg for the PlayMakers Repertory Company. In 2017, Jiayun and Shanghai-based choreographer Fan Jiang founded *The Three Bowls Co-op*—a performance group that experiments with new storytelling mediums and technological possibilities in theatre and performance. At the Academy for Theatre and Digitality in Dortmund (Germany), Jiayun is currently developing her latest project, *FXKE*, a performance installation on dis/information dissemination and public engagement in the post-truth era.

List of Figures and Online Resources

Cultural Studies

Gabriele Klein
Pina Bausch's Dance Theater
Company, Artistic Practices and Reception

2020, 440 p., pb., col. ill.
29,99 € (DE), 978-3-8376-5055-6
E-Book:
PDF: 29,99 € (DE), ISBN 978-3-8394-5055-0

Elisa Ganivet
Border Wall Aesthetics
Artworks in Border Spaces

2019, 250 p., hardcover, ill.
79,99 € (DE), 978-3-8376-4777-8
E-Book:
PDF: 79,99 € (DE), ISBN 978-3-8394-4777-2

Nina Käsehage (ed.)
Religious Fundamentalism
in the Age of Pandemic

April 2021, 278 p., pb., col. ill.
37,00 € (DE), 978-3-8376-5485-1
E-Book: available as free open access publication
PDF: ISBN 978-3-8394-5485-5

All print, e-book and open access versions of the titles in our list
are available in our online shop www.transcript-publishing.com

Cultural Studies

Ivana Pilic, Anne Wiederhold-Daryanavard (eds.)
Art Practices in the Migration Society
Transcultural Strategies in Action
at Brunnenpassage in Vienna

March 2021, 244 p., pb.
29,00 € (DE), 978-3-8376-5620-6
E-Book:
PDF: 25,99 € (DE), ISBN 978-3-8394-5620-0

German A. Duarte, Justin Michael Battin (eds.)
Reading »Black Mirror«
Insights into Technology and the Post-Media Condition

January 2021, 334 p., pb.
32,00 € (DE), 978-3-8376-5232-1
E-Book:
PDF: 31,99 € (DE), ISBN 978-3-8394-5232-5

Krista Lynes, Tyler Morgenstern, Ian Alan Paul (eds.)
Moving Images
Mediating Migration as Crisis

2020, 320 p., pb., col. ill.
40,00 € (DE), 978-3-8376-4827-0
E-Book: available as free open access publication
PDF: ISBN 978-3-8394-4827-4

**All print, e-book and open access versions of the titles in our list
are available in our online shop www.transcript-publishing.com**

GPSR Authorized Representative: Easy Access System Europe, Mustamäe tee 50, 10621 Tallinn, Estonia, gpsr.requests@easproject.com

www.ingramcontent.com/pod-product-compliance
Lightning Source LLC
Chambersburg PA
CBHW081653120626
46550CB00010B/2889